Integrating Children's Literature through the Common Core State Standards

Integrating Children's Literature through the Common Core State Standards

Rachel L. Wadham and Terrell A. Young

LIBRARIES UNLIMITED™

An Imprint of ABC-CLIO, LLC

Santa Barbara, California • Denver, Colorado

Library of Congress Cataloging-in-Publication Data

Wadham, Rachel L., 1973–

    Integrating children's literature through the common core state standards / Rachel L. Wadham and Terrell A. Young.
      pages cm
    Includes bibliographical references and index.
    ISBN 978-1-61069-608-1 (pbk : alk. paper) — ISBN 978-1-61069-609-8 (ebook)
1. Reading (Elementary)   2. Children's literature—Study and teaching (Elementary)   3. Language arts (Elementary)—Standards—United States.   4. Reading comprehension.   5. Children—Books and reading—United States.   I. Young, Terrell A.   II. Title.
    LB1573.W18 2015
    372.4—dc23   2015008164

ISBN: 978-1-61069-608-1
EISBN: 978-1-61069-609-8

19 18 17 16 15   1 2 3 4 5

This book is also available on the World Wide Web as an eBook.
Visit www.abc-clio.com for details.

Libraries Unlimited
An Imprint of ABC-CLIO, LLC

ABC-CLIO, LLC
130 Cremona Drive, P.O. Box 1911
Santa Barbara, California 93116-1911

This book is printed on acid-free paper ∞

Manufactured in the United States of America

Contents

1 What Are the Common Core State Standards?

In 2009 the landscape of education changed with the development of the Common Core State Standards (CCSS). Since their initial development and the subsequent implementation efforts, the Core has had both its advocates and its detractors. No matter how the Core is characterized, the reality is that the CCSS has had and will continue to have a major impact on education. The effort to develop standards and accountability measures is really nothing new for the field of education; however, the development of the CCSS did represent some rather radical shifts in thinking, as it created standards philosophically grounded in research that could be applied across state lines.

Believing that essential reform in education was needed to make American students more globally competitive and to ensure that students were prepared for the demands of 21st-century colleges and workplaces, several groups initiated a joint effort to create a common set of research-based educational standards. The National Governors Association Center for Best Practices and the Council of Chief State School Officers led the effort. These two groups also worked with Achieve Inc., an education reform group based in Washington, D.C. The Bill & Melinda Gates Foundation, the Charles Stewart Mott Foundation, and other private groups provided funding. The impetus for this work was grounded in the long-term movement toward accountability and standards-based reform that began in the early 1990s. During the early period of this movement, states created their own standards and worked under various systems of accountability, many of which were federally mandated through the No Child Left Behind Act. Finding these efforts lacking and with the act showing its age, these school and state government leaders began to seek out a way to create a more universal set of standards that all states could adopt. The work of this group to reexamine educational benchmarks and devise new approaches for assessment resulted in the CCSS that were released in June 2010. As of January 2015, 43 states and the District of Columbia have individually and voluntarily committed to the adoption of the English language arts (ELA) and mathematics standards in varying combinations.

The history, present, and future of the Core is a very complex issue, and providing a complete picture of its development and implementation is not within the scope of this book. A close reading of the Core documentation will provide much of this information for those with interest. Additionally works such as *Something in Common* by Rothman and *Common Core Meets Education Reform* by Hess and McShane are suggested as reliable and comprehensive resources. Since the philosophy and ideas that inform the Core are clearly outlined in these and other works, here is offered only clarifications for several important issues surrounding the Core that will inform the philosophy and ideas to be outlined in this book.

It is significant to clarify that the Core is only a set of standards. At its most basic, a standard is a statement or rule that helps us ensure quality. The implication is that in applying a standard, a certain level of quality will be met. There have been and always will be standards for manufacturing, business, government, and even education. No matter what their realm is, standards are intended to provide a foundational level of quality. This all holds true for the Core. As stated in the CCSS documentation, these standards are designed to provide a clear statement of what students are expected to learn in grades K–12 in regards to reading, writing, speaking, listening, and mathematics.

Aimed at professionals, such as teachers, administrators, and librarians, and other stakeholders, including support staff, parents, and the community, the Core shows us what outcomes we can expect for quality student learning. The Core is not by definition or application a curriculum or pedagogy. The Core outlines only the outcomes of performance, meaning they describe what students ought to be able to do (make inferences from a text, for instance), but they do not describe how teachers should reach this goal (curriculum), how it should be taught, or what tools should be used (pedagogy).

Understanding what the Core is and what it is not is important for building the context of this book. This book will use the standards as a basis to build a vision of what curriculum and pedagogy could potentially look like when implemented in a classroom. Here is provided one interpretation of the Core using the versatile tool of children's literature as a foundation.

Because the Core only outlines standards that should be met, the reality is that the Core leaves much room to interpretation. The interpretation of the standards into actual curriculum and pedagogy that can be implemented into the classroom is left up to individual teachers, schools, and districts. In fact, one of the most fundamental aspects of the Core is how much stock it puts into the discretion of teachers to create their own classrooms. The Core clearly states in a variety of ways throughout its documentation that it is up to teachers to apply their professional knowledge, judgment, and experience to determine what tools and applications will be the most helpful for them and their students as they work toward meeting the goals of the Core.

Although many have misinterpreted the Core by saying that it advocates for certain texts and tools, there is nothing further from the truth. The standards do not define how a teacher should teach or what they should teach with. The Core builds only a robust system for judging and applying texts and tasks of all varieties into all classroom situations. It is then up to individual teachers and schools to apply these standards in a way that is best suited to the contexts in which they work. The potential to use a wide range of techniques and tools in the classroom is an exciting prospect, but it can be a little daunting. The purpose of this book is to help bridge that gap between excitement and fear and to provide a vision of just how the Core can be interpreted and applied using trade books written for children as a fundamental tool.

The potential of the Core to create dynamic and engaging classrooms that will build the skills students need to engage in 21st-century colleges and workplaces is outstanding. It only remains to determine how they can best be implemented and interpreted. It is easy to believe that under the direction of passionate, creative, and engaged professionals, implementations of the Core can provide us with the right set of conditions to create the quality learning environments that all teachers strive to achieve.

Bibliography

Hess, F. M., & McShane, M. Q. (2014). *Common Core meets education reform: What it all means for politics, policy, and the future of schooling.* New York: Teachers College Press.

Rothman, R. (2011). *Something in common: The Common Core Standards and the next chapter in American education.* Cambridge, MA: Harvard Education Press.

2 The Anchor and Grade-Level English Language Arts Standards

The English Language Arts (ELA)/Literacy Standards of the Common Core Standards articulate benchmarks for all the fundamental literacy skills. These skills include reading literature and informational texts, foundational skills, writing, speaking and listening, language (which covers skills associated with the grammar, usage, and mechanics of the English language), and literacy in history/social studies, science and technical subjects. This last set of skills articulates one of the fundamental philosophies of the Core: these crucial literacy skills must be developed through an interdisciplinary model. This means that building students' literacy abilities should no longer be confined to just the realm of ELA. The Core provides encouragement for integrated approaches that incorporate literacy into all the content areas, including social studies and the sciences. The Core addresses this integration in the separate skill standards for grades six through 12 that outlines a set of 10 standards each for history and social studies, and science and technical subjects. These standards address literacy skills that are necessary in these particular disciplines in these grades. The lack of content area standards for grades K–5 should not be taken as an indication that literacy integration is not necessary in the early grades. It is only an indication that in these grades the integration is easily addressed though the basic Anchor Standards, and it is not until later grades when other discipline-specific skills come into play.

The ELA standard's main intent is to ensure that when students graduate from high school they will have all of the literacy skills they will need to succeed in college and career. To make sure that this happenes, the authors of the Core began at the end. They determined what fundamental skills a high school graduate would need for college and career readiness, and these skills formed the foundation or anchor for all the standards. For example, authors of the Core looked at the kinds of texts that students would be reading in college and then went backward to determine what types of texts students should be able to read in elementary school. It is very significant that the Core started at the end in order to decide what students needed to do. By looking at the skills that students needed for college and careers and then mapping backward from that point to see where students should start, the authors of the Core created a very unique structure for the standards. This is important because it means that everything in the Core is connected. So what students learn in kindergarten then builds on what's next in first grade and so forth into college. Skills and abilities in the Core are carefully scaffold from one to the next so that no one individual skill is isolated. This also allows students to have a great deal of practice with any one skill, unlike a pattern seen in many previous standards where a skill was taught and then abandoned only to be reintroduced many years later.

To convey this scaffold structure, each section of literacy skills, reading, writing, speaking and listening, and language starts off with its Anchor Standards. In total there are 32 Anchor Standards: 10 for reading, 10 for writing, 6 for speaking and listening, and 6 for language. The Anchor Standards apply to all grade levels and content areas in that they articulate the overarching skills that will be required of students. Starting with these ending Anchor Standards the authors of the Core then worked through these skills from 12th grade to kindergarten to articulate how each of these anchor skills should be applied in each grade. These grade-specific skills are then expressed in Grade-Level Standards. The Grade-Level Standards are intended to provide the proper scaffolding needed for students to ultimately reach the Anchor Standards. Thus the skills expressed in the kindergarten standards are then meant to prepare students to master the skills articulated in the first-grade standards and so forth. The standards show a very strong connection between the Anchor Standards and each Grade-Level Standard in that they all use the same language and expressions. Because of this, reading the standards often feels like reading the same thing over and over again; however, there are very subtle and exact differences in how each of the Anchor Standards is expressed at each grade level. While the exact application of the skills may look slightly different at each grade level, all the skills outlined in the standards are inexorably linked since they all return to the main skills offered in the Anchor Standards. To engage with the standards teachers will need to not only understand their Grade-Level Standard but also how these standards connect to the Grade-Level Standards both before and after them and ultimately to the Anchor Standards.

In its overview of the research, the authors of the CCSS state that evidence has shown that current educational approaches have not done enough to build college- and workplace-ready students who are independently able to apply the literacy skills needed for success in these venues. The overall intent of the Core is to ensure that students have learning and teaching environments that will give them those skills. For the ELA standards, college and career readiness means that students have mastered important skills related to reading, writing, speaking, and listening. While these groups of skills have been and will always be important, the Core places emphasis on how these abilities should be applied in the 21st century. The focus is on the patterns of thinking and communication that all students will engage in throughout their lives and into the future. In the Core there is less emphasis on mastery and restatement; instead the focus is on the processes and the how and why of fundamental skills. For example, the Core places emphasis on methods involved in creative thinking and synthesis rather than on rote comprehension and fluency. Ultimately the Core defines literacy as more than reading and writing, as it also puts an emphasis on communication, collaboration, creativity, problem solving, technology, citizenship, information literacy, and life skills.

These skills are the more complex aspects of education. Sadly, current educational approaches often tend to focus more on what could be considered lower levels of thinking. Considering Bloom's taxonomy (Bloom, 1956) as a hierarchy of learning processes, current approaches to teaching and learning literacy skills might likely be found at the very lowest levels of recall and comprehension. However, these lower level skills are not those that are necessary to compete in 21st-century environments. Skills for the conditions found in modern colleges and workplaces require higher order skills such as analysis and synthesis. The Core asks teachers to focus more on these higher order complex skills. This does not mean lower order skills will be abandoned, for comprehension and knowledge skills are still fundamental; however, the Core encourages a diversification of practice to ensure that skills are being taught and assessed at all levels.

Teaching and learning under these expectations have the potential to be something very different than what teachers and students might have experienced in the past. Each classroom is going to have to discover for itself what works. However, in this book it is the contention that children's literature is the perfect tool for implementing both the Anchor and Grade-Level Standards and that it meets all the expectations of the Core. Beginning with the Core's expectation for increasing complex texts and then moving through its philosophies for instructional approaches and pedagogies children's literature serves as an excellent tool for teachers. From this basic understanding of the Core offered here, the plan is to build a greater depth of understanding of just how the Core might work with children's literature. While this in reality is only one way to implement the Core it is hoped that professionals will see the great power of books and reading in their classrooms so that as the Core moves forward children's literature becomes an integral part of any Core classroom.

Bibliography

Bloom, B.S. (1956). *Taxonomy of educational objectives, handbook I: The cognitive domain.* New York: David McKay Co Inc.

3 Text Complexity and the Core

The Core purposefully avoids suggesting any pedagogy, curriculum, or tools that should be used to implement the standards, with one exception. The Core very clearly advocates for one tool—texts. Texts, of all varieties and formats, are the essential tool that the Core requires. One common misconception of the Core is that it requires students to read certain texts and text types. This misconception stems from the fact that the Core articulates a list of text exemplars in Appendix B. However, this exemplars' list is not a definitive list of what students should read. It is only designed to serve as a guidepost to help teachers apply the structures for judging texts that the Core outlines. The Core's intent is to provide an outline that teachers can then use and apply to their own classroom situations. Because it is possible to apply the structures that the Core outlines to any text at all, teachers can and should use the Core to judge a wide range of texts to determine their suitability for the needs of their own students and classrooms. Let's see how children's literature can be analyzed according to this outline offered in the standards. The main focus here will be on children's fiction and nonfiction in traditional print formats. However, it is important to note that the Core is equally applicable to all text types, even multimedia formats, including video, audio, and digital texts. Anchor Standard 7 emphasizes this fact when it very clearly states that students should be able to use media in diverse formats that represent textual, visual, and quantitative ways of expressing information. The widest possible range of texts will be important components to any implementation of the Core so in future examples multimedia texts will be offered in addition to the wide range of children's literature.

As noted, texts are a fundamental tool to applying all the Core Anchor and Grade-Level Standards; however, the application of texts is most obviously stated in Anchor Standard 10. This standard articulates the need for students to comprehend both fiction and nonfiction texts at proficient levels. Anchor Standard 10 and each of the associated Grade-Level Standards provide a structure for students to increase their reading comprehension, fluency, skill, and ability steadily in each progressive grade. The end goal is to have students who are prepared to engage with the types of texts that will be required in college and the workplace. The Core provides a structure of scaffolding that beginning in kindergarten will progressively raise students' ability to the levels needed for college and workplace readiness. In each grade the Core intends that increasingly complex texts are used to engage students with the standards. This concept of text complexity is pivotal to the Common Core. Understanding how the Core views complexity and how it is applied in a classroom context is an important first step in applying the Core standards to children's literature.

The Core portrays text complexity as an intricate process by defining complexity as an interaction between several components. The first set of components, the quantitative and qualitative dimensions, applies to the specific qualities of a text. The quantitative dimension provides a number derived from a mathematical formula that indicates the relative simplicity or complexity of a text. The qualitative dimension informs professionals about the inherent structural qualities of a text that contribute to its difficulty that cannot be reduced into a numeric representation. The Core then extends its definition of complexity to include a second set of components, the reader and text dimension. These dimensions extend the definition for complexity outside of the text itself to include forces outside a text that impact complexity. This helps to extend the understanding of complexity by acknowledging that the readers themselves and the tasks they engage in do interact to create a complete vision of complexity. The reality is that quantitative measures, qualitative structures, readers, and tasks are all significant parts of what makes a text complex. The Core acknowledges this by creating a structure to judge text complexity that is balanced to represent each of these dimensions. This approach will most likely be nothing really new for most teachers who already have lots of experience with judging texts from a number of angles. The Core's three-tiered model of text complexity only serves to articulate in a concrete way what we already do to evaluate texts to find the best fits for classroom instruction.

The Core's model for judging text complexity is visually portrayed in its documentation as a pyramid. At the base of the triangle are the reader and task dimensions, and on each side are the qualitative and quantitative dimensions. Placing the reader and task dimensions at the base may have just been a coincidence on the part of the Core's designers; however, it seems that placing these dimensions at the foundation communicates something important. Professionals understand what an important role readers themselves play in making meaning during the reading process. Because of this, as they build curriculum they try to select texts that meet the needs of their students. For example, they might work to find a text that matches their students' interests, knowing that a text that is interesting to a reader will be more likely to be read. Professionals also know that certain texts are best suited for the teaching and learning of certain tasks. They select texts that match to the needed skill set, and then provide authentic learning experiences for their students to engage with the text. It seems that the reader and task dimensions already play a large role in the text selection teachers already do, so seeing it presented as the foundation for judging texts just confirms the professional expertise that is already in practice.

Overall the balance of the three-tiered model of text complexity provides professionals with a strong context for judging texts. However, some implementations of the Core have failed to acknowledge the balance required in judging all the dimensions together by defaulting to the use of only the quantitative dimension. Sadly the Core documentation itself leads to some of this confusion. The Core states emphatically that each of the dimensions is of equal importance. It further states that professionals should always apply several quantitative measures and that a qualitative measure can easily override these numbers. However, the Core documents only offer a rather vague description of the reader and task dimension. For example, in Appendix A where the text complexity model is outlined, four full pages are dedicated to the application of the quantitative and qualitative perspective, but only a few paragraphs that are about half a page are focused on readers and tasks. These brief explanations of these dimensions further narrow the scope by only focusing on a certain set of reader characteristics that address reading ability and the fact that teachers will need to support readers who are not at the appropriate grade level. Additionally, in the outlines discussing the exemplar texts the reader and task dimensions are further glossed over by offering only a single sentence, compared to one paragraph for the quantitative dimension and four paragraphs for the qualitative. This sentence essentially leaves the job of analyzing these dimensions up to the teachers themselves. While an exciting application of the Core's intent to put teachers at the forefront of determining curriculum, tools, and pedagogy, the vague mentions of these two important dimensions offer very little guidance. Additionally, this vague approach fails to truly capture the importance and intricacy of these crucial elements of complexity.

Because they are lacking in sufficient commentary, it seems that professionals are relying mostly on the easily accessible quantitative numbers and the more completely explained qualitative elements. A reliance on only one or two elements was never the intent of the Core, and sadly it can lead to some very interesting implementations of the Core. For example, one school library organized and color coded its collection according to Lexile levels, and then only allowed students to check out and read books that fell in the exact level they had tested at. There was even a teacher who would not use any text in his classroom that did not exactly meet the predetermined Lexile level required by the Core. Most professionals will see lots of problems with these two examples, realizing that there is no cut and dried solution for any educational situation, especially when it comes to reading and texts. Failing to notice the other elements of the model and how all three interact to create an appropriate vision for measuring text complexity can certainly lead to a wide range of problems. However, these issues can be avoided if the balanced approach the Core advocates for is more fully understood and applied. The first step in applying the three-tiered model of text complexity in practice is to see it in use. This book offers one such application by showing how teachers can apply and integrate a balanced vision of all of the dimensions of the model in the judgment of children's literature. To best equip readers with the knowledge needed to make sound decisions based on all of the dimensions of text complexity, let's take a deeper look at each one.

The Quantitative Dimension

The quantitative dimension is probably one of the most universally used dimensions, but it is also one of the most commonly misunderstood ones as well. To see how this might be consider these two books:

1. *The Wee Free Men* by Terry Pratchett (2006): This book is written by British author Terry Pratchett, who is most famous for his adult books in the *Discworld* series. This book, one of his titles in the series aimed at a younger audience, contains Pratchett's signature wit and his extensive use of figurative language, symbolism, metaphor, and analogy. The atmosphere of the work is further enriched by the colorful characters of the Wee Free Men who speak in a Scottish brogue.
2. *The Berenstain Bears and the Trouble with Chores* by Stan and Jan Berenstain (2005): This is a picture book featuring the classic Berenstain Bears. In this title the little bears are having trouble doing their chores so Mama Bear decides to stop cleaning and the rest of the family has to deal with the consequences.

Comparing these two books based on this information, which of the two do you think represents a higher level of complexity? Most professionals find that of the two *The Wee Free Men* would be ranked at a much higher complexity level. Now compare the books on only the quantitative dimension, the Lexile level. *Both* the titles have a Lexile level of 680L. This means that both these books would be considered appropriate for a second or third grader according to the levels outlined in the Core documentation. It seems fairly obvious that few second or third graders would be able to really comprehend Pratchett's work, and in fact with its complex figurative language and dialect use *The Wee Free Men* would tend more toward a middle or high school band. Additionally, there are those who might find *The Berenstain Bears* inappropriate for third graders, with many indicating that this book is appropriate for those as young as preschool. Using the Core Lexile levels alone gives a very unrealistic vision of the complexity of these books. This simple example helps to shed light on just how complex, intricate, and misleading the quantitative dimension of text complexity can be. This does not mean however that these numbers are not helpful, just that they have problems that need to be fully understood in order for them to be applied appropriately.

Assessing the Quantitative Dimension

The development of mathematical or quantitative formulas to measure the "readability" of a text has had a long history. The movement to develop these formulas began in the 1920s as teachers and other professionals decided that they needed to have an easy way to assess texts. They needed these formulas because the 1920s saw a rise in the number of children of varying backgrounds attending school as child labor and compulsory schooling laws were enacted. With a wide range of new students entering their schools professionals were eager to have an easy way to assess if children were going to be able to read the textbooks that were used in the classroom. While not the only reason, one of the most significant reasons these formulas were developed was to find a way to make texts easier to read in order to meet the needs of these diverse populations. Also during this time the process of teaching children to read was dominated by sight approaches to learning, and phonics instruction was less popular. A sight approach requires that students learn to recognize words as a whole instead of phonetically deconstructing them. With this approach texts needed to represent a difficultly level that matched this pedagogic style. Use of this pedagogy also encouraged researchers to discover ways to assess texts so they could identify those with the simplest words that could be sight read with ease (Zakaluk & Samuels, 1988).

As researchers examined the issues surrounding the readability of texts, they looked at a variety of variables. For example, in their work Gray and Leary (1935) came up with 24 variables that were found to impact a text's readability. However, researches soon realized that many of these elements were difficult to measure. They also discovered that a large number of variables made the process of assessing readability very complex. To address these issues, the majority of the research at the time focused on only two variables of readability: semantic and syntactic difficulty. These two variables are easily quantifiable in that they can be reduced to numbers and then a mathematical formula can be applied to reveal interesting information about a text. Expanding from the initial research in the 1920s, later research into readability continues to build on this foundation, and while some researchers are exploring how other variables can be used, the majority of formulas used today still rely only on semantic and syntactic variables.

There are many readability formulas in use today, some of the most popular include:

- Flesch–Kincaid formula—developed by J. Peter Kincaid and Rudolf Flesch as part of a contract with the U.S. Navy in 1975 and it is still widely used today by word processing programs like Microsoft Word (Burke & Greenberg, 2010; Trollinger & Kaestle, 1986).
- SMOG (Simple Measure of Gobbledygook)—developed by G. Harry McLaughlin in 1969, this formula has been widely used to assess materials related to health education (Burke & Greenberg, 2010; McLaughlin, 1969).
- Coleman–Liau index—developed by Meri Coleman and T. L. Liau in 1975 for evaluating textbooks (Coleman & Liau, 1975).
- Gunning fog index—developed by Robert Gunning in 1952 to assess business documents, newspapers, and magazines (Gunning, 1952).
- Coh-Metrix—development of this formula began in 2004. It is one of the first to try to add other elements into the formula in order to measure the overall cohesion of a text (McNamara, Graesser, McCarthy, & Cai, 2014).
- Dale–Chall readability formula—developed by Edgar Dale and Jeanne Chall in 1948, this formula is widely used to assess scientific research and is considered by many to be the most reliable and validated formula (Dale & Chall, 1948; School Renaissance Institute, 2000).
- ATOS/Accelerated Reader—developed by Judi and Terry Paul in 1984, this formula was designed to support the Accelerated Reader Program that is used widely in many schools (School Renaissance Institute, 2000).
- Lexile—developed by A. Jackson Stenner and Malbert Smith in the 1980s in an effort to create a formula that could assess a student's reading level and then match it to the appropriate texts (Smith, 2000; Stenner, 1999).

Each of these formulas approaches the task of measuring readability in a slightly different way, but they all share some commonalities. Each of these formulas takes a text, defines the semantic and syntactic variables, and then uses a mathematical formula to derive a number that indicates the relative reading difficulty of the text. Beyond these basic commonalities, readability formulas do have some variances that create significant differences that are helpful to understand in order to correctly apply these numbers to an analysis of complexity.

First, the formulas vary in how they define the semantic and syntactic variables. Semantics is the focus on the words in a text and is most often measured by assessing word length, word familiarity, or word frequency. Syntax focuses on the structure of language, and it is most often measured by sentence length or the average number of words in a sentence. Each formula uses a slightly different focus to ascertain the measure of these variables. For example, the Flesch–Kincaid formula uses the average number of syllables per word and the sentence length to calculate its number. On the other hand, the Coleman–Liau index uses the number of letters per word and the number of sentences overall to calculate. Because each formula is measuring something slightly different, the application of different formulas can often yield very different results. For example, *Black Ships before Troy* (1993) by Rosemary Sutcliff, which is a retelling of Homer's *Iliad*, has a Lexile level of 1300L, which is on the high end of the 9–10th-grade band or middle of the 11–12th-grade band. On the other hand, the ATOS level is 6.8, which indicates its suitability for the later part of sixth grade. At best this is a discrepancy of two or three grade levels, at worst it reveals a six-year divide. With such a wide disparity in results it is essential to never base leveling decisions on one formula alone. Consulting a variety of formulas gives a more complete picture and in the end provides a better sense of where the middle of the road rankings are. In addition to the variance that different definitions of the semantic and syntactic variables bring to formulas, it is important to note some of the inherent difficulties with these measures themselves. The reality is that the semantics and syntax of a text don't necessarily make a text harder or easier to read. This is the case because language is contextual, relying both on the denotation (the literal meaning) and connotation (the idea or feeling invoked) of the word to convey meaning. Even a simple word like "dog" (denotation) can be made much more complex if it acts as a symbol to convey the idea of loyalty (connotation). What meaning is intended depends entirely upon the context of the text. It is necessary to have the words and ideas surrounding that one word in order to ascertain if the meaning is literal or figurative. Because words really only have meaning in context, when we strip out the context things become unclear. This is just what quantitative formulas are doing: they are stripping words and sentences of their context to only measure their structure. This is one of the major limitations of the quantitative dimension in that it reduces the complexity of a text to only two variables that may or may not give a true indication of the real complexity level of a text. To illustrate this point, researchers show that if a simple sentence is analyzed it will come back with the exact same analysis if the words were jumbled and striped of their grammatical context. So a sentence like the one above, "What meaning is intended depends entirely upon the context of the text," when stripped of its grammatical context "meaning what the text entirely intended depends is context upon the of" would be assessed at the exact same quantitative level, but to a reader the second sentence is incompressible (Trollinger & Kaestle, 1986; Zakaluk & Samuels, 1988). In the end because a measure of semantic and syntactic variables only gives a portion of the picture, other dimensions must be included in any analysis to compensate.

Second, these formulas vary in how they express their level. Some formulas, like SMOG, are designed to automatically indicate at what grade level a text would be readable. These formulas are easily applied in classrooms because the number is direct and easy to interpret and apply to the context used in schools. For example, a SMOG number of 5.4 would indicate that the text is readable at a fifth grade level, or more specifically a fifth grader in their fourth month of schooling. However, other formulas, like Lexile, result in a singular number that is less directly applied. With these formulas, usually a higher number indicates a more difficult text. For example, a Lexile level of 500L would indicate the text is easier to read than one scored at a 1300L. While these numbers indicate a relative level of readability, they do not indicate a specific grade level. These numbers need a chart or translation to show how the number is interpreted grade by grade. The Core includes such a chart that indicates grade-level bands for Lexile levels. So referencing the Core chart found in Appendix A, a 500L indicates a book in the second–third-grade range and a 1300L would indicate about a 10th- or 11th-grade complexity level. Understanding how each formula expresses its level is important since some levels will need to be translated into another form so that all the formulas can be compared to one another.

Lastly, one of the main differences in the formulas is that they can vary in how much of the text they analyze. For ease of use, many of these formulas analyze only a portion of a text. Some recommend taking a sample of the text as small as 100 words. Reducing the text to a sample is really for the sake of convenience. Since most of these formulas must be applied by a computer, it is often difficult to obtain or create a full digital copy of a text, and so smaller samples are easier to access. While using a portion of the text makes these formulas easier to use, it also creates some problems. Relying only on a selection of a text can lead to an effect related to sampling error. For example, some portions of a text automatically rate lower in complexity. Dialogue, for example, almost always quantifies at a low level of complexity no matter how complex the text is overall. So if a section of dialogue is selected to represent the text, then the text will most likely come out with a lower number. In fact, a study found that analyzing only sections of a text resulted in the Lexile scores varying as much as 10 grade levels across the text (Hiebert, 2009). To combat the sampling error inherent in selecting only a portion of the text, it is recommended that several random portions are selected for analysis so that an average is better ascertained. However, the very best way to combat this error is to derive a number using the whole text. Formulas like ATOS/Accelerated Reader and Lexile have created pathways to access the full digital texts so these formulas tend to be much more accurate because they avoid these errors. However, when full digital versions of the texts are not available or the ATOS and Lexile formulas have not been applied, professionals will need to rely on formulas that use only a sampling.

Strengths of Quantitative Measures for Texts

While all readability formulas share the same intended outcome, each represents different assumptions about the purpose and application of measuring readability. Each formula was developed for its own reason. Some formulas were developed by researchers interested in attacking an intellectual problem. Others were developed to support a product. So while they may all look and act slightly differently as a whole, quantitative measures of texts do have their strengths. Readability formulas are widely available and in most cases very easy to use. This makes them a very good place to start the process of assessing text complexity. The objective and dependable information they offer create a good foundation for teachers to match texts and readers, promote independent choices, and evaluate progression.

Readability Formulas Help Match Readers and Texts

There is a sweet spot when it comes to reading. This is especially true for readers who have yet to master the decoding skills necessary for a sense of fluent, easy reading. Especially for struggling or beginning students, studies have shown that successful reading experiences come when children find that sweet spot with a text that is not too challenging but at the same time not too easy. Texts that are too complex or challenging only serve to frustrate readers. Facing this frustration can lead to poor reading experiences that can then lead to an overall negative feeling about reading itself and even a negative perception of one's own ability as a reader. These poor experiences are the ones teachers strive to avoid, so in the end matching a reader's ability level with the level of complexity of a text at just that right sweet spot is important (Allington, 2012). The quantitative dimension provides a good starting point for making this match. Good testing can fairly easily provide a solid quantitative level for almost any reader. This level can then be matched to a similar or comparable quantitative level for a text. In fact, some formulas, like Lexile, partners with publishers and test makers to create assessments that rate individual readers on the same scale as texts are rated. These two numbers (the Lexile Reader Measure and the Lexile Text Measure) are easily correlated. Even without this direct correlation most of the formulas can easily connect reader ability and text complexity. Using scores to match readers and texts is a simple way to find that sweet spot for any reader. By connecting them to that spot, the potential for successful reading experiences is heightened and it helps to ensure that students are engaging with texts that are challenging enough to stretch them but not so difficult that they are turned away.

Readability Formulas Help Students Make Independent Choices

Readability formulas are a great tool for teachers and librarians to use when matching complexity levels to reader's abilities; however, they can also be a great tool for students themselves as they self-select their own texts. As students try to navigate the complex world of texts having a benchmark through which they can judge a text's suitability for them as readers is very helpful, knowing this measure can help them locate books that would suit them. However, while these quantitative measures can be helpful to students they can also be detrimental. Students should be taught how to self-select texts on a variety of criteria. Any good reader knows that it is possible to read and enjoy things both above and below one's reading level. Even with this knowledge, there are times that schools have applied readability formulas in a way that limits or biases students in a very specific direction. These are those schools that only allow children to read texts on their level to exclusion of all other texts. For readers way above the expected reading level this bias serves to funnel them to texts that may be developmentally inappropriate or prevent them from reading and enjoying things that their peers are reading. For readers with a lower skill level this bias can serve to have them looking at texts that they would consider to be too young for them and that they don't want to read because they expect shame from their peers who are reading grown-up books. There is such a wide range of texts out there, and any action that biases a reader against a certain grouping of texts can set a reader up for some measure of failure. So when instructing students to self-select texts it is important to also help them understand that readers select texts for a variety of reasons. Finding texts that match personal interests and needs are just as important as texts that match one's reading abilities. Students need to learn how to select books based on their own preferences for genres, themes, and ideas as much as they need to know what the quantitative level of the text is. Most readers can do this quite easily and have the abilities to find texts that fit their needs, and they also know how to abandon texts that don't match those needs. For readers who don't possess these skills, relying on quantitative measures is a good place to start helping them self-monitor their reading selections. However, this should not be considered the only pathway to finding texts. Students should also be guided by knowledgeable teachers and librarians who can help them learn to select texts based on a wide range of criteria.

Readability Formulas Help Evaluate Progress toward Upper Ranges of Complexity

Fundamental to the Core is the idea that students will progress upward by engaging with increasingly complex texts each year until they reach the level where they are ready for college and the workplace. Because this progression is a fundamental part of the Core, being able to assess this progression is essential. An easy way to assess upward movement is through the use of the quantitative dimension. Teachers can use these measures to not only assess students' increasing ability, but they can also show that texts used in the classroom increase in difficultly. A list of quantitative measures of the texts used in an individual classroom or across the school can be easily matched to the charts and ranges out-lined in the Core to show movement toward the upper ranges of complexity. The quantitative dimension's simple numerical representation of complexity provides a clear and easy way to show upward progress. Remember, however, that while the Core advocates for increasingly complex texts over the years, it does not say that every text used at a specific grade level has to be at that grade level's range complexity. In fact, in several places the Core notes that a wide range of texts needs to be used to meet the standards. This means that texts with a high, low, and middle range of complexity should be used together in order to create the environment that will move students upward. The understanding of complexity as outlined by the Core should not serve as a bias toward texts; it should instead serve as an opportunity to expand the range and variety of texts used in classroom. For example, pairing a picture book with a read-aloud section from a very complex text in a first-grade classroom will serve to address the Core's expectations. Even using a complex nonfiction text in connection with an easier selection of fiction in a sixth-grade class fills the Core's expectations and also allows students to explore the immense breadth and depth of quality texts available to them.

Limitations of Quantitative Measures for Texts

The quantitative dimension with its clear and easy representation of readability is certainly a nice way to assess complexity. However, these formulas also have some important limitations. Some of these limits have already been brought to light, and it is important to consider all of these as the quantitative dimensions are applied. Some limitations are inherent in the formulas themselves. For example, while there is a wide range of readability formulas, they may or may not be easy to access. Lexile provides an online database that is freely accessible, so the Lexile level of texts that have been added to this database is quick to access. However, not all texts are in this database, so other steps are required for texts not represented such as utilizing their Lexile Analyzer, which, after registration, allows users to input up to 1,000 words of text. The biggest barrier to utilizing the analyzer is that it requires digital text so the text in a digital form has to be obtained or created. This can be a challenge if the only option is to key text into a computer.

Other limitations are inherent in the texts themselves. When you reduce a text to its semantic and syntactic variables, all texts begin to look a lot alike. However, they clearly are not. A nonfiction text has a very different purpose and approach than a fiction text. A text written in the 1800s will evidence a very different context for its grammar and language than a text written today. In his study, Hiebert (2009) illustrates this difference when he compares a novel with a Lexile score of 1100L and a biology textbook with a score of 1130L. Comparing by the Lexile level alone, these books would land pretty much at the same level of complexity. However, a closer study shows that the textbook contains more new words than a reader would be likely to encounter during one semester of learning a foreign language. Thus, the vocabulary demand of the textbook is much greater than that of the novel. Texts are certainly not created equal, and sadly the quantitative dimensions can easily mask these differences. This is why other measures such as the qualitative dimension are necessary components in assessing complexity.

Still other limitations of the formulas are inherent in readers. Teachers understand that when it comes to reading, a lot of factors come into play in the interaction between a text and its reader. A reader's interests, likes, dislikes, personality, motivation, and other characteristics are all important. These factors can often trump any quantitative ranking. For example, consider the sixth grader whose reading ability tested at a second-grade level who tackled and completed the first book in the *Harry Potter* series (an 880L, about a fifth- or sixth-grade level) because all his friends were reading it. A text clearly out of range of his level was successfully navigated just because of interest. A reader's characteristics may or may not match his or her quantitative ability. There has yet to be a magic formula invented that can perfectly match a reader with a text. Even though there are those who believe that the quantitative dimension is that magic answer, it is not. In fact, some researchers, the authors of this book among them, believe that once a reader has reached a certain level of decoding ability then readability formulas begin to lose their effectiveness entirely. Since the formulas measure the characteristics of a text that are connected with one's ability to decode language, once a reader has developed decoding skills, other skills take precedence. Once a reader knows how to decode, other skills such as interpreting textual cues or other comprehension strategies take over. Since quantitative formulas don't measure the cohesion of a text, once a reader can decode words and sentences, the formula alone does not give an accurate picture of a text. In fact, many researchers indicate that these formulas are best used for readers in fourth grade or below. This is because confidence in decoding happens in about the third grade, and once that is in place, optimal comprehension and learning are measured beyond the semantic and syntactic characteristics of a text (Zakaluk & Samuels, 1988).

Even though they have their positives the many limitations of the quantitative dimension reveal some significant issues that should not be ignored. This is why the Core has made it clear that there are other important dimensions of complexity that need to be considered in order to create a full picture of complexity. In fact, the Core explicitly states that other dimensions, particularly the qualitative dimensions, can and should override the quantitative measures. Only by considering a wider range of measures can the limitations of the quantitative dimensions be remediated. Perhaps in the future researchers will develop more robust formulas that take into account some of the current limitations we face. For example, Danielson and Lasorsa (1989) suggest that formulas should be developed that take into account the inherent changes in the complexity of language over time. Their contention is that texts such as Jane Austen's *Sense and Sensibility*, originally published in 1811, which has Lexile level of 1160L should not be compared to Jodi Picoult's *Plain Truth*, published in 2001, that has a Lexile level of 780L. Language has just changed too much in the intervening time, they contend, and making this comparison is unfair to both texts. However, until the time that formulas are created that address the quantitative dimension's limitations, assessing the complexity of a text will require the application of all three tiers of the Core's model.

Examples and Applications of Quantitative Measures

Overall, applying the quantitative dimension is a relatively easy task. The Lexile and ATOS/Accelerated Reader formulas are probably the most widely accessible, and some view them as the most accurate because they assess the whole text in most cases. Both measures have free online databases that contain a wide range of texts. For texts not in their databases, both provide a free service where digital texts can be input for analysis.

Lexile: https://lexile.com/
Lexile Analyzer: https://lexile.com/analyzer/ (registration required)
ATOS/Accelerated Reader Book Finder: http://www.arbookfind.com
ATOS Analyzer: http://www.renaissance.com/products/accelerated-reader/atos-analyzer

Other formulas are easily calculated using free online tools:

Free Text Readability Consensus Calculator: Gives numbers from seven popular formulas including Flesch–Kincaid formula, SMOG, Gunning fog index, Coleman–Liau index, and Automated Readability index:

http://www.readabilityformulas.com/free-readability-formula-tests.php

OKAPI!: Calculates the Dale–Chall readability index:

http://www.lefthandlogic.com/htmdocs/tools/okapi/okapi.php

Readability Calculator: Calculates the Flesch–Kincaid grade level, SMOG, Coleman–Liau index, and Automated Readability index:

http://www.online-utility.org/english/readability_test_and_improve.jsp

Text Readability Scores: Calculates the Flesch–Kincaid grade level, SMOG, Coleman–Liau index, Gunning fog index, and Automated Readability index:

https://readability-score.com/

Words Count: Readability: Provides numbers for the Flesch–Kincaid grade level, SMOG, and Gunning fog index:

http://www.wordscount.info/wc/jsp/clear/analyze_readability.jsp

Using these resources an analysis of a text on the quantitative dimension might look something like this:

Half a Chance by Cynthia Lord. Scholastic Press, 2014.
    Flesch–Kincaid grade level: 3.7
    SMOG: 4.1 (fourth grade)
    Coleman–Liau index: 6 (sixth grade)
    Gunning fog index: 5.6 (text scale, fairly easy to read)
    Dale–Chall readability index: 7.13 (ninth or tenth grade)
    ATOS/Accelerated Reader: interest level: middle grade, grade level: 4.5
    Lexile: 690L (second/third grade CCSS equivalent)

These numbers represent quite a wide range of grade levels from second to tenth. However, the most common numbers seem to settle around the fourth grade. So a final analysis would place this text at a fourth- or fifth-grade complexity measured by the quantitative dimension.

The Qualitative Dimension

The second part of the three-tiered model of text complexity is the qualitative dimension. This dimension is designed to consider the structure and cohesion of a text. The qualitative level works to assess the parts, ideas, structures, and characteristics that make a text complex. This variable defines the characteristics of a text beyond the semantic and syntactic variables that holistically create the textual form. Because texts vary in their approach, purpose, expectations, and outcomes, each text has its own characteristics that make it more or less complex. Additionally, texts also have an artistic sensibility and so they must also conform to the rules and patterns that go into making this art form. All these elements that make up the qualitative dimension need to be considered when assessing complexity. Some of these characteristics and rules are tangible and they can be easily outlined and discussed. But when it comes to the qualitative dimension there are also intangibles that can't be concretely identified. These "you know it when you see it" characteristics just exist and seem to come to light when texts are analyzed by those who have had a lot of professional experience. All these factors make the qualitative dimension impossible to measure without human intervention. This part of the model requires a critical look at a text with a trained eye.

Even with the intangible aspects, the qualitative dimension can be structured to allow for a more concrete analysis. The Core offers one such outline in Appendix A as it outlines the four factors it considers to be part of the qualitative dimension. This outline provides a good foundation from which qualitative analysis can begin. However, the Core's broad strokes can be added to and refined in order to create a more comprehensive construction for qualitative analysis. By building on the factors in the Core, an overall assessment of the characteristics and structures of a text provides a comprehensive look at qualitative complexity. While engaging in this comprehensive analysis it is important to consider the following elements that make it very different than a quantitative analysis.

Qualitative Analysis is Assessed along a Continuum

Unlike the quantitative dimension that strives to pinpoint a text's complexity down to a very specific number, even going so far as noting a particular month of schooling, the qualitative characteristics are less exact. An analysis of qualitative characteristics will only reveal a text's relative location along a continuum of complexity. This range can vary from lower level complexity to a higher level. The overall intent here is to show approximately where a text falls in relation to the low and high ends of that range. The result of qualitative analysis will only then be a general idea of the range of complexity; it will never offer a specific grade or age level.

Qualitative Analysis Considers Text Type

In a quantitative analysis the resulting numbers are meant to be compared to each other, no matter the type of text being analyzed. However, since the qualitative dimension considers a range of complexity, it is important to take into account how that analysis is impacted by the text type. For example, a picture book is almost always going to be less complex than a classic adult novel. These two extremes might constitute two ends of the complexity spectrum on the quantitative side. However, in a qualitative analysis it is unfair to compare one text type to another extreme. Because the qualitative characteristics create a wide range of purposes and functions, the qualitative analysis should also consider these separate and distinct types. So with qualitative analysis, one consideration should be not only for where the text falls on a continuum of different texts, but also where it would fall on the continuum compared to similar texts. For each text a consideration for where it falls from the range of beginning readers to difficult adult texts is then balanced by a consideration of its relative complexity against other texts that are the same (i.e., beginning readers, picture books, chapter books, etc.). These two complexity ranges can vary widely. In comparing a picture book to an adult book the complexity of the picture book would be on the lower end. However, if this same picture book was compared to other picture books then it might be found that this book was of a higher complexity than most picture books. Thus in the final result it might be found that the book is of high complexity because it was compared to other similar texts, and from that viewpoint it was found to be more complex.

Qualitative Analysis Will Not Always Reveal the Same Level of Complexity for All Characteristics and Structures

While quantitative analysis results in one number that represents the whole text, a qualitative analysis often shows different levels of complexity depending upon which characteristics or structures are being assessed. The construction of a text and how a creator puts together all the characteristics and structures that make it up will not always result in an equal level of complexity on all measures. For example, a creator may make a text with a lot of figurative langue so the text is very complex when it comes to the detail of its style and language. However, the same text might go into very little depth with its theme by sticking to only the most commonly known ideas, so in this case the text would be less complex as measured by that structure. To get a complete picture of qualitative complexity each characteristic and structure should be measured alone, then using these individual ranking a complete picture of the overall complexity level can be obtained. Additionally, knowing both a rating for the individual characteristic and structure and the text as a whole becomes especially significant when the task dimension of complexity is added later on.

   With this basic understanding of the elements of qualitative analysis, the first step in applying this model is to assess the qualitative elements of a text and to define the characteristics creating complexity in all texts. After defining these characteristics the next step is to apply these characteristics to the structures that make up a text.

Textual Characteristics and Complexity

Texts are created using a number of characteristics that impact their complexity. These characteristics are analyzed in order to ascertain a calculation for the qualitative dimension. There are six qualitative characteristics of texts: detail, development, depth, didacticism, design, and dialogue.

Detail

Textual detail relates to the particular descriptions and language used in the text. Here complexity is gauged by a sense of the number and level of details used to convey the textual structures. The amount of detail used is one of the most important indicators of complexity because it engages all the text structures. Also textual detail is an important part of the Core itself. The standards focus on textual evidence and students' ability to use supporting detail to analyze and make inferences from texts. Thus understanding how detailed a text is connects not only to the qualitative dimension, but it also impacts the task dimension which will be discussed later. Overall, the less detailed a text is, the lower it will be on the complexity scale. The assessment first focuses on language when considering detail. Extensive detail often makes use of complex and figurative language, so considering how much figurative language is used in a text shows a level of detail complexity. Additionally, when considering detail it is important to assess if the details serve to make the text more clear or if they tend to make the text more symbolic or ambiguous in some way. For example, figurative language that is used to convey symbols is much more complex than figurative language that is used to make only basic comparisons. The way detail is conveyed can also be very important. If the detail is being conveyed in a conversational or explicit way then the text will be less complex than if the detail is expressed from an academic or scholarly stance. Lastly, especially when considering children's literature it is important to note that detail refers not only to language but also to visual representations. Note that the level of detail of artwork or illustrations should also be part of the qualitative analysis of illustrated texts.

To assess the characteristic of detail consider the following questions: How much detail is used to convey the text structures? How much figurative language is used in the text? What is the purpose of the details? Do the details make the text clearer or ambiguous? How are the details being conveyed? What level of detail is contained in the visual structures of the text?

Development

Textual development is the characteristic that connects all of the pieces of a text together as it progresses from start to finish. Here complexity is gauged by a sense of the ambiguity, connectedness, and precision of the textual structures over the course of the text. All texts must have a beginning, middle, and an end. Developmental characteristics reveal themselves as a text works to get from one of these points to the other. For some texts the development from point to point is direct and clear, and these texts would be considered less complex. On the other hand, if the development is convoluted or twisted in any way then the text is going to be more complex. For example, if a text has a character that develops simply through a problem to a climax then the text will be less complex than if the character revisits pervious emotional states or has added problems that also must be resolved as part of the character development. Any development that is unexpected or unusual overall tends to make the text more complex. In children's literature these kinds of uncommon developmental progressions are oftentimes expressed in an unexpected structure or organization. Creators of texts often use different kinds of structures in order to help readers navigate an unconventional development. For example, flashbacks that show a development outside of a standard chronological order can be put in a different font. Additionally, if the creator chooses to address two different points of view that make the development more complex, then characters' names may be put at the beginning of a chapter to indicate this change. These organizational structures can indicate that the development is uncommon and thus indicate a higher level of complexity. However, if too many of these structures are used then they can also lower complexity because they give the reader the needed clues to navigate the text, thus making it less difficult. So assessing these features includes evaluating how these structures support the navigation of the text and how that support raises or lowers the complexity.

To assess the characteristic of development, consider the following questions: How does the creator of the text get where he or she is trying to go? Do the authors move directly from one point to another or are there twists and turns? Are there any features or text structures that guide a reader through an unconventional approach? How do these features support the overall text?

Depth

Textual depth is the characteristic that addresses the complexity of the thought or intent of the text. Here complexity is gauged by a sense of how profound the text is. The Core expresses the characteristic of depth as levels of meaning. The intent here is to determine how many layers of insight a text has, or how many questions a text tries to answer. Here the expectation is that the more levels of meaning there are and the more questions are addressed, the more complex the text becomes. But depth goes beyond just the layers of meaning; it also has to do with how distinctive that meaning is. An approach that is fresh, new, or addresses little-known insights brings a greater level of complexity to the text than if the text just expresses everyday thoughts. A text can also have distinctive depth when it uses an unconventional structure or approach. When something unexpected is encountered in a text design, organization, or structure, the text's complexity is raised. When considering depth it is often important to take into account a text's genre or format. Genre plays a big role in the way a creator constructs a text. Remember that not all texts share the same level of complexity, so the need to compare both across and within formats also impacts the analysis of genres. For example, if the comparison was between a piece of literary fiction that debates a complex social issue and a straightforward family story then the depth scale would certainly be tipped to the piece of literary fiction. However, if two family stories were compared then the difference in depth would be shown more vividly for one or the other. This effect is especially true with certain genres, such as science fiction. Some consider science fiction in general to have less depth than, say, a work of realistic fiction. Comparing across genres is not always accurate since they have different purposes, so in a case like this comparison with other works of science fiction would give a more accurate picture of the true depth of a work. Lastly, as noted in the discussion of detail, with children's literature it is important to note that depth refers not only to language but also to visual representations. Illustrations or graphics in a text should be judged for depth right along with the text.

To assess the characteristic of depth consider the following questions: How profound is the text? What kinds of questions does the text raise? How many layers of meaning do the language and illustrations have? How fresh and new is the approach? Is there something unexpected about the text? How does this text compare to other texts both of different and of the same genre? What depth do the illustrations give to the text?

Didacticism

Textual didacticism is the characteristic that shows the overall purpose of a text. Here complexity is gauged by a sense of the instructive purposes of the text. The Core notes that an explicitly stated purpose makes a text less complex than an obscured or indirect purpose. Those texts with an explicitly stated purpose most often tend to inform or instruct. Texts with the intent to teach or instruct often show high levels of didacticism. Highly didactic books tend to be at a lower level of complexity. This is because texts with an instructional purpose tend to strip out figurative language and other details to such an extent that they become less complex. Additionally, instructional texts often include many developmental structures designed to help readers navigate the text. These structures, such as bolding and defining difficult vocabulary, or explicitly conveying a plot point by explaining to the reader what is expected, tend to lower the complexity of a text. Additionally, highly didactic texts may not only show a lower level of complexity, but can also impact the quality of the text structures. In general, highly didactic books also tend to be of lesser quality in the long run. Think, for example, about the old Dick and Jane basal readers by Gray and Sharp. While highly purposeful in their teaching approach, these texts are often considered of lesser quality because of their dry story line and stilted use of language. On the other hand consider Dr. Seuss's early readers including *The Cat in the Hat*, texts that are generally considered to be of much higher quality than Dick and Jane. Seuss's focus on story, his use of playful language, and his engaging characters and plot raise quality while at the same time eliminating any overt didacticism of the text. As teachers, part of our purpose in assessing texts is to not only look at the complexity level but also assess quality, an issue that will be addressed more in upcoming chapters. But for the purpose of this discussion it is important to understand that since teachers will only want to use the highest quality texts in the classroom, didacticism can also be a good indicator of quality as well as complexity.

To assess the characteristic of didacticism consider the following questions: What is the intended purpose of the book? How explicit is that purpose? Does an instructional purpose reduce the complexity of the text? What structures assist in navigating the text? How do these structures convey the texts' purpose?

Design

Textual design is the characteristic that addresses the complexity of the structures of the text including the font, format, organization, and illustrations. Here complexity is gauged by a sense of how complex the text is physically. Design plays a large role in text complexity. How a text is constructed and laid out can make it harder or easier to read. For example, texts with a very dense text block with little white space and a very small font size are going to be more complex than a text that's in a large font with lots of room around it. One need only look at texts of increasing complexity to see how this works. Beginning readers have large font sizes and lots of white space. Novels for more advanced readers have a smaller font and less room around the text block. The organization of a text can also impact complexity. If a text is organized in an expected way, such as dividing the plot up into chapters, then the text is going to be less complex than if it was organized is some unusual way. For children's literature, illustrations will also play a big role in the design considerations. The visual elements of a text are very important and should be considered when addressing all the characteristics of the text, especially those of detail and depth. However, the purpose of the illustrations should also be considered as part of the design characteristic. Illustrations and graphics in a text can serve very different purposes. Some illustrations are there to just add visual interest and do very little other than reiterate the words directly. Other types of graphics add to or extend the text beyond itself. These types of illustrations add depth to the text, and in most cases they must also be "read" in order to gain the full meaning of the text. In this way illustrations can extend or enhance the setting, characters, or plot; they can provide an alternative viewpoint or interpretation; or they can even tell another story altogether. Visual elements that extend the text beyond its anticipated scope or those that add additional information to the text will tend to make the text more complex.

To assess the characteristic of design consider the following questions: How is the text constructed? How large is the font? How dense is the text? How is the text organized? Is the organization unusual? What role do the graphics in the text play? How do the illustrations support the words? What kind of information do the illustrations give? Do the graphics or illustrations make the text unique in any way?

Dialogue

Textual dialogue is the characteristic that connects texts to things outside itself. Here complexity is gauged by a sense of how the text engages, extends, or matches with elements outside of the one individual text. Since texts do not exist in isolation, it is necessary to consider how other forces impact complexity. As Keene and Zimmerman (2007) note, texts make a lot of connections. These connections can include those made between the text and the reader, the text and other texts, and the text and the world outside the text. The more connections a text can make the higher the complexity level will be. For example, if a text can only make a connection between readers and their lived experiences the text would be less complex than if the text could connect to the life of readers, other texts, and an important world event. Of foremost consideration when assessing complexity is to consider how a text impacts a reader. The Core addresses this issue when it addresses a text's knowledge demands. Almost every text expects that readers will come with some kind of background knowledge or experience. Many texts assume that a reader will have the necessary background when he or she approaches the text. Texts that make these assumptions will become more complex for those readers who do not have this background. Kelly Gallagher (2009) gives one example of how this works when he includes an example of a paragraph that outlines the events of a baseball game. Because of its specialized terminology and slang, this paragraph is very complex for an individual who does not already have an intimate knowledge of baseball. So what the text expects the reader to know and what the reader brings to the text impact its complexity. This element connects with the reader dimension, which will be discussed later, because the level of knowledge brought to a text varies between individuals. However, when assessing the text alone it is possible to make some general judgments about the knowledge demands of a text. A text that requires a lot of background knowledge that would have to have been built from sources outside the text will usually be more complex than texts that provide that background. Additionally, texts that exhibit diversity in any of the text structures, including plot, setting, or point of view that is beyond the experience of most readers will also be more complex. Texts that extend readers' experiences will most likely also make connections with other texts and the world at large. The more a text can extend beyond itself to address topics in the same or different ways than other texts or to tackle important issues happening around the world, the more complex a text will be. Those texts that have a distinctive point of view or that capture an idea that is unusual in comparison to other texts or other world views will also be more complex. These kinds of connections are an important part of the Core, since several of the standards ask for students to make just these kinds of connections. Particularly, Anchor Standard 9 asks students to compare texts that address similar topics or themes. So identifying and using this text characteristic will be important not only in assessing complexity but also in identifying texts to use in classroom tasks that address the standards.

To assess the characteristic of dialogue consider the following questions: What kind of knowledge does this text expect a reader to bring? How does the text match or extend a reader's experience? How similar is this text to other texts? What kind of dialogue can this text have with other texts? What world, social, or other extended issues does this text address? What kinds of connections can be made between the text and readers or the text and the world?

Textual Structures and Complexity

To make a text, creators use a number of standard structures. Considering the six characteristics that were outlined earlier allows professionals to assess the way a creator applies these structures to make a complex text. For example, an assessment of detail will look at all the structures, from plot to characters, to see how each detail is expressed in each one. As with the characteristics it is possible that one structure will show a deeper level of complexity than another. For example, it is possible that in a work of fantasy a creator will go into a great deal of depth in describing a setting while at the same time he or she may use less depth for the characters. Here an individual assessment by each characteristic with each structure may be needed in order to obtain an overall balanced assessment of the complexity of a text. While it is certainly possible to go through each structural element to assess it on each characteristic, this exacting approach may or may not be necessary. The exactness needed in the assessment will depend on the how and where the text is being used. An anchor text, for example, that will be used throughout a lesson will most likely need a closer analysis than a text that will only be used as an accessory text. Additionally, how extensive the assessment of the qualitative characteristics is will depend on individual needs and circumstances. If, for example, a quick assessment is called for then less comparison will be possible, but if more time is available then more attention can be paid. In general it is recommended that all the textual structures should be considered in conjunction with all the textual characteristics. To show how this might be done, let's first look a little more closely at the text structures. While the traditional text structures are most likely familiar and this examination will be a review for most, looking at these elements in the context of complexity is certain to add dimension and insight to the application of these structures. While the language to describe text structures is most often used in the context of fiction, these structural elements relate equally to nonfiction. Even though words like plot, setting, and character have probably not been considered in connection with informational texts, the reality is that their context does apply to all texts. In this context and with these definitions, consider that all texts, no matter their format or context, share these same structural elements.

Plot

Plot is defined as the sequence of events in a text that take it from beginning, to middle, to end. Plot is essentially what happens in a text. Plot can be represented by the chronological order of events as might be found in fiction or a work of biographical nonfiction to a topical organization that might be found in an informational text.

To assess the complexity of plot through the textual characteristics consider the following questions: How detailed is the plot? How does the plot develop? Is it linear or does it jump around? How does the plot create depth of thought or purpose? How didactic is the plot? How much of the plot is intended to be instructional? What design elements (including illustrations) does the creator use to express the plot? How does the plot connect to the reader, other texts, or the world?

Setting

Setting is defined as when and where the text takes place. The setting can be entirely imaginary as in a work of fiction, or it can be entirely connected to a real time or place as it would be in an informational book. Some texts will have more than one setting; others will maintain the same setting throughout.

To assess the complexity of setting through the textual characteristics consider the following questions: How detailed is the setting? How does the setting develop? Is there more than one setting or is the same one maintained throughout? How does the setting create depth of thought or purpose? How much depth does the setting offer to the other textual structures? How does the setting impact the instructional intent of the text? What if any design elements (including illustrations) does the creator use to express the setting? How does the setting connect to the reader, other texts, or the world?

Character

Character is defined as the people or things that exist in a text. Characters can be real, as they would be in a biography, or imagined, as they would be in a fictional text. Characters can be human or they can be animals or things. Nonhuman characters can exist both in fiction and nonfiction texts. A nonfiction book about a scientist studying frogs will have just as many animal characters as a picture book with personified bears.

To assess the complexity of character through the textual characteristics consider the following questions: How detailed are the characters? How do the characters develop? Is their development straightforward or is it multifaceted? How much depth is given to the development of both primary and secondary characters? How do the characters create depth of thought or purpose? How much depth do the characters offer to the other textual structures? How didactic are the characters? Do the characters convey an instructional purpose? What design elements (including illustrations) does the creator use to extend the characters? How do the characters connect to the reader, other texts, or the world?

Point of View

Point of view is defined as the perspective through which the text expresses its ideas. The point of view can come from the characters themselves or it can be expressed in the agenda or intended point of the author. Point of view also contains the intent or even bias of the author in some cases. This is especially true for works of nonfiction where authors have a particular vision or purpose to convey.

To assess the complexity of point of view through the textual characteristics consider the following questions: How detailed is the point of view? How does the point of view develop? Are there multiple points of view or just one? How much depth is given to the development of these points of view? How does the point of view create depth of thought or purpose? How much depth does the point of view offer to the other textual structures? How didactic is the point of view? Does the point of view convey an instructional purpose? What design elements (including illustrations) does the creator use to extend the point of view? How does the point of view connect to the reader, other texts, or the world?

Theme

Theme is defined as the truth or message that the text is attempting to address. The theme tells the reader what the text is about. Theme expresses the meaning or objective of the text. Texts can have both primary and secondary themes. Themes can also be explicit and stated purposely or they can be implicit and only discerned by an individual reader.

To assess the complexity of theme through the textual characteristics, consider the following questions: How detailed is the theme? How does the theme develop? Are there multiple themes or just one? How much depth is given to the development of the theme? How does the theme create depth of thought or purpose? How much depth does the theme offer to the other textual structures? How didactic is the theme? Does the theme convey an instructional purpose? What design elements (including illustrations) does the creator use to extend the theme? How does the theme connect to the reader, other texts, or the world?

Conflict

Conflict is defined as the essential problem or issue that the text addresses. The four main types of conflict are identified as man versus man, man versus nature, man versus society, and man versus self. Conflict is what creates tension in the text. Both fiction and well-written nonfiction will have this tension; without it the overall effect is a flatness that makes texts dull.

To assess the complexity of conflict through the textual characteristics consider the following questions: What type of conflict does the text have? Is there more than one main type of conflict? How detailed is the conflict? How does the conflict develop? It is straightforward or intricate? How much depth is given to the development of the conflict? How does the conflict create depth of thought or purpose? How much depth does the conflict offer to the other textual structures? How didactic is the conflict? Does the conflict intend to convey an instructional purpose? What design elements (including illustrations) does the creator use to extend the conflict? How does the conflict connect to the reader, other texts, or the world?

Style

Style is defined as the way in which the creator conveys his or her purpose. There are four basic styles for texts: argumentative, descriptive, persuasive, and narrative. Each style has its own conventions and approach. All will use the text structures in a different way to convey their message, and the techniques the author uses will be the things that convey the style. For visual forms also style applies; however, the number and extent of styles will vary depending upon the media used for any illustrations.

To assess the complexity of style through the textual characteristics consider the following questions: What is the basic textual style? What is the basic visual style? How much detail does the author use to convey his or her style? How does the style develop over the course of the text? What depth does the style add to the text? How does the style create depth of thought or purpose? How much depth does the style offer to the other textual structures? Is the style intended to be didactic? Is the style inherently instructional? What design elements (including illustrations) does the creator use to convey the style to the reader? How does the style connect to the reader, other texts (in the same or different style), or the world?

Tone

Tone is defined as the attitude that the creator makes for the reader. The tone is conveyed through the creator's choice of style and how he or she decides to approach the purpose of the work. Tones intend to convey some type of emotion or basic feeling, from happy to sad or serious to comic. Tone is conveyed both in words and pictures. Thus, both text and illustrations can have a tone and this tone can be the same or different from one another.

To assess the complexity of tone through the textual characteristics consider the following questions: How detailed is the tone? How does the tone develop? Are there multiple tones or just one? Does the text and illustrations have the same or different tones? How much depth is given to the development of the tone? How does the tone create depth of thought or purpose? How much depth does the tone offer to the other textual structures? How didactic is the tone? Does the tone carry an instructional purpose? What design elements (including illustrations) does the creator use to extend the tone? How does the tone connect to the reader, other texts, or the world?

Language

Language is defined as the denotation and connotation expressed by the creator's word choice. Words convey a literal meaning in addition to feelings and ideas that extend beyond the primary meaning. The literal meaning is discovered in a dictionary. The connotation is expressed through the use of figurative language. The use of imagery, personification, metaphor, motif, allegory, irony, symbolism, and other figurative devices are part of a text's language structures. In addition to word meaning, language also relates to the form of language. The language structure also includes the use of dialects or language expressive of a particular part of the world.

To assess the complexity of language through the textual characteristics consider the following questions: How complex are the denotations of the words used? How complex are the connotations of words used? Are any dialects or other language forms used? How detailed is the language, particularly the figurative language? How does the language develop? How does the language create depth of thought or purpose? How much depth does the language offer to the other textual structures? How didactic is the language? Does the language convey an instructional purpose? What design elements (including illustrations) does the creator use to extend the language? How does the language connect to the reader, other texts, or the world?

Knowledge Requirements

All texts require some form of background knowledge of the reader. In order to fully comprehend a text, readers need to have the knowledge the text requires. This does not mean that a text cannot be read or enjoyed without this knowledge; it only means that the text will be more comprehensible with it. Knowledge requirements are one structural element that is explicitly outlined in the Core.

To assess the complexity of the knowledge requirements through the textual characteristics consider the following questions: How detailed are the knowledge requirements? How much does the text expect the reader to already know? How much knowledge does the text allow the reader to develop? Are there multiple knowledge requirements or just one? How much depth of knowledge does the text require the reader to have? How do the knowledge requirements create depth of thought or purpose? How much depth do the knowledge requirements offer to the other textual structures? Can the knowledge required be obtained through instruction? What design elements (including illustrations) does the creator use to extend the knowledge requirements? How do the knowledge requirements connect to the reader, other texts, or the world?

Construction

While the other text structures are inherent in the way the words are put together on the page, construction is inherent in the physical packaging of the text. Construction deals with all the physical aspects of a text including the font, the layout of the text on the page, the way the text is organized, the illustrations, and other packaging elements including the binding, paper quality, and any other ways texts are constructed.

To assess the complexity of the construction through the textual characteristics consider the following questions: What design elements does the creator use to make the text? How much detail was put into the construction? How detailed are the fonts? How many fonts are there? How does the layout support the text's ability to develop the other text structures (i.e., plot, setting, character, etc.)? How is the text organized? Are there multiple organizational constructions or just one? How much depth does the construction (such as font, layout, organization, or illustrations) bring to the text? Does the construction add to the depth of thought or purpose? How does the construction interact with the other textual structures? How does the construction connect to the reader, other texts, or the world?

Strengths of Qualitative Measures for Texts

A qualitative assessment of texts provides a broad and comprehensive view of a text. This is the greatest strength of the qualitative dimension: it takes into account every element that makes up a text. This offers a more complete view of the text than that offered by quantitative measures. Because texts are so much more than their semantic and syntactic variables, in order to attain a sense of how the cohesion, purpose, and the functions of a text's characteristics impact complexity it must be assessed on this dimension. At the same time, the qualitative dimensions provide a more comprehensive measure; it provides a more granular one as well. Texts are made up of many different characteristics and structures, and not all of these will show equal levels of complexity. Having the ability to assess each characteristic and structure separately for complexity is especially important for teaching texts. Certain parts or structures of the texts will connect well with certain instructional purposes, and knowing the complexity level of each of these will allow for texts to be better matched to instructional outcomes. For example, Anchor Standard 2 asks students to identify a central idea or theme, so to apply this standard in the classroom, a text that shows a certain level of complexity on the thematic structure would be an ideal choice. For this, standard complexity in plot or character may be less important of a consideration. Qualitative measures allow both a comprehensive and granular assessment of a text that gives professionals much more useful information than the quantitative dimension.

Limitations of Qualitative Measures for Texts

The qualitative dimension certainly adds to the vision of text complexity. However, that does not mean that this dimension is perfect. One of the most significant limitations of the qualitative dimension is that it is rather subjective. Unlike the quantitative dimension, which provides an exact number, assessment of the qualitative characteristics and structures is up for debate. While there will certainly be some consensus, it is possible that two individuals will come up with two different assessments. Individual interpretations and applications can create a wide range in understandings of complexity levels.

To address this limitation, it is suggested that professionals bring in others to help assess texts. Discussion can help everyone come to a shared consensus on a complexity level. However, it is also important to note that even though consensus is good, a lot of assessment will remain up to one's individual teaching needs. As noted, the Core puts a premium on teacher professional judgment, something that is particularly important for the qualitative dimension. As long as teachers can concretely articulate their assessment and connect it to the standards being taught, even individual assessments will have validity.

Another limitation of the qualitative dimension is that it does require some experience to apply. To understand how the characteristics and structures of a text work, professionals will need to have at least a basic understanding of how these elements interact. Happily, most teaching professionals already have this experience built from previous coursework or practice, so this limitation should not be significant for most. However, experience also comes into play in another way. In order to make accurate comparisons between texts, one must have a lot of experience with a lot of different texts. An assessment of several of the characteristics depends not only upon an understanding of an individual text, but also on an understanding of how a text fits in with others in the same format or genre. Because of this, a wide and broad understanding of all types of texts that can be used to support the Core is essential. This limitation may already be addressed for most professionals; however, there are a select few who may need to broaden their reading background in order to make quality assessments on the qualitative dimension.

One of the most significant limitations of the qualitative dimension is that it takes time. This is the case because to truly assess a text, it must have been read. This makes it harder to assess longer texts because the assessor first has to read the entire text before he or she can engage in an assessment. However, the focus here is children's literature so a great majority of these texts are brief and can be easily read. Additionally, this limitation can be addressed through constant reading, which will also build the broad experience professionals need with a wide range of formats and genres. It is suggested that when a text is completed, a few brief moments should be set aside for taking notes on the complexity of all the characteristics and structures. This practice will build the arsenal of texts that professionals can draw on. Online systems like Goodreads.com (https://www.goodreads.com/) and Shelfari. com (http://www.shelfari.com/) that allow readers to keep databases of books read with places for comments and other ratings prove to be good sources for teachers to store this information for later consumption. Additionally professionals can rely on each other to divide and conquer. One need not read every text when others can join in the reading.

Even though reading an entire text is recommended it is not always necessary; a great deal of information about texts is available online. Accessing this information is easy, and it can provide a great deal of information that can help professionals to assess a basic level of complexity. Book reviews from professional sources like the *School Library Journal* (http://www.slj.com/), *Publishers Weekly* (http://www.publishersweekly.com/), *Kirkus Reviews* (https://www.kirkusreviews.com/), and *Booklist* (http://www.booklistonline.com) are good options. These sources can provide some information about one reviewer's perception of the characteristics and structures of a text. Additionally, there are a great many nonprofessional review sources. Sources like Amazon, Barnes and Noble, Goodreads, and Shelfari allow users to post their own reviews. These reviews are often more comprehensive than professional reviews, and they also provide a wide range of viewpoints. Other personal views can be obtained from blogs or other online sources. Searching the title or author of a text in an Internet search engine will bring up these sources. Lastly, publishers will often provide a wide range of information about their texts. Looking at publisher's websites or printed sources can also provide a wide range of information that can be used to assess complexity. While not an entire substitute for actually reading the text, all of these sources can help provide what is needed for a quick qualitative assessment.

Examples and Applications of Qualitative Measures

Since the qualitative dimension is less exacting than the quantitative, the application of this measure can take a lot of different forms. There are a wide variety of charts and rubrics available online that can assist teachers in making this assessment. One such structure will be offered here; however, this by no means intends to indicate that this is the only method. Professionals are encouraged to seek out the method that best suits their needs, no matter if that is the one here in this book, others, or the one they create on their own. All these methods will be compatible. Since all methods will be based in the qualitative dimension of the Core and connected to the characteristics and structures of texts, each one will draw on the same theory. In the end, many may find a combination of methods to be useful or different methods may be used in different situations. For the purpose of this text, a qualitative evaluation looks at each of the textual characteristics and how they are manifested in the textual structures. After assessing the structures, an overall assessment of the range of complexity for each characteristic can be determined. As noted before this assessment will vary across characteristics and structures since no two elements need be equally complex. From there overall and individual assessments can be placed into a complexity range, based on the questions offered earlier or using a rubric such as this:

	Beginning Complexity	Midrange Complexity	Higher Complexity
Detail	Simple, basic detail that is not ambiguous.	A more advanced level of detail that only contains a mild level of ambiguity.	Sophisticated, complex detail that has a great deal of ambiguity.
Development	Direct and clear progression with an expected approach.	Mostly direct and clear, but shows some ambiguity in its progression with a somewhat unexpected approach.	Indirect and ambiguous progression with an unexpected approach.
Didacticism	Has a clear and explicit purpose and is structured for easy navigation.	Purpose is not conspicuous but is still relatively easy to discern. Some structures help navigation.	Obscured or vague purpose with structures that complicate navigation.
Depth	Light text with a single level of meaning raising few questions in a standard approach.	A moderate text with several levels of meaning raising a few questions that have a few new approaches.	Profound text with multiple levels of meaning raising many questions that has a fresh and unconventional approach.
Design	Basic construction, layouts, and font with an organization that supports the text with no surprises.	Higher level of construction and layout with some complex fonts with an organization that supports the text but has a few surprises.	Indispensable construction with complex fonts and layout with an organization that is integral to the text with many surprises.
Dialogue	Limited connections to other experiences, texts, and ideas.	Some connections to other experiences, texts, and ideas.	Extensive connections to other experiences, texts, and ideas.

After each characteristic is assessed an overall complexity range for the entire text can be determined. Notes on the comparison and assessment can be recorded in a chart such as the one below. Using this format as a basis the analysis of a text on the qualitative dimension might look something like this:

Half a Chance by Cynthia Lord. Scholastic Press, 2014.

	Commentary	Assessment
Detail	Extensive detail in setting descriptions, because they are described as if taking a photograph. Tone is friendly and typical of a family story, but is added to because of the detailed language. Uses quite a lot detail in the language with extensive figurative language (metaphors, many connected to photography), but it is unambiguous. Secondary characters (associated family members) lack in details.	Midrange complexity
Development	Organized in a very straightforward manner. Characters develop in small ways as the plot progresses, some secondary characters are not developed extensively. Set in one place and progresses day-to-day over the course of a summer. Plot development is expected. Only one point of view, everything seen through the eyes of the main character.	Beginning complexity
Didacticism	Purpose is to explore the life and thoughts of the main character; reader must connect the thoughts and come to their own conclusions. Theme is about family and learning to move on; the theme is woven in throughout and is not didactic in any way.	Higher complexity
Depth	Style is narrative in nature, not much depth to that form as plot and setting are simple. Not a lot of knowledge required, almost all is basic universal experiences. However, there is greater depth in the theme as the main character's separation from her father contrasts with her friend's gradual loss of his grandmother. This also adds to depth in the conflict which comes as the two relationships are understood better.	Midrange complexity
Design	Larger text font with more white space, text blocks, no other font, or construction issues not typical of a chapter book, no illustrations.	Beginning complexity
Dialogue	Conflict is not out of the ordinary; flow and format follow traditional lines for realistic fiction. Connects to other texts with themes of conservation and family loss. Has connections to photography as an art form.	Midrange complexity

Combining this information, this text seems to come out at a midrange complexity level, about fourth or fifth grade overall. The theme and language are particularly complex structures, so this text would be ideally used in connection to standards that address those elements.

The Reader and Task Dimensions

The first two elements the Core uses to judge text complexity relate to the text itself. These elements measure a level of complexity for only the textual elements. The quantitative and qualitative dimensions are designed to consider the text in some kind of vacuum where only that work exists. However, the act of reading requires something more than just the text itself. Firstly, it requires a reader. The interaction between text and reader creates a whole new context by which to judge the complexity of a text because oftentimes what a reader brings to a text is just as important as what the text itself contains. Secondly, in classroom situations texts also interact with the tasks they are being used for. How tasks are constructed and applied can also impact complexity, making it another important consideration. Because both readers and tasks play an important part in complexity, the Core wisely places them at the foundation of its three-tiered model of text complexity. These elements are underrepresented in the discussion of the model in the Core. The Core documentation leaves them mostly up to professional judgment. However, these two dimensions are so important for assessing complexity that it is important to fully understand their scope and application.

The Reader Dimension

Without readers, texts would be lifeless works of art. It is a reader who brings life to a text. Reader response theorists like Louise Rosenblatt (1995) show how reading is an important interaction between a reader and a text. Through this interaction both the text itself and the reader play a role in making meaning. Because meaning making happens when a reader engages with a text and fundamental to the Core is teaching students to make meaning from texts, the reader becomes a very important consideration. Since the ultimate goal is to understand complex texts, as Anchor Standard 10 requires, it is understandable that both the text's characteristics and the reader's characteristics need to be considered when determining a text's complexity. Additionally, while it is possible to assess the complexity of a text using both the quantitative and qualitative elements only, that analysis lacks some significant value until it is applied to a reader. If readers are expected to advance through increasing levels of complexity, then it is not only significant to understand where the texts are but also at what state the readers themselves are. The understanding of a reader's beginning and subsequent stages is the knowledge that allows us to identify and progress through the levels of complexity required by the Core. A wide range of reader characteristics impact the assessment of complexity. In particular, development pathways and cognitive abilities, emotional and social needs, motivation, interest, and experience should be considered when assessing the reader dimension.

Reader Development Pathways and Cognitive Abilities

A child's reading development is the first important consideration in the reader dimension. Learning to read builds on a foundation of basic communication skills that children start developing at a very young age. As they begin to prepare to enter school, children expand these communication skills into the basic skills required for reading. These skills grow into the ability to decode the written word. As decoding is mastered, the skills relating to comprehension and fluency take precedence. From there a sense of mastery and competence begins to develop. The whole process of learning to read is a complex one, and while its specific intricacies are beyond the scope of this book, it is important to know that developmental needs are directly connected to an assessment of complexity. The age range of children from kindergarten to sixth grade represents a wide range of development. Even within these grades there will be a wide range of cognitive abilities. While the Core outlines a very general outline for increasing complexity that will apply to the most perfect application of the model, there will always be outliers and exceptions. Having knowledge of developmental needs and cognitive abilities is the only way to address these exceptions. To assure that Anchor Standard 10 for increasing complexity is met professionals must first know where the student is academically. For one student at a particular developmental stage certain texts may be complex; however, for a student at a higher developmental stage the same text may be considered less complex. While texts hold their own inherent complexity level, this level can be raised or lowered depending upon the reader's development and cognitive abilities. Matching texts to students' developmental needs ensures that the text is at just the right level of complexity for that student. From there students can progress through the higher levels the Core requires.

When speaking of developmental pathways and cognitive abilities text complexity needs to be first matched to the reader's decoding abilities. The ability to decode has to do with understanding phonics and text structures. Beginning or poor readers will need texts that are easier to decode with shorter, simpler words and textual and grammatical structures. More advanced readers will have the ability to decode more complex texts. Some aspects of decoding words can be addressed through quantitative measures of text complexity; however, not all of them will be addressed there. It is important to remember that these measures only look at word and sentence length, but even short words may be difficult to fully decode if they carry symbolic meaning or if the student does not have the background knowledge necessary to understand them. Because of this understanding, both the qualitative and quantitative complexities of texts are essential to matching the right text to the right reader at the right level of complexity.

Overall, developmental needs will be most easily addressed for those students who are considered "normal" or on grade level. Developmental needs are more challenging to address for those students who are on the extreme ends of the continuum. For students who are reading below grade level or those reading well above reading level, assessing complexity is the only way to ensure that students are finding the right books. As was noted, research shows that in order to be successful students need to find that sweet spot of reading that allows them to feel confident about what they do but at the same time challenges them (Allington, 2012). Finding that spot is dependent upon knowing where a student is developmentally, and then selecting the texts that will challenge that level at the perfect level of complexity. As students develop cognitively they will then be able to move upward in the levels of complexity.

The Core Standards themselves build in some developmental progression as they ask students to increase understanding of basic text structures throughout the grades. However, beyond that structure professionals will need to address their student's developmental needs in their own way throughout the assessment of complexity levels. By addressing a child's developmental and cognitive needs, professionals can create an important connection between texts and readers. Children are very responsive to the world they inhabit, and they most often want to read texts that connect to their experiences and concerns. Selecting texts that meet a reader's developmental needs creates an environment that is more conducive for a reader to connect with a text. A connection with a text provides just the right conditions for students to be able to make meaning from a text, and if they can create meaning they can meet the expectations of the Core.

Reader's Emotional and Social Needs

Reading development as considered thus far connects to a child's physical and cognitive development. However, another important consideration is connected to students' psychological development. While much of the professional focus should be on the cognitive development of students, as caring and engaged teachers it is important for us to also pay attention to their emotional and social needs. Reading should be a safe place for students. Even for the youngest, reading can be a very emotional experience. Every student is going to be at a different level of maturation, and this level can impact the assessment of text complexity. For a text that extends beyond a student's level of psychological development, that text is going to be more complex. For example, a text that addresses a budding romance between a boy and a girl is much more developmentally appropriate for the psychological level of an older child. This example may seem fairly obvious; however, this principle can be applied more broadly. For example, a child who has experienced the death of a parent is much more psychologically likely to be able to empathize with a text about a similar event. Students without this experience may not be ready to engage with such a text. This effect happens because, as Zakaluk and Samuels (1988) outline, the readability of a text is based upon an interaction between a text and the resources the reader brings. It is up to professionals to assure that this interaction happens in an emotionally supportive environment. As noted, quantitative formulas don't in any way assess the content of a book. The result is some stunning mismatches between texts and readers, for example, a text with adult-level content that is graded for a second grader. The Core's exemplar text *The Grapes of Wrath* (1939) is a great example of this. Even though a second grader may be able to decode such a text, they most likely would be psychologically unable to handle it. This is why the reader dimension is so important; it can belay such mismatches, because in addition to the qualitative, professionals will be considering the reader's emotional and social needs.

In assessing texts for complexity on this level the detail, development, and didacticism of the text's meaning, theme, and conflict are of paramount importance. Within these elements concepts should be presented at the right level for students' social and emotional development. This concept is particularly evident when considering texts with tough or controversial subjects. For example, a kindergartener will have a certain understanding and ability to process the emotional constraints of a concept like death at a much different level than a sixth grader. So in this case, a book like *The Heaven of Animals* by Nancy Tilman (2014), which deals with the grief over losing a pet, would be much more developmentally appropriate for a kindergartener. On the other hand, a work such as *Scribble: a Dog Story, a Ghost Story, a Love Story* (2004) by Richard Jennings, which deals with the same topic but from the perspective of a 12-year-old, would be more developmentally connected to the emotional needs of a sixth grader. This same concept, however, does not need to only connect to harder issues: the same concept can be applied to almost any topic. For example, a complex scientific topic like gravity requires texts that also match a student's social and emotional developmental level. Here a book like *Gravity* (2014) by Jason Chin, which deals with the concept with large graphics and accessible word choices, would be accessible at the emotional level of a first or second grader who needs to engage with the complex concept. *Zero Gravity* (1994) by Gloria Skurzynski, in contrast, deals with the topic on a more abstract level, an approach which is more appropriate for the emotional development of students in the older grades. Just like connections made through developmental needs, addressing emotional and social needs creates just the right conditions for students to be able to make meaning from a text so they can meet the expectations of the Core.

Reader Motivation

Reader motivation is a very complex topic. Psychological, social, and educational research has been striving for decades to help unravel its mysteries. Especially when it comes to a complex task like reading, it is even more difficult to determine if and how someone will be motivated to do something. Despite the overall lack of clarity there are a few things that are clear. Motivation plays an important role in student's choice to read, how much effort they put into reading, and how much they enjoy the task of reading (Ulper, 2011; Wilson & Kelley, 2010). On the other hand, a lack of motivation can prevent students from engaging in reading, and without the proper motivation students will read at much lower levels than those who are motivated (Allington, 2012).

There are many factors that create the conditions where students are motivated toward reading. Forces inside a student such as self-perception, developmental needs, and psychological makeup are important in creating motivation. A student's perception of his or her own ability to read and engage in tasks associated with reading is one of the most critical elements for success (Gambrell, Palmer, Codling, & Mazzoni, 1996; Wilson & Kelley, 2010). Students who see themselves as good readers enjoy reading and are more motivated to read. Additionally, good readers will stick with reading longer even when conditions may not be ideal or when they find the tasks or texts they are engaged with to be very difficult. Students who consider themselves to be less able readers tend to disregard reading altogether. When they do read, they will struggle more with texts and they will be less likely to stick with texts they find difficult. This contrast between how self-perceived good and poor readers react to reading is an important consideration when addressing text complexity. Since students who view themselves as good readers are more likely to stick with texts even if they find them difficult, a higher level of complexity could be used for these students. In these cases, even if a text is too difficult, the students' self-efficacy and motivation take over and compensate for some of the complexity. For those who regard themselves as less-able readers, the compensatory factors don't exist. If a text is too complex, most of these readers will become overly frustrated. For these readers texts need to be at a more compatible level to their own development so they will have a stronger chance to engage with texts in a positive way. Finding the balance between a student's motivation and text complexity can be tricky since feelings of self-efficacy are not always constant. Certain situations or tasks can change students' perceptions. Even some texts can change a student's motivational level. For example, texts that students find interesting can override a lack of motivation for most students. Many teachers may have experienced this effect when even the most reluctant readers devoured the *Harry Potter* series during the height of their popularity. While some great motivational situations like this come naturally, professionals can also build motivation in their students by creating ideal classroom situations.

Professionals can use their understanding of reader's motivation to their advantage by selecting texts and creating conditions that will be motivating to their students. Creating classroom structures that are motivational is the best way to assure that both proficient and reluctant readers are motivated to engage with a wide variety of texts. Classroom environments often build extrinsic motivations by using motivators such as grades or rewards, but they should also strive to build intrinsic motivations. In order for students to become the independent readers of complex texts that the Core requires, they will need this intrinsic motivation. Extrinsic motivators have some benefits, but research has shown that their use, especially with children, needs to be approached with caution because they can backfire. Research suggests that extrinsic motivation is best used when a student has little interest in a task or lacks basic skills. After those skills have been built and intrinsic motivation starts to take over, rewards should be slowly removed (Brown, 2007). Research also clearly shows that when rewards are used they should be connected to the task at hand, for example, to reward reading, things like books or bookmarks that connect to the task should be the prize (Gambrell, 1996). Moving from extrinsic to intrinsic motivators is essential because it is only when a student is motivated by their own internal motivation that they will be willing to stick with hard tasks longer, and in the end they will be more satisfied with their ability and outcome of those tasks (Wilson & Kelley, 2010).

There are many ways to create classroom environments that leverage students' motivation in a way that will engage learning so that professionals can lead students' through learning outcomes. Gambrell (1996) outlines six factors that increase motivation: teachers who serve as models of reading, availability of lots of texts in a classroom, ability to choose, a broad familiarity with a variety of texts, chances to interact socially with books, and classroom philosophies that reflect the value of reading. Teacher and reading advocate Donalyn Miller (2012) also supports a large reading volume, time set aside for reading, activities that support reading, choice, and reading aloud as motivational factors for classrooms. All of these conditions build reading motivation and are fully compatible with the Core. Professionals are encouraged to explore these strategies and find those that work for them in their own classroom situations.

In addition, there is one really strong motivator for students, and that is to use children's literature. Authentic texts that connect to a reader's interests and experience are much more motivational than texts that are dull and bland. In fact, research has shown that authentic texts are also much more instructionally useful because they use real language in real-life situations in a context that connects to learning outcomes (Berardo, 2006). There is little doubt that children's literature is significantly more motivational to students than other texts. Sadly, there are professionals who don't always pick the types of texts that serve to motivate their readers. There are those who discount the types of reading that kids like to do by overlooking important texts like graphic novels or looking down on genres like fantasy in favor of texts they find to be more instructionally sound. When kids' reading preferences are disregarded, it is much more difficult to engage students in the kinds of learning they need to meet the requirements of the Core. Today there are so many wonderful texts available that there is something available for every reader and for every instructional situation. The best way to motivate readers is to embrace the widest possible range of texts so that just the right ones for each reader can be identified. Building motivation with the right texts then allows for just the right conditions to establish students' intrinsic motivation. From there it is possible to create the types of independent readers the Core wants to see.

Reader Interest

If you think about the books you personally select to read, chances are that all your choices connect with things that interest you. If you have an interest in history, science, or other topics, you will read books connected to that interest. Readers of all ages tend to do this very same thing. Readers just prefer to read texts that interest them. When texts lack interest to a reader they become lackluster and boring, making it harder to read and often impossible to finish. This simple fact plays an important part in motivating readers to engage with texts but it also plays part in assessing text complexity. For a reader who has an interest in the subject of a text may also find it to be less complex. This can be true because having an interest may mean that the reader already knows something about the topic and can easily navigate the vocabulary and context necessary to read a work. Additionally, it can mean that a reader is so interested in a text that motivational factors kick in so they are willing to stick with a text longer. In this case a text might be very complex but a reader is more likely to stick with it and work through navigating the complexities because it is of interest to them. So a reader's interest level can either serve to raise or lower the complexity level of a text depending upon the characteristics of both the text and the reader. Making a connection between a text and a reader's interests is another important step toward building independent readers. A text connected to a reader's interests is more likely to build the important kinds of personal connections that allow a reader to find pleasure in a text. Professionals know that reading in and of itself should be a pleasurable experience and it is up to them to guide their students to this understanding. Helping students have good experiences with texts builds not only their positive self-perception of themselves as readers but also positive impressions of the act itself. Good experiences help readers find the inherent pleasure of reading and so they are more likely to do it again. Thus connecting a text to a reader's interests creates the right conditions to build both the independent and lifelong readers who are college and workplace ready.

Professionals will find that interests do not always match reading level. For example, a recent report about what kids are reading found that overall third grader's favorite book was a title from *The Diary of a Wimpy Kid* series by Jeff Kinney (Renaissance Learning, 2014). This title has a Lexile level of 1060L (sixth–eighth grade) and an ATOS rating of 5.6. This means that third graders have a strong interest in a book that is quantitatively two or more grade levels above their reading ability. Additionally, fourth, fifth, sixth, seventh, and eighth graders all had this book listed as one of their favorites. So for all these grades, but one, this book is either below or well above the perceived level of the text. Many professionals have probably seen this effect firsthand as they observe a reader with a very low reading level engaging with a text way above their level just because of interest. As is shown here, interest can easily trump reading level. In fact, interest is probably the one factor that can make a text less complex for a reader in an instant. This is not a perfect situation however. Interest cannot overcome every reading difficulty, but it certainly can do a lot. Weighing how far a professional can push this effect depends upon knowing the students and their overall motivational level. With this understanding, professionals can find just the right level of complexity to match any reader's abilities and interests.

Reader Experience

In the discussion of the qualitative dimension, part of the outline discussed the fact that texts require some level of knowledge of a reader. While this discussion considered the text in isolation, it is now time to consider the role the reader plays in the transaction. For as Rosenblatt (1995) and Bleich (1975) show, what a reader brings to a text is as important as what the text offers. Everything students read is somehow impacted by their previous experience and knowledge. Even adult readers sometimes experience how a lack of background knowledge impacts reading ability. For example, recently one of the authors was required to read some documents relating to copyright law. It was found to be extremely difficult reading because the author lacked the necessary background with the legal language and context of the documents. Although the words themselves were comprehensible, the overall text was made more complex because of what the reader brought to the text. Because of this effect, being able to comprehend a text depends as much on a reader's ability to understand the context of the text as it does on the reader's ability to decode the words. For readers whose experience matches the knowledge base the text requires, that text may be less complex. For readers without the needed experience a text may be more complex. This raising or lowering of a text's complexity can be connected to any knowledge required by any of the text structures. Plot, setting, theme, characters, conflict, and all the other text structures can require some kind of knowledge of a reader. Consider, for example, a text set on a farm that uses the language and context of that setting. For a student who has never left a large city, the disconnect between their lived experience and the context of the text may prove to make the text more complex.

Readers build much of this experience before they even enter our classrooms or during the times they are not in school. Professionals will need to pay attention to how these outside experiences impact a text's complexity for a reader. However, professionals also have the ability to build some of the necessary experience students need as part of their daily learning outcomes. Since part of what teachers do is build experience for students, doing the same thing to help students access texts is very natural. For example, reading a simple text that builds background knowledge before reading a more complex text on the same subject is a good approach. In assessing complexity it is important to consider first what a reader already brings to the text. This assessment alone will indicate a certain level of complexity. Additionally, professionals should then consider if and how deficits in readers' knowledge can be addressed. This may mean guiding readers to other texts first before others are introduced. It could also mean that teachers can design tasks that address the students' needs, a strategy that will be addressed further in the remainder of this book.

Examples and Applications of Reader Characteristics

The reader dimension is very individualized. The only way to truly apply this dimension is to have a real reader to consider. Professionals will best know their own students and be able to best determine how each of the reader characteristics can impact each text. Because this book lacks a pool of real readers to draw on, in this application of the reader dimension it is only possible to make broad generalizations. For real classrooms this kind of analysis will prove to be more specific than the one offered here; however, this example should show how the reader dimension could apply to a text.

Half a Chance by Cynthia Lord. Scholastic Press, 2014.

Development and cognitive ability	The text's language is at a fairly basic level of decoding so most students with a basic level of confidence should be able to decode the text. However, the text does have a large amount of figurative language so much of the text carries some symbolic meaning. This language is very connected to the main character's interest in photography. It creates in words the idea of the visual images the main character is capturing. This raises the developmental complexity of the text, but it is still within the reach of most readers who are confident with decoding.
Emotional and social needs	The text addresses some difficult emotional issues, including trying to impress one's parents and dealing with the decline of an older relative. These two elements could impact the complexity of the text for some children. The text also has a budding romance between the main girl character and a secondary boy character. While the context is just a level of puppy love and some jealousy in regards to the relationship the boy has with another friend, there is no physical contact or any indication of anything more. For students who have not reached an emotional level that anticipates romance this relationship could be easily read as no more than basic friendship. For those with more emotional understanding of romance this relationship could be interpreted as something more. For those with more emotional context there is an added complexity to these characters that will not be there for children without that context.

Motivation	The text is a fairly typical family story which will connect to many of the lived experiences of a wide range of students. This connection should increase the reading motivation for some students and lower the text's complexity for them as well. Lord is also a Newbery Honor Award winner so some motivation for the text could be built through this connection, especially for readers who have experienced the author's other texts.
Interest	Students who enjoy family stories or realistic fiction will find interest here. There is also a strong connection to photography in the text so any student who enjoys art or photography will find interest in this text. For students with these interests, this text should be less complex. However, the text describes the setting, plot, and characters in such a detailed way that students without this interest should also be able to connect with the text without any negative effects on complexity.
Experience	Students who have fathers who travel for work, students who have moved a lot, and/or students who have been close to a grandparent who has declined or had Alzheimer's or dementia will have some experience that will help them connect with the book. For students with this background the complexity level will be lessened. However, the demand is such that even readers without these experiences will be able to connect with the text. The overall level of experience required by the text is such that it will be accessible to a wide range of readers.

Overall the demands this text will place on readers is minimal. Most readers in the fourth or fifth grades will have the development and cognitive ability, emotional and social needs, motivation, interest, and experience to engage with this text. There are some emotional and experience elements that either increase or decrease the complexity of the text depending upon the reader being considered.

The Task Dimension

The second dimension outside of the text that impacts the assessment of complexity is the task dimension. Tasks relate to any curriculum, activity, or pedagogy through which students engage with the texts and the standards of the Core. Professionals have already spent years of training and development building the skills they need to address the task dimension. The skills to create lesson plans and units, to study and learn to implement new pedagogies, or to assess our students and make changes as needed are all abilities that professionals already possess. The implementation of the Core does not change any of these processes to any great degree. The process of identifying standards, creating a learning outcome, selecting texts, designing a unit made up of interconnecting activities, and designing proper assessments under the Core is no different than what teachers did under other standards. The only difference is that the approach will be based on a slightly different philosophy that is drawn from the Core, an issue that will be discussed fully in the next chapters. Since the Core puts a strong emphasis on teacher expertise, the implementation of tasks under the Core is also left up to teachers. Many schools and districts will have already begun the process of building their own curriculums based in the Core. None of what this book has to offer should be incompatible with any of these efforts. The purpose here is not to change anything that is already being done but to add to it. In the remaining chapters the aspects of pedagogy and other task applications will be addressed; however, here it is important to consider how tasks impact an assessment of complexity.

As with the reader dimension the application of the task dimension can also raise or lower a text's complexity. How a text is used in instructional situations will change the inherent complexity of any text. For example, if only an excerpt of a very complex text is used, the text automatically becomes less complex overall. On the other hand, using the whole text will make it more complex. There will also be a difference when we consider who will be reading the text. If a text is used for whole-class reading then it may be necessary to select a text that is less complex than would be optimal from some readers. No one text will remain at the same complexity level in all situations. It is up to professionals to determine how the complexity of a text fits into their own curriculum needs. Considering the purpose of a lesson and how that purpose connects to the lessons tasks is the first step to matching the complexity level of a text to overall outcomes. For example, consider the purpose of the lesson that will help students determine the meaning of nonliteral language (Grade Level 3 Reading Literature Standard 4). For this lesson writing tasks will be used. For this lesson the teacher will need to select a text at the level of complexity that matches their students' level of development in regards to the writing tasks. Such a text would likely have a high level of complexity in its detail of language. The qualitative assessment of the text will have revealed this level, making it easy for the teacher to find just the right text. So to apply the task dimension, teachers must carefully select texts that fit with their readers' capacities and connect to the structures that are being taught.

As teachers assess reader's capacities in order to design tasks, Vygotsky's (1962) concept of the zone of proximal development comes into play. This philosophy suggests that teachers need to design tasks that address students' level of development. If a task is too simple or too complex, optimal learning cannot take place. What teachers are striving for is the place where students are engaging with tasks that stretch them just a little but at the same time allow them to complete the task because they have the support of a more knowledgeable expert. Teachers are the experts who provide this support to guide students through the tasks they have set. The optimal point is for the texts and tasks used in instruction to be at the student's own zone of proximal development. Assessing their students will allow teachers to find this zone for their own classrooms. However, because teachers will work with a wide range of children they will no doubt face the challenge of finding the zones for a very diverse group. No two readers will be alike, nor will they bring the same experience and knowledge to every text. Because of this, it is important to remember that every reader will need support to engage with the texts at one time or other. The Core documentation makes special note of struggling or reluctant readers and their need for support as they outline the three-tiered model. As teachers design tasks, it will be especially important to ensure that the right level of scaffolding is provided to help these students engage with complex texts.

Scaffolding texts to bring students up to appropriate levels can be done in many ways. One of the most direct ways is by making connections. Connections between a reader's experience, between other texts, or between world events can support students by building up their knowledge. The interesting corollary to making these connections is that not only do they develop the necessary background knowledge students need, but at the same time they can also raise the complexity of any text. When texts speak to other texts or other themes outside the texts, then more depth is added to all the texts and themes. This added depth increases complexity. Additionally, making connections is also a great way to address the Core's call to include more nonfiction in all the content areas. Making connections to nonfiction opens up a lot of possibilities to benefit students. Using all types of texts, including fiction, nonfiction, digital, and other non-book formats, engages our students in the wide range of issues and ideas. This kind of engagement is just what the Core is asking teachers to do to ensure that students are college and workplace ready.

The implementation of the Core provides teachers with the impetus to look very critically at all the aspects of instruction in order to determine how well they work. This time of change provides a great opportunity to explore and consider how a wider range of texts and tasks can be used to meet the expectations of the Core. Teachers have a wide range of options open to them, and among these options children's literature will be a prime component. In the remainder of this text the task dimension will be further explored by delving into the scope of children's literature and showing exactly how these texts can be integrated into the curriculum and pedagogy used in the classroom to address the standards of the Core.

Examples and Applications of Text Characteristics

As with the reader dimension, the task dimension requires a real classroom with real students for full application. Because this book does not have a specific classroom context to draw on, it is only possible to address this dimension in general ways. Here is offered one way in which the assessed grade level complexity of the text can be applied in a classroom. Further, a second example of how the text's complexity could be raised through the application of a task is also offered. Additional examples of how tasks and texts can be connected will be offered in subsequent chapters of this book.

Half a Chance by Cynthia Lord. Scholastic Press, 2014.

The text has been assessed at about a fourth-grade level. To directly connect the text to this grade, an identification of a standard at that grade level that connects to the text can be found. For example, the text could be used to address Fourth-Grade-Level Standard for Reading Literacy 3, which asks students to describe in depth a character in a story with details from the text. To connect a task, the students could be asked to identify passages where the author reveals the main character's thoughts. Using these passages the students would then make a PowerPoint that introduces this character to the class using the character's thoughts to develop a description of the character.

To increase the level of complexity of the text, teachers might draw on the complex figurative language that is used in the text. The connection here is to the main character's hobby of photography. Part of the structure the author uses is to frame this in the context of a contest. Kids are given words, and they need to take photographs that convey those words. A task that extends this contest could be used to address Sixth Grade-Level Standard for Reading Literacy 4 to define the figurative meaning of words. Students could pick one metaphor or other passage of figurative language from the text, and then draw an image or take a photograph that captures that piece of figurative language from the text. They could then explain how the image conveys the same meaning and tone the author of the text intended.

Conclusion

The three-tiered model has now been completely broken down into its component parts. This discussion should have provided a concrete vision for professionals of how this model works and how it can be applied to texts. This model certainly can and should be applied to the widest possible range of texts, including children's literature. In fact, one of the most exciting things about the Core is that its model allows teachers to defend and use a wide range of texts that will serve as the foundation for wonderful teaching environments. It is acknowledged that teachers will encounter a wide range of readers and classroom situations, and that even this comprehensive view of the model will not be able to address every issue. However, through an application of their own skills and enthusiasm teachers will certainly be able to use the Core in amazing ways to address every student's needs. Times of change can be stressful and without a doubt the implementation of the Core and its model of complexity is one of those stresses. However, change can also be dynamic and exciting. The implementation of the Core is a thrilling opportunity because it gives us the language and structure to analyze and use a wide range of texts. This vision of the Core provides for addressing complex texts is just the beginning. Now let's move on to see just how appropriately complex texts of children's literature can fully meet the demands of the Core.

Bibliography

Allington, R.L. (2012). *What really matters for struggling readers: Designing research-based programs* (3rd ed.). Boston, MA: Pearson.

Austen, J. (1811). *Sense and sensibility*. Whitehall, London: Thomas Egerton.

Berenstain, S., & Berenstain, J. (2005). *Berenstain bears and the trouble with chores*. New York: Harper Festival.

Berardo, S. A. (2006). The use of authentic materials in the teaching of reading. *The Reading Matrix, 6*(2), 60–69.

Bleich, D. (1975). *Readings and feelings: An introduction to subjective criticism.* Urbana, IL: National Council of Teachers of English.

Brown, L. V. (2007). *Psychology of motivation.* New York: Nova Publishers.

Burke, V., & Greenberg, D. (2010). Determining readability: How to select and apply easy-to-use readability formulas to assess the difficulty of adult literacy materials. *Adult Basic Education and Literacy Journal, 4*(1), 34–42.

Chin, J. (2014). *Gravity.* New York: Roaring Book Press.

Coleman, M., & Liau, T. L. (1975). A computer readability formula designed for machine scoring. *Journal of Applied Psychology, 60*(2), 283–284.

Dale, E., & Chall, J. S. (1948). *A formula for predicting readability.* Columbus, OH: Bureau of Educational Research, Ohio State University.

Danielson, W. A., & Lasorsa, D. L. (1989). A new readability formula based on the stylistic age of novels. *Journal of Reading, 33*(3), 194–197.

Gallagher, K. (2009). *Readicide: How schools are killing reading and what you can do about it.* Portland, ME: Stenhouse.

Gambrell, L. (1996). Creating classrooms cultures that foster reading motivation. *The Reading Teacher, 50,* 4–25.

Gambrell, L., Palmer, B., Codling, R., & Mazzoni S. (1996). Assessing motivation to read. *The Reading Teacher, 49*(7), 518–533.

Gray, W. S., & Leary, B. E. (1935). *What makes a book readable: With special reference to adults of limited reading ability, an initial study.* Chicago, IL: The University of Chicago Press.

Gunning, R. (1952). *The technique of clear writing.* New York: McGraw-Hill.

Hiebert, E. H. (2009). *Interpreting Lexiles in online contexts and with informational texts.* Retrieved from http://www.apexlearning.com/documents/Research_InterpretingLexiles_2009–02%281%29.pdf

Jennings, R. (2004). *Scribble: A dog story, a ghost story, a love story.* New York: Houghton Mifflin Harcourt.

Keene, E., & Zimmerman, S. (2007). *Mosaic of thought: The power of comprehension strategy instruction* (2nd ed.). Portsmouth, NH: Heinemann.

McLaughlin, G. H. (1969). SMOG grading: A new readability formula. *Journal of Reading, 12*(8), 639–646.

McNamara, D. S., Graesser, A. C., McCarthy, P. M., & Cai, Z. (2014). *Automated evaluation of text and discourse with Coh-Metrix.* Cambridge, England: Cambridge University Press.

Miller, D. (2012). Creating a classroom where readers flourish. *Reading Teacher, 66*(2), 88–92.

Picoult, J. (2001). *Plain truth.* New York: Washington Square Press.

Pratchett, T. (2006). *The wee free men.* New York: HarperTempest.

Renaissance Leaning. (2014). *What kids are reading and why it matters.* Retrieved from http://doc.renlearn.com/KMNet/R004101202GH426A.pdf

Rosenblatt, L. M. (1995). *Literature as exploration.* New York: Modern Language Association of America.

School Renaissance Institute. (2000). The ATOS[TM] readability formula for books and how it compares to other formulas. Report. Madison: Wisconsin School Renaissance Institute, Inc. (ERIC document reproduction service no. ED449468). Retrieved from EBSCOHost ERIC database.

Skurzynski, G. (1994). *Zero gravity.* New York: Bradbury Press.

Smith, R. R. (2000). How the Lexile framework operates. *Popular Measurement, 3*(1), 18–19.

Steinbeck, J. (1939). *The grapes of wrath.* New York: Viking Press.

Stenner, A. J. (1999). Instructional uses of the Lexile framework (ERIC document reproduction service no. ED435976). Retrieved from EBSCOHost ERIC database.

Sutcliff, R. (1993). *Black ships before Troy: The story of the Iliad*. New York: Delacorte Press.

Tillman, N. (2014). *Heaven of animals*. London: Feiwel & Friends.

Trollinger, W. V., & Kaestle, C. F. (1986). Difficulty of text as a factor in the history of reading. Program report 86-13. Madison: Wisconsin Center for Education Research. (ERIC document reproduction service no. ED312652). Retrieved from EBSCOHost ERIC database.

Ulper, H. (2011). The motivational factors for reading in terms of students. *Educational Sciences: Theory and Practice, 11*(2), 954–960.

Vygotsky, L. S. (1962). *Thought and language*. Edited and translated by E. Hanfmann and G. Vakar. Cambridge, MA: MIT Press.

Wilson, N. S., & Kelley, M. J. (2010). Are avid readers lurking in your language arts classroom? Myths of the avid adolescent reader. *Reading Horizons, 50*(2), 99–112.

Zakaluk B. L., & Samuels S. J. (Eds.). (1988). *Readability: Its past, present, and future*. Newark, DE: International Reading Association.

4 Children's Literature and the Core

The term "children's literature" encompasses a wide range of texts in many formats and genres, so in order to contextualize this vast area it is important to first begin with a definition. To articulate a brief yet comprehensive definition of children's literature, however, proves to be a challenging task in no small part because this definition can vary greatly between individuals and has changed and evolved over the years. For some scholars their working definition of children's literature encompasses anything read and enjoyed by children between birth and 18 (approximately). This definition, however, is very broad and can include not only texts many might term "young adult," but also books written for adults but read by children. Such a definition seems to leave the lines between children's literature and literature for other audiences quite blurry and opens the selection of texts to a broad range of developmental needs. This kind of definition it seems then only serves to confuse the issue of what children's literature really is. So in order to narrow the scope it is necessary to define the span of the field by identifying the important aspects of the texts that make children's literature unique. While there are many characteristics of the field the aspects of point of view and marketing are most connected to the expectations of the Core. Thus, the definition of children's literature offered here is *A work that represents an entirely child's point of view that is mainly marketed to that same audience.*

The defining feature of children's literature, without a doubt, is that these texts tell their story from a child's point of view. Texts that fall into the children's category feature not only child protagonists but also child perspectives on the world. So, by this definition, books such as *To Kill a Mockingbird* (1995) by Harper Lee, which features a six-year-old protagonist, would not be considered children's literature because the story is told by the adult looking back at her childhood. Because the text looks back it does not offer a child's perspective, but that of an adult who is now analyzing what happened. While texts like these do have child protagonists, they are not told from the point of view of a child; rather, they are retellings of memories rendered by an adult looking back at life. As a result, these books feature analysis or insight about events or characters that comes from an adult's reflections on the past, and thus they do not represent an entirely child's point of view. On the other hand, texts like Kristin Levine's *The Lions of Little Rock* (2012), which looks at race relations from the point of view of a 12-year-old, not only has child characters but also makes use of the child's point of view by embodying a typical child's feelings, language, and ideas about the issues.

As noted in the discussion of text structures, even though textual elements are usually directly associated with fiction, the aspect of point of view is critical to consider for all texts. For fiction the point of view will most certainly be tied to the protagonist and the other character viewpoints the author chooses to address. For nonfiction, on the other hand, point of view is connected to how information is presented to the intended audience. Authors of nonfiction choose the audience to which their information will be addressed. With this choice the information is then structured to meet the needs or expectations of this community. So in nonfiction the point of view for children's literature will be one that is most connected to the feelings, ideas, experiences, and expectations of that age group. So it may well be that a nonfiction text is speaking about adults or events that adults were mostly involved in. This means that these texts are unlikely to have childhood experiences entirely at their center. However, nonfiction texts like this can still be children's literature if the author has chosen to represent the information in a way that would engage a real child's point of view. For example, a picture book like *Sit-In, How Four Friends Stood up by Sitting Down* (2010) by Andrea and Brian Pinkney emphasizes an adult's determination, a feeling that is certainly shared and understood by children. Additionally, the Pinkneys use food metaphors and bold strokes of color to illustrate these feelings all of which are aspects that connect to ideas that children are developmentally attuned to. So no matter what its form or genre is the representation of a child's point of view will be one defining characteristic of children's literature that also offers important connections to the Core. Assessing the purpose of point of view is part of Anchor Standard 6. Additionally, point of view also plays a role in the other Anchor Standards that assess characters and other text structures. So point of view is not only an important part of the definition of children's literature but it is also integrally connected to any implementation of the Core.

While point of view is paramount in identifying a piece of children's literature, in today's market publishers also play a very strong role in categorizing books. This role may not be as strong a defining characteristic as point of view; but it certainly does impact the makeup of a field. When a house publishes a book, it decides which audience that book is best marketed to, and their designation clearly holds a lot of power since publishers target certain librarians, readers, and booksellers to help them promote and market their works. These decisions clearly influence whether or not certain texts make it into the hands of children. So how a text is marketed is also an important consideration in the definition of children's literature. The role of publishers, however, is not always clear and the process by which decisions are made can often seem arbitrary, especially at the upper ends of the market which direct texts to older children. For example, Markus Zusak's *The Book Thief* (2006), was originally published in Australia as an adult book. When it was published in the United States, however, it was marketed to a much younger audience because U.S. publishers clearly saw an audience as young as 12 as suitable for this title. It is also important to note that despite the fact the publishers try to dictate the market, in actuality the market does not always follow their instructions. This has been true for works such as J. K. Rowling's *Harry Potter* series, which has likely had as many adult readers as child readers. Nevertheless, even with these challenges, marketing plays a significant role in which books end up being read by children so this aspect is also integral to a definition of the field.

Additionally, including the role of the publisher as part of the definition for children's literature is also important in the context of the Core. Because the Core defines the idea of text so broadly to include a wide range of texts it is important to designate between them by defining their mode of publication. How a text is published or produced inherently builds into it characteristics that create complexity that have been previously discussed as part of the design aspect. Furthermore looking at what audience a publisher considers to be the best marketing match for a text can go a long way in helping determine a basic complexity level for any text. Publishers know their texts, and their age or audience designations can provide a lot of basic information that further complexity analyses can be built on.

For the purpose of this book we are only including under our definition of children's literature those texts that are further defined as trade books. Generally trade books are defined as books published by commercial publishers that are intended for a wide audience. Trade books do not have an intended instruction component nor are they designed exclusively for classroom use. Trade books contrast with textbooks that are designed for a specific purpose and audience inside a classroom. The Core connects its definition of texts to a trade book context as well in its articulation of the exemplar texts. From stories such as Patricia MacLachlan's *Sarah, Plain and Tall* (1985) to read-alouds like Kevin Henkes's *Kitten's First Full Moon* (2004), a majority of the texts offered perfectly fall into the category of children's trade books that has been defined here. This does not mean, however, that the only texts important to the Core are those that follow the traditional mode of publication that trade books do. The standards advocate for a wide range of diverse media and formats. This includes not only trade books, but poems, drama, stories, articles both from news and scholarly sources, documents both primary and secondary, media including video and audio, and even other forms of multimedia texts which imbed both text and visual formats. This wide range of texts is essential for addressing the standards outlined in the Core; however, for our purposes here the term children's literature will also be synonymous with the term trade book.

A Brief History of Children's Literature

Stories of all forms and genres have always been a part of children's lives. From the beginning of humanity children shared the stories about mankind's history and culture that were told around them. So on some level children's literature has always existed. However, there was no real distinction of audience because these stories were designed to be consumed by both adults and children. It was not until the 1600s that stories for a definite children's audience emerged and a distinctive and separate genre of children's literature evolved. Most scholars agree that the first clear-cut piece of children's literature was the *Orbis Pictus* which was originally published in 1658. A digital version of the text can be viewed at http://www.gutenberg.org/files/28299/28299-h/28299-h.htm (Comenius, 1887). Illustrated with lavish woodcuts this textbook was designed to educate children about the natural world. During this early period most of the texts published for children did have some kind of instructional purpose. Many were designed like the *Orbis Pictus*, to be more like the basal readers used in schools today. Others were designed to instruct children in perfect moral or religious behavior. This connection to the instructional purpose for texts pervaded the field of children's literature for decades, that is until John Newbery and active folklorists changed everything.

In the 1740s a man named John Newbery began publishing. Newbery, for whom the famous children's literature award given by the American Library Association is named, believed that children deserved to be entertained not just taught. His first book for children, *A Pretty Little Pocket Book*, came out in 1744, while it still has its moralistic overtones it also includes fun poems for each letter of the alphabet accompanied by woodcuts of children playing. A digital version of the text can be viewed here: http://lcweb2.loc.gov/cgi-bin/ampage?collId=rbc3&fileName=rbc0001_2003juv05880page.db (*A Pretty Little Pocket Book*, 1787). Newbery's publishing efforts set a whole new tone for the field of children's literature allowing the fun and playful side of children's books to come out. During this same time, folklorists like Charles Perrault who worked from 1697 to 1703 and Jacob and Wilhelm Grimm who worked during the early 1800s also changed the face of children's literature. An early version of Perrault's famous work *Tales of Mother Goose* (1901) can be found at http://www.gutenberg.org/files/17208/17208-h/17208-h.htm. Early examples of the Grimm bothers' works can also be found at http://www.gutenberg.org/ebooks/author/971. Many of these stories collected from oral versions were those that had been a part of children's lives since the beginning of time. However, when they began to be collected and written down, they became associated with the world of children, and from this point on the idea of fairy and folk tales almost exclusively conjures up the idea of childhood. These significant impacts heralded in a new world for the field of children's literature that extended into the 1890s. This era of refinement saw a rise in publications for children, many of which are still loved favorites today, such as Lewis Carroll's *Alice's Adventures in Wonderland* in 1865 (a free online version can be found here: http://literature.org/authors/carroll-lewis/alices-adventures-in-wonderland/) and *Little Women* by Louisa May Alcott in 1868 (a free online version can be found here: http://www.gutenberg.org/ebooks/37106). Other classics from this same time period included the following:

- *The Adventures of Tom Sawyer* by Mark Twain, 1876—An online version can be found at http://www.gutenberg.org/files/74/74-h/74-h.htm (Twain, 1884).
- *The Adventures of Pinocchio* by Carlo Collodi, 1883—An online version can be found at http://www.gutenberg.org/ebooks/500 (Collodi, n.d.).
- *A Child's Garden of Verses* by Robert Louis Stevenson, 1885—An online version can be found at http://www.gutenberg.org/ebooks/19722 (Stevenson, 1916).
- *The Jungle Book* by Rudyard Kipling, 1894—An online version can be found at http://www.gutenberg.org/files/236/236-h/236-h.htm (Kipling, 1894).

The turn of the century saw the development of a uniquely American brand of children's literature, beginning in 1900 with the publication of *The Wonderful Wizard of Oz* by L. Frank Baum, the first modern fantasy to be written by an American. In 1928 the first American picture book *Millions of Cats* was written and illustrated by Wanda Gág. These efforts by American authors and illustrators became so important that in 1922 the John Newbery Medal (http://www.ala.org/alsc/awardsgrants/bookmedia/newberymedal/newberymedal), the world's first prize for children's literature, was established by the American Library Association. Sixteen years later in 1938 the Randolph Caldecott Medal (http://www.ala.org/awardsgrants/randolph-caldecott-medal-), which recognizes book illustrations, was established. Both of these awards that recognize outstanding contributions to American children's literature are still awarded annually.

The 1950s and 1960s were marked by a grand expansion of the field to more adequately address a wide range of ages and cultures. Considered by many to be the first novel of the category of children's literature that we now term young adult published in 1951, *Catcher in the Rye* by J. D. Salinger engaged an older age range of readers. The needs of beginning readers were also addressed in 1957 when *The Cat in the Hat* by Dr. Seuss along with *Little Bear* by Else Holmelund Minarik created the beginning reader picture book. In 1962 *The Snowy Day* written and illustrated by Ezra Jack Keats was the first picture book to feature an African American protagonist to win a Caldecott Award. During this period the field also began to break other taboos and barriers. Texts like *Where the Wild Things Are*, written and illustrated by Maurice Sendak (1963), and *Harriet the Spy* by Louise Fitzhugh (1964) were controversial in their time because of their realistic depictions of children's feelings and family situations. Other books like *Are You There God? It's Me, Margaret* by Judy Blume (1970) directly addressed taboo subjects like maturation and religion for the first time.

The 1970s and 1980s brought with them a wider acceptance for a broader range of text formats and forms. For example, concept books were born in 1972 with *Push-Pull, Empty-Full: A Book of Opposites* by Tana Hoban. In 1981 *A Visit to William Blake's Inn: Poems for Innocent and Experienced Travelers* by Nancy Willard, illustrated by Alice and Martin Provensen was the first book of poetry to win a Newbery Medal. In 1983 *Sugaring Time* by Kathryn Lasky, with photographs by Christopher Knight became the first photo essay to win a Newbery Honor Medal. *Lincoln: A Photobiography* by Russell Freedman was the first photobiography to win a Newbery Medal in 1987. *Joyful Noise: Poems for Two Voices* by Paul Fleischman was the first choral poetry text to win a Newbery Medal in 1988. In 1990 *Color Zoo* (1989) by Lois Ehlert was the first engineered picture book to win Caldecott Honor Medal. Additionally, the important role of nonfiction was acknowledged in 1990 when the first nonfiction book award, the *Orbis Pictus* was established by the National Council of Teachers of English (http://www.ncte.org/awards/orbispictus).

The modern era of children's literature still continues to build on its strong heritage established in the 1600s. However, even as they draw on the past authors and illustrators today are breaking even more barriers. In 2007 *The Invention of Hugo Cabret* by Brian Selznick changed the field's understanding of format with its unique combination of picture book and novel elements. Also in 2007 *The Arrival* by Shaun Tan stretched the understanding of what should work with an audience of children with his wordless picture book. Even newer formats like graphic novels are also engaging readers in innovative ways. From nonfiction graphic novels like *Primates: The Fearless Science of Jane Goodall, Dian Fossey, and Birute Galdikas* by Jim Ottaviani and Maris Wicks (2013) to graphic novels for the youngest readers like *Chick and Chickie Play All Day!* by Claude Ponti (2012), new texts continue to expand and redefine the field. Today there is no shortage of inventive and exciting texts that are sure to engage a wide range or readers while at the same time being suitable for all kinds of classroom applications. So now is the time to delve into this amazing field to see how all these texts can provide powerful results when paired with the Core Standards.

The Power of Children's Literature in the Classroom

Even though textbooks have proven to be a staple for literacy endeavors in the classroom, research has shown that authentic children's literature is by far one of the best tools teachers can use. Studies have shown time and again that children's books in the classroom create just the right environment for students to thrive. In the age of the Core where texts form the basis for all literacy endeavors both in ELA and other content areas, the need for authentic children's texts is even greater. For many the power children's literature has in the classroom to engage students in their learning may be overtly obvious and no further evidence is needed. However, for those who need more proof either for themselves or to help them convince other professionals what a strong role children's literature can play, let's take a closer look at the research. By highlighting a few of the hundreds of studies available, it is clearly obvious that:

The use of children's literature is connected to greater reading and writing achievement:

- Cohen (1968) compared second graders in classes who were taught with basal readers to classes where children's trade picture books were used and read aloud. It was found that students in the classes that used picture books showed a significant increase in reading achievement including word knowledge, reading comprehension, and vocabulary development.
- Larrick (1987) found after engaging with a program that immersed English language learners in kindergarten with children's literature, by the end of the year that students were reading above grade level and only 3 of the 350 students failed to pass their reading comprehension tests.
- Baumann and Ivey (1997) found in a yearlong study of their literature-based classroom instruction that their students' reading level improved and they also built better word identification skills, showed increased fluency and comprehension, and became better writers.
- Cantrell (1999) found that students in classrooms that had teachers who implemented recommended literacy practices, among them the frequent use of children's literature, significantly outperformed, in both reading and writing, those students whose teachers did not implement such strategies.
- Wilson, Martens, Arya, and Altwerger (2004) showed in their study of second graders that students who used literature had no advantage over those given explicit phonics instruction through textbooks, and the group that used literature showed greater gains in reading comprehension.
- Reis, Eckert, McCoach, Jacobs, and Coyne (2008) found that after 14 weeks students in the test group who had high interest literature read aloud to them and then were supported with follow up higher order thinking questions had statistically significantly higher gains in reading fluency than those in a control group who did not engage with literature.

Children's literature provides the right kind of models to engage students with authentic language and literature:

- Durkin (1961) concludes that learning to read is much like learning to speak, so in order to learn to read well students need experiences with whole texts that serve as ideal reading models.
- Lancia (1997) in an action research study of his second-grade classroom found that literature served as an inspiration and that it influenced his students to be better writers because they had good role models on which to base their own writing.

Children's literature provides strong connections to content areas:

- Guzzetti, Kowalinski, and McGowan (1992) in a study of sixth graders who used literature as part of a unit on China showed significant gains in concept acquisition over those who used only textbooks.
- Smith, Monson, and Dobson (1992) found that students in classrooms where historical novels were read were able to recall 60 percent more information, including historical details and main ideas, about U.S. history than those students who used only textbooks.
- Morrow, Pressley, Smith, and Smith (1997) showed that when literature was integrated into science instruction the students scored significantly higher in tests of both literacy and science skills.
- VanSledright and Kelley (1998) found that using biographies, historical fiction, and other historical literature with fifth graders not only increased their interest in the subject but also led to signs of their emerging ability to do critical reading and to engage in advanced historical thinking.
- Van den Heuvel-Panhuizen and Van den Boogaard (2008) found that picture books were able to engage children in mathematical concepts even without explicit instruction or prompting.

Children's literature encourages students to engage with a diversity of perspectives and ideas:

- Pate (1988) found that students who engaged with multicultural texts had less negative ideas about people who were different from themselves.
- Holmes, Powell, Holmes, and Witt (2007) found that students often pick books to read that have characters who have different racial backgrounds than themselves, leaving them to conclude that multicultural books can build bridges between racial groups.
- Lohfink and Loya (2010) found that Mexican American third graders demonstrated higher engagement when culturally relevant picture books were used for class book discussions.
- Ghiso, Campano, and Hall (2012) show that because children's literature is an important part of children's intellectual and imaginative development it is important that students have the opportunity to interact with texts that cross social, cultural, and linguistic boundaries.

Children's literature leads to higher reading motivation and engagement:

- Trelease (1985) notes that interaction with a wide range of real reading materials not only gives students a reason to read but also helps them want to read.
- Pachtman and Wilson (2006) found that the proximity of and access to books was the most valued characteristic of classroom reading programs, and having lots of books was what motivated their fifth-grade students to read.
- Ness (2009) found that one of her student's reading fluency improved dramatically when humorous children's literature was used mostly because of her engagement with and motivation to read those particular texts.
- O'Sullivan and McGonigle (2010) review research that shows that the emotional power of children's literature serves to engage readers, and engaging with texts through writing and talking increases students' reading motivation.

The use of children's literature builds a positive attitude toward reading:

- Fader and McNeil (1976) found that boys who were allowed to read lots of books and were not asked to do any classroom assignments associated with them had gains in self-esteem and had lower levels of reading anxiety.

- Tunnell (1986) found that after seven months of reading children's literature children in a class that included children with reading difficulties developed better attitudes toward reading and showed higher levels of self-efficacy toward their own reading ability.
- Baumann, Hooten, and White (1999) found that the use of trade books in a fifth-grade classroom not only lead students to read more but they also valued reading more and demonstrated a greater appreciation for books and reading.
- Alden, Lindquist, and Lubkeman (2003) found that a literature-rich classroom supported with literature-based activities leads to a marked increase in students' reading motivation.

The use of children's literature is linked to increased reading volume which is linked to higher reading ability:

- Hepler (1982) found that over a year the behaviors of students in a literature-based classroom changed so that they read more, were more engaged, and were better able to discuss and interact with what they read.
- Greaney (1980) reports that many studies find that there is a strong relationship between the amount of leisure reading students do (which presumably is mostly children's literature) and their level of academic attainment.
- Allington (2012) found that the students who read the most have the highest reading ability, so increasing reading volume is one of the best ways to help struggling readers.

What Children's Literature Brings to the Core

All of the findings in these research studies clearly show that children's literature has great power when it is an integral component of any classroom. These reasons alone could offer enough support for the use of children's literature; however, the connections children's literature can make to the Core add another perspective. Children's literature is a natural fit for the expectations of the Core. With its diverse range of formats and complexity levels, its ability to address a wide range of skill levels, and its opening of a wide range of choices, there is little doubt that children's literature can serve as a foundation for any Core implementation.

Children's literature is one of the most diverse fields of literature today. With a range of formats from picture books to graphic novels, there is something for everyone. The Core Standards place a premium on text and text types when they ask for students to be able to integrate information in diverse media and formats. Because the Core asks for the widest possible range of texts it seems logical to implement the standards with literature that also has the widest possible range of texts, children's literature.

Children's literature also offers the widest possible range of complexity levels. Again, because the Core places such great importance on students being able to read and comprehend complex texts it seems logical that a foundation for the Core would be texts that represent a broad range of levels. From texts designed for prereaders to those designated for mature confident readers children's literature offers the best range and fit for the Core. Textbooks are designed to address one individual complexity level throughout, so with texts like this it is impossible to mix and match. Mixing texts is essential because it is unlikely that every student in the same class will be at the same level. In order to meet every student's needs a wide range of texts is needed. Additionally, the Core never states that students have to read texts of all the same complexity level. Nor do they say that because a student is at a certain reading level they should only read texts that match or exceed that same level. The Core only states that students should be able to read increasingly complex texts. So this does not mean that every text used for every task needs to be at the same complexity level. Nor does it mean that students will be required to read a small range of texts that meet some perceived need. What this means is that students should engage with a wide range of texts and that overall throughout their 13 years of schooling they will ultimately be asked to come to a point where they can read and comprehend texts of a complexity level appropriate for college and the workplace.

Without a doubt the Core requires engagement with a wide range of texts. This idea should be somewhat obvious especially with an understanding of the reader and task dimension outlined in the previous chapter. Since readers and tasks can impact a text's complexity level a clear understanding of who is reading a text and what task they are going to be engaged in is essential. This understanding helps professionals to realize that throughout the school day some tasks will require lower complexity texts, others will need higher ones. As the readers progress this balance will change and shift. It is up to the professionals to determine how the concept of complexity will be applied in their classroom. For example, Szymusiak, Sibberson, and Koch (2008) note that many professionals' instinct is to select a complex text to teach a skill to their students. However, it may be that a complex text is not what is needed. For example, if a skill is being taught for the first time then most often a text of a lower level of complexity is better. When trying to learn something new students can be overwhelmed by a complex text in a way that can easily prevent them from learning what is being taught. However, once a skill has been adequately developed students can then apply that skill to a complex text very easily.

The wide range of children's literature available makes it possible for teachers to be able to find just the right kinds of texts they need to suit any teaching endeavor. Having this wide range of texts to select from is important for teachers wishing to implement the Core. First, having a range of choices is important for teachers because the Core requires a wide range of texts. At the most basic level the Core makes a distinction between literature and informational texts offering grade-level standards of each type. So one of the fundamental requirements of the Core is that students will engage with both fiction and nonfiction in ELA and other content areas. Within the standards different formats or genres are often specifically referred to. These suggestions are ones that will work particularly well with the skills of that standard. For example, standard 2 for reading literature in the third grade explicitly asks students to engage with fables, folktales, and myths from diverse cultures. To implement the standard these forms will provide the best connection. Expanding this to other requirements for specific forms, types, and genres; it is clear that the Core requires students to read all types of texts. The field of Children's literature addresses every type, format, and genre the Core requires so this body of texts provides all the choices teachers will need. Secondly, a variety will also be necessary to teach the standards as teachers address differing complexity needs and skill levels. No one complexity level will meet the needs of all students or tasks all the time. Happily the wide range of children's literature provides the kind of variety teachers will need to address all levels of complexity for their students and tasks. From selecting a single text to choosing a group of texts to be used for instruction the range of children's literature makes it possible for teachers to find just the right texts as they apply the structures of the three-tiered model of text complexity. From that point teachers who know their own classrooms will be able to meet the needs of their readers and tasks by selecting texts that address their instructional outcomes. No matter how this process of matching texts with readers, standards, and tasks happens in each individual classroom, children's literature will give teachers just the right choice of texts.

It has been noted that having a range of choices is an important part of why children's literature is good for teachers, but having a choice of texts is also important for students. The aspect of choice is a very important part of learning. Cambourne (1995) notes that students who don't have any input into how their learning happens often feel powerless and lack motivation. These feelings lead to apathy and poor engagement in the learning process. Building in some form of choice into instruction has been found to be one of the best ways to combat these negative feelings. Giving students choices imparts to them a sense of control over their own learning which then allows them to have greater confidence in their own abilities. Providing choices, in order to engage students and build self-efficacy, is certainly compatible with the Core. In the end what the Core wants is readers who can engage with texts independently and proficiently. This level of skill certainly can't be reached by a student who lacks confidence in his or her own reading ability. Just as children's literature provides teachers with a wide range of choices, the same scope is provided to students. Access to this wide range of choices supports students in both assigned and independent reading. Teachers can use children's literature to build lessons and activities for both types of reading in a way that can give students a choice of texts. From allowing students to choose from a suite of texts for a lesson to providing some level of choice with assigned texts there are many ways in which choice can be built into assigned reading. Independent reading is a natural place for student choice. Choice in independent reading is also a great opportunity to help students build important skills that are characteristic of the kind of independent readers the Core seeks to build. Among other skills independent readers know how to select texts to meet their own reading interests and needs. By choosing their own books students are given the opportunity to test the bounds of their reading interests and to find texts that are just the right fit for them. Like any skill independent reading behaviors need to be practiced and the wide range of children's literature allows students the right tools to practice honing their skills as readers. Overall children's literature offers direct connection to many readers' needs thus providing a great connection for both teachers and students to meet the needs of the Core.

Even though the wide scope of children's literature provides strong connections to the Core, one misconception about the Core is that it requires certain texts. This misconception stems from the fact that the Core outlines exemplar texts to illustrate how the three-tiered model of text complexity can be applied. These texts are only offered as examples. They are not intended to be the only texts students read, and in reality, a student need not read any of the texts on these lists to meet the requirements of the Core. The Core encourages teachers to use their professional judgment to select from the widest possible range of texts. Sadly even though the Core advocates for the widest possible range of texts its selection of exemplar texts does not always show the same breadth. As Calkins, Ehrenworth, and Lehamn (2012) find the classics serve as the basis for the exemplar text lists and modern children's literature takes a backseat. However, because the exemplar lists are by no means designed to be proscriptive teachers do not have to take its biases at face value. Teachers need to find the right tools for their teaching. Not every text is going to be suited to every standard or learning outcome. Finding just the right texts to meet the standards will entail performing a critical analysis not only of the text's complexity but also of how the text's structure and ideas fit into the needs of the readers and tasks to which they will be applied. To meet the needs of the Core an assessment of complexity will come first. This assessment will allow teachers to meet the expectations of Anchor Standard 10 directly. The assessment will also help reveal the best uses for the text with the qualitative analysis revealing characteristics and structures that can be connected to other standards. There is little doubt that children's literature will meet the rigors of this process and in the end prove to be a fundamental tool for implementing the Core. With the strong research backing it up and the strong connections to the Core it is clear that professionals will judge children's literature to be a very strong part of how the Core Standards should be taught.

Selecting Children's Literature for Classroom Use

In the previous chapters the three-tiered model of text complexity was outlined. This model serves as a foundational tool for assessing children's literature that teachers will use in the classroom. However, while the Core places a premium on increasing complexity, when selecting texts for classroom use teachers will also need to assess texts on other criteria not so explicitly outlined in the Core. First and foremost teachers will need to find texts that are of the highest quality. Understanding what a quality text looks like is an important part of selecting texts for the classroom.

Assessing Quality

Assessing quality has always been one of the fundamental tasks underlying text selection. While teachers may also consider other aspects of texts including popularity and appeal, determining the quality of a text should serve as the basis for a wide range of decisions. This does not mean that teachers should only use texts that are of the highest quality. All quality levels can be useful. For example, many of the preservice teachers the authors work with assume that texts like the classic series *Nancy Drew* are inappropriate for classroom use because of their low quality. However, these texts have a wide range of uses. From doing character maps to talking about cause and effect in plot, these texts' clear structures provide just the right fit for students to engage with complex skills before a student moves on to other more complex texts. Just because these texts are seen as low quality does not mean that they are incompatible with classroom activities. However, it is still important to note that with all other things being equal, it is more likely that teachers will use quality books over lower quality ones.

The Core's definition of complexity and the concept of quality are not necessarily the same. Complexity is defined as how difficult the text is to decode and interpret. Quality on the other hand has to do with how well the author and publisher of the book did their job. However it is important to note that while we cannot confuse complexity and quality, they are connected. Books of higher complexity tend to also be of higher quality. This is because when an author does something particularly well, like construct a well-envisioned setting, for example, the complexity of the work is also heightened because this element makes the text more difficult to interpret. It is also true that the areas referred to as subliterature where professionals tend to find lower quality also has lower complexity. The use of figurative language, for example, in this literature, is very trite, thus the complexity of this work is lowered. The job of a teacher in applying the Core, then, is twofold. It is first to identify and use those items that are of the highest quality for their classrooms and then second to determine how those quality indicators translate into complexity. While in some situations, such as when a text is selected for a class read-aloud, it may not be necessary to directly make the transition to complexity. In other situations, such as when a text is used for an activity connected to the standards, an explicit translation may need to be made between these two elements. The good news is that the characteristics of quality and complexity turn out to be the very same thing, even if their interpretation varies somewhat. Characteristics of quality are the same ones that would be considered when assessing the qualitative dimension of the three-tiered model of text complexity. When assessing quality it is only necessary to look at these characteristics from a slightly different viewpoint. Let's take a brief look at how the textual characteristics change when used to assess quality.

Detail

Texts with less detail tend to be of lower quality. Without sufficient detail texts lack interest and excitement which makes them of lower quality. Quality texts will use details to connect the text structures in interesting ways. They will also use language in ways that are exciting and out of the ordinary. This means that quality books will often use figurative langue, especially when it adds something unique to the text.

Development

Texts of lower quality will have straightforward and simple development. Additionally, lower quality texts may at times develop in ways that make no sense or are unclear. On the other hand higher quality texts will have intriguing and innovative development that carries the reader through the text. Quality texts will also develop clearly, and even when developments surprise the reader they will be well planned and integrated.

Depth

Lower quality texts will be dry and lifeless, and this is most often connected to the lack of depth. Shallow texts that only use the textual structures in very base and expected ways will be of lower quality. Higher quality texts will use the textual structures in fresh and surprising ways. Quality texts will engage a reader's mind at such a depth to create new insight for the reader.

Didacticism

As noted previously texts that have an explicit instructional purpose often tend to be of lower quality because they are dry and stilted. When an author is trying to convey a very specific moral or purpose this focus tends to obscure the textual structures which usually makes didactic texts of lower quality. Texts designed to balance purpose and structure tend to result in better texts that are of higher quality. While quality texts may have an instructional purpose, those with highly didactic focus tend to be of lower quality overall.

Design

Texts of lower quality tend to have lower quality design. From the use of lower quality paper and binding, low-quality texts usually display low-quality construction. Additionally, low-quality texts tend to have straightforward and unsurprising organizations. Quality texts tend, on the whole, to have higher levels of design—a fact that seems logical when it is considered that editions of Shakespeare often have bindings of leather but editions of *The Babysitter's Club* series are less likely to be treated so well. Along with construction quality texts also tend to have interesting and engaging organizational structures designed to draw readers in.

Dialogue

Texts that do not connect with other texts or the world at large will be of lower quality. While lower quality texts may naturally connect to a reader's life and experience they often connect to only a certain small subset of readers. Lower quality texts are often trying to engage a certain type of reader only, for example, most lower-quality texts will not cross gender barriers only connecting to either boys or girls. Quality literature, however, will connect broadly with other texts and the world. It will also address more universal experiences and is more likely to connect to the widest possible range of readers.

As with the application of the characteristics while assessing complexity, to assess quality each of these characteristics will be applied to each of the text structures. Plot, setting, character, point of view, theme, conflict, style, tone, language, knowledge requirements, and construction should each be assessed with the textual characteristics to find out how well the authors and illustrators did their job. In applying the text characteristics to the structures professionals should look for authors and illustrators who use the text structures in ways that are clear, believable, fresh, universal, original, consistent, novel, appropriate, and creative. Texts that have these qualities will be of high quality. While each of these qualities can indicate a level of quality individually, part of assessing quality is to determine how the characteristics, structures, and qualities interact as a whole. Texts are the sum of their parts, so how structures connect and interact will reveal a full understanding of quality. For example, as an author uses detail to describe a setting with clarity his or her words will then also impact the depth the author will use to create a believable plot. Most professionals should already have a basic level of confidence with quality assessments like this. However, for those who require more, additional information on assessing quality can be found in *A Critical Handbook of Children's Literature* (2012) by Lukens,

Smith, and Coffel and other textbooks such as *Children's Literature Briefly* (2012) by Tunnell, Jacobs, Young, and Bryan.

Special Considerations for Quality Informational Texts

In addition to these general quality indicators it is also important to note that when selecting informational texts, professionals need to consider several additional characteristics in a way that is unique to these texts alone. Quality informational texts are interesting and appealing; they compel readers to keep reading and make the information more memorable. The following criteria are important when selecting informational texts in general, but are particularly significant for science books.

Accuracy

Accuracy is generally considered to be the most important criterion of informational texts since their purpose is to introduce the reader to factual content on a given topic. Another reason that accuracy is so important, particularly in science literature, is because children often verify their results and conclusions based on their personal inquiries with what is published in trade books. So assuring that information in these texts is accurate will assure that children are not led astray by poor information. Professionals should also note that outdated information or missing information can be just as problematic as incorrect facts, so accuracy should be defined quite broadly. To determine if a text is accurate professionals should first look at the author's qualifications. Qualified or very informed authors are less likely to include inaccurate information. Readers can also look to the author's notes, references, acknowledgements, and appendices to help determine accuracy. A good example of accuracy is found in *Eye to Eye* (2014) by Steve Jenkins. Beginning with four pages about the variations of eyes, the book explains the different types of eyes, how eyes have evolved, and how most animals rely on sight more than any of their other senses. The information Jenkins provides is accurate and compelling as it invites readers to meet and learn about animals with more than 100 eyeballs, or to discover eyeballs that are the size of a basketball.

Style

Authors need to write in a manner that students will find interesting and engaging. An engaging style is particularly important for informational texts. The facts, dates, people, places, and other tidbits of information that make up informational texts can easily become dry and unappealing. Even when they are not presented that way many students find it hard to connect with nonfiction because of previous experiences they may have had in the classroom. Many students find history to be boring, for instance, not because history is inherently boring but because of the way it has been presented to them. Informational texts need to combat these perceptions and present information in a highly engaging way. In addition to having an engaging style, quality informational texts will often include little known facts, unusual viewpoints, fascinating comparisons, and first-person accounts to capture students' interest (Tunnell et al., 2012). Overall these factors will be the things that will engage readers with the information presented. As noted engagement is then what will allow students to build understanding and appreciation for what they are learning. Again a fine example of quality style in an informational book is Steve Jenkins's *Eye to Eye* (2014). As is the case with all of Jenkins works, the book is filled with interesting snippets; this text supplies readers with enough information about its topic, eyes, to be able to supply trivia on demand.

Design

As noted considerations of design are important for all texts, but they are particularly significant for informational texts. In fact, Appendix B of the Core notes that visual elements are most important in both informational texts and texts for young readers. Effective design results in attractive, readable text that appeals to students. Beyond that, design actually facilitates children's access and understanding of information. Design plays an important part in capturing readers' attention and keeping it engaged throughout the text (Tunnell et al., 2012). Once again, in *Eye to Eye* (2014), Steve Jenkins meets all the requirements of quality design. The torn- and cut-paper collage illustrations capture the creatures and their eyes in such a way that they are sure to lure young readers in with its incredible detail and ornate colors.

Scope and Availability

Classrooms and libraries should be the places where children are encouraged to explore many kinds of books. As professionals implement the Core they can utilize books in their instructional routines, encourage children to read for pleasure, and recommend books to keep kids reading or to nudge them out of their reading ruts. Thus, it is important that adults working with children be familiar with books across the range of children's literature. To this end let's highlight the various formats and genres of children's literature.

Format

Children's books can be published in a variety of formats. The **picture book** traditionally has one or more illustrations on each two-page spread. Traditionally picture books were always 32 pages in length. Today these books can be much shorter or longer. For instance, the 2014 Caldecott Medal winning book, *Locomotive* (2013) by Brian Floca, features 64 pages of evocative, poetic text about a family traveling in 1869 on the newly completed Transcontinental Railroad. Picture books can be any of the genres—nonfiction, realistic fiction, historical fiction, traditional literature, modern fantasy, or science fiction.

Chapter books are typically longer in length than picture books and are most often characterized by their organization, which is into chapters. However, chapter books can vary greatly in length, beginning chapter books like *Frog and Toad are Friends* (Lobel, 1970) are good examples of a shorter chapter books. Fictional chapter books, such as Liesl Shurtliff's *Rump: The True Story of Rumpelstiltskin* (2013), are usually referred to as novels and tend to be longer in length. Like picture books, chapter books can be fiction or nonfiction and come in any genre. For example, nonfiction chapter books like *Red Madness: How a Medical Mystery Changed What We Eat* (2014) by Gail Jarrow exhibit the length required and are organized into chapters.

Other typical formats of texts that connect to the Core include poetry, drama, short stories, and graphic novels. **Poetry** is a form that is designed to convey emotions through language that is organized into a certain style and rhythm. Poetry can come in short formats like the picture book *Mirror, Mirror: A Book of Reversible Verse* (2010) by Marilyn Singer. It can also come in longer forms more akin to chapter books. For example, verse novels are chapter books written in verse instead of prose. Novels in verse are not limited to fiction; for example, a verse novel *Three Rivers Rising: A Novel of the Jamestown Flood* by Jame Richards (2010) recounts the impact of a real event. **Drama** is a form that conveys a text intended to be performed. There are many pieces of drama that are designed to be performed and read by children. Texts like *Theatre for Young Audiences: 20 Great Plays for Children* (1998) by Coleman Jennings provide great compilations for texts in this category. In addition, other texts extend the form of drama by telling the stories of plays in visual formats. These texts change the form into a traditional narrative format, so while they do not provide the same structure of dramatic scripts they do provide strong connections to the stories. In this category texts, like *Tales from Shakespeare* (1998) by Marcia Williams, serve as excellent bridges to the actual plays. **Short stories** are fully complete stories but they are shorter than those that would be presented in a format like a novel. Short stories offer variety to classroom instruction, and because of their length they allow more texts to be read by students in a short amount of time. Texts like *Dragons at Crumbling Castle and Other Tales* (2015) by Terry Pratchett offer a wide range of stories that are suitable for many classroom situations. In addition to these formats, currently **graphic novels** are a popular trend in publishing. Graphic novels resemble comic books and are considered a type of sequential art. According to McTaggart (2008) once a comic book is longer than 50 pages and is bound in soft or hard cover rather than stapled, it is considered a graphic novel. Fictional graphic novels abound, and an interesting trend today is the retelling of chapter books in graphic novel forms, such as Neil Gaiman's Newbery Award winning book *The Graveyard Book* (2008) which has been reformatted into a graphic novel by P. Craig Russell (2014). Also as with novels in verse, graphic novels are not limited to fiction. For example, *Around the World* (2014) by Matt Phelan recounts real stories of people who traveled around the world on bicycles.

Fiction

Fiction has long been a staple for reading instruction, reading aloud, and classroom book collections. The Core recognizes what fiction has to offer children, while calling for an increasing amount of informational text. Despite misconceptions both fiction and nonfiction are critical pieces of the Core. Fiction describes imaginary events, people, and places. While entirely imaginary some fiction represents events and people that could exist. Other forms represent aspects that could never exist in the real world. Fiction is further subdivided into genres that define additional aspects and characteristics.

Genres

Genres represent categories of stylistic criteria that indicate a fiction's distinctive style, form, and content. Understanding genre categorizations is helpful when groups of texts with similar characteristics are needed. While there are many ways to break down the genres, for the purpose of this text four general groupings are identified: traditional literature, modern fantasy and science fiction, realistic fiction, and historical fiction. The point in approaching genres from this stance is that the concept of genres is a very fluid one. For example, some more specific categories like adventure, mystery, or horror can easily cross between general categories. The characteristics of adventure can easily be found in both realistic fiction and modern fantasy. Historical fiction can also contain the characteristics of mystery or horror. This mixing of genres is especially evident in publishing today. It is becoming harder and harder to pinpoint a text as one specific genre. While most texts connect with a dominant genre, very few will be clearly identified as one genre or another at a specific level. Pinpointing genres just becomes too hard when we delve into the specifics since too many particulars serve only to engender more confusion not less. To eliminate some of this confusion general categories serve the purpose here. For those who wish a more specific treatment of genres, texts such as those previously recommended including Lukens et al. (2012) and Tunnell et al. (2012) are suggested.

Traditional Literature

Traditional literature can be defined as the stories of people. These stories were passed by word of mouth from generation to generation with no known tellers or authors. As retellers publish the stories in written form, they complete the metamorphosis from folklore to folk literature. There are many sub-genres of traditional literature including the following—fables, fairy tales, folktales, legends, myths, and religious stories.

Type	Definition	Characteristics	Example
Fables	Brief stories meant to teach a lesson.	• Single incident plots • Animal characters with human characteristics • Impersonal names such as "hare" and "tortoise" • Explicit or implicit morals	*The Lion and the Mouse* by Jerry Pinkney. Little Brown, 2009.
Fairy tales	A folk tale that includes magic or enchantment.	• Set in the distant past • Includes fantasy and supernatural • Characters are clearly defined as good or evil • Problems that need to be solved • Happy ending based on the resolution of the problem	*Rapunzel* retold and illustrated by Paul O. Zelinsky. Dutton Children's Books, 1997.
Folktales	An anonymous story told orally within a people or culture.	• Simple and straightforward story • Flat characters representing human qualities • Clear-cut problems and conflicts • Good is usually rewarded and evil is punished	*Mufaro's Beautiful Daughters: An African Folktale* retold by John Steptoe. Lothrop, Lee & Shepard, 1987.
Legends	A famous story often about historical figures or events that cannot be authenticated.	• Contains real historical characters and events • Features exaggerated elements	*Parzival: The Quest of the Grail Knight* by Katherine Paterson. Lodestar Books, 1998.
Myths	A story that offers supernatural explanations for the way the world works.	• Contains characters that are Gods or humans that have superhuman qualities • Offers explications for natural or social phenomena • Reflects on human weaknesses and strengths	*D'Aulaires' Book of Greek Myths* by Ingri and Edgar d'Aulaire. Doubleday, 1962.
Religious Stories	Stories of religious events and people.	• Connected to religious traditions • Often drawn from religious texts including scripture • Intended to convey moral ideals	*The Story of Esther: A Purim Tale* retold by Eric A. Kimmel, illustrated by Jill Weber. Holiday House, 2011.

Modern Fantasy and Science Fiction

Both modern fantasy and science fiction contain story elements not known in today's universe. In fantasy, those elements come about by magic while in science fiction those elements are extrapolated from scientific fact. Fantasy comes in many forms and types from novelized fairy tales such as *Jack: The True Story of Jack and the Beanstalk* (Shurtliff, 2015), to a story where water has magical possibilities such as *The Water Castle* (Blakemore, 2013), to a young girl rescuing a boy who has been imprisoned for 300 years by an evil snow queen in *Ophelia and the Marvelous Boy* (Foxlee, 2014), to a terrifying tree that haunts the people living in the sourwoods in *The Night Gardener* (Auxier, 2014).

Authors of science fiction create futuristic stories that may someday be possible. These authors begin with scientific principles and imagine what might happen as certain conditions or events evolve. Science fiction is published more often for young adults than for children. Yet, sometimes there are even science fiction books published for the very young such as David Wiesner's (2013) *Mr. Wuffles* where a cat finds a new toy that turns out to be a spaceship filled with Aliens. In a middle-grade book, *The Fourteenth Goldfish* (Holm, 2014), 11-year-old Ellie discovers that the teenager who shows up at her house is actually her grandfather who has discovered how to reverse the aging process. Dystopian fiction trilogies, which most categorize as science fiction, are a popular publishing trend in books for young adults sparked by Suzanne Collins' *The Hunger Games* (2008), *Catching Fire* (2009), and *The Mocking Jay* (2010).

Realistic Fiction

Realistic fiction contains story elements that could possibly happen. Realistic fiction, while entirely imaginary, could just as easily exist with characters, plots, and settings that could be real. Just as real life encompasses many different aspects, realistic fiction covers a wide range of experiences: from works that deal with problems children face such as dealing with complicated family issues in *The Thing about Luck* (Kadohata & Kuo, 2013), to stories that talk about children's growth to adulthood with the beginnings of romantic feelings in *The Boy on Cinnamon Street* (Stone, 2012), to stories that talk about children's day-to-day adventures at home and at school in *The Waffler* (Donovan, 2013), to a story where children face extreme adventures such as those in *Hatchet* (Paulsen, 1988), to stories where children are drawn into adventure by mysterious circumstances in *Under the Egg* (Fitzgerald, 2014).

Historical Fiction

Historical fiction contains story elements that could possibly happen but these stories are set in the historical past. Historical fiction is the one genre that can cross between the imaginary and the real. Some texts like Konigsburg's *A Proud Taste for Scarlet and Miniver* (1985) feature real people but at the same time fictionalize their experiences. On the other hand some texts, like *Bud, Not Buddy* (Curtis, 1999) represent entirely imaginary contexts. Historical fiction is not limited to a certain time period or place. All eras and locations can and will be represented by historical texts: from medieval times found in texts like *The Midwife's Apprentice* (Cushman, 1995), to representations of ancient cultures such as *A Single Shard* (Park, 2001), to stories that come from the historical past but whose themes are just as applicable today such as *Crispin: The Cross of Lead* (Avi, 2002), to stories about familiar events such as *Out of the Dust* (Hesse, 1997), to slightly more modern connections like those found in *Countdown* (Wiles, 2010).

Nonfiction

In the age of the Core Standards, nonfiction has become synonymous with informational text. While there may be those who see some distinction between these terms the reality is they are interchangeable, and both can and will be used to describe this body of work. In contrast to fiction, nonfiction describes real people, places, and events. Informational books are based on facts and their intent is to expose and inform readers about those facts. Reading nonfiction is important for two reasons. Nonfiction, particularly expository text, is critical to school learning and becoming college and career ready. Another equally important reason is that children tend to have a sense of awe and wonder. Nonfiction fuels their curiosity, and finding answers to their questions leads to satisfaction with learning new things they didn't know previously. Thus, many children prefer reading nonfiction to fiction.

Types of Nonfiction

A variety of different types of nonfiction are available in children's trade books. There are six general categories of nonfiction: narrative, expository, combined, hybrid, procedural, and argument texts.

Narrative Nonfiction

Narrative nonfiction is accurate information written like a story, with a well-defined beginning, middle, and end. Like stories, these books are generally read sequentially from the beginning, even though some formats like narrative nonfiction picture books are not always paginated (Young & Ward, 2012a, 2012b). Because of its connections to fictional narrative actual information in these texts is often conveyed with literary devices. This allows narrative nonfiction to offer rich curricular connections to the standards through all content areas. For example, art and social studies are both enriched by Kathleen Benson's (2015) *Draw What You See: The Life and Art of Benny Andrews*, which informs young readers not only of Andrews' life and art, but also of his efforts to promote the civil rights of women and artists of color.

Many excellent informational stories convey scientific information through characterization. Lita Judge's *Born in the Wild: Baby Animals and Their Parents* (2014) provides information as it characterizes how wild baby animals are fed, sheltered, and cared for by their parents. Lynne Cox even goes so far as to give her real-life animal a human name; *Elizabeth, Queen of the Seas* (2014) is the fascinating true story of an elephant seal living in the Avon River, which flows through Christchurch, New Zealand. Children relish thinking about a 2,000-pound mammal blocking traffic as she returns to her Christchurch home after misguided humans have made two attempts to relocate her nearer to other elephant seals. Much of the nonfiction children's literature published today is, like the adventures of Elizabeth, told in narrative style.

Expository Texts

Expository texts give information as information rather than as a story. These books are written with text structures such as cause and effect; comparison and contrast; description, problem and solution; question and answer; and sequence. Many expository trade books introduce children to navigational devices that enable them to find information quickly without reading the entire book; these include tables of contents, indexes, page numbers, and headings. Expository writing may resemble what children will find in textbooks: the style and tone are more straightforward and objective, and specialized vocabulary, often critical to comprehension, may be introduced with definitions embedded in the text or supplied with a glossary. For example Susan Campbell Bartoletti's book *Hitler Youth: Growing up in Hitler's Shadow (2005)* explains the roles that boys and girls unknowingly played in promoting the Nazi regime. Bartoletti's straightforward tone and her use of many direct quotes engages readers in this unique view of Nazi Germany. Added structures like a table of contents and index also help readers navigate the text.

Combined Text

A combined text is typically told as a narrative but includes expository sections to provide explanations of certain aspects of the story. Katherine Roy's *Neighborhood Sharks* (2014) is a notable example of a combination text. Roy tells the fascinating story of how the great white sharks return to their hunting grounds in the Farallon Islands 30 miles from San Francisco's Golden Gate Bridge. The sharks' hunt is fascinating and enriched as Roy adds expository information that describes how seals are nature's perfect food for hungry white sharks to help them get the energy they need. Expository sections that follow explain how shark's body, head, high-definition vision, endless teeth, and projectile jaws make it a deadly hunter and apex predator of the ocean. Child readers are already fascinated with sharks, but through this text they will learn more about them and why and how scientists study these large and powerful predators.

Hybrid Texts

Hybrid texts combine both fiction and nonfiction and are typically referred to as informational storybooks. These books are usually shelved in the nonfiction section of the library since their primary purpose is to explain. The best-known informational storybooks are Joanna Cole's *Magic School Bus* series.

In one case, *The Magic School Bus and the Climate Challenge* (2010), there are three storylines—the fantasy story of the magic school bus taking students on a field trip from the Arctic to the Equator, the dialogue, and the student reports that are expository text. In Molly Bang and Penny Chisholm's *Buried Sunlight: How Fossil Fuels Have Changed the Earth* (2014), the Sun actually narrates the story of how fossil fuels are formed and how humans are quickly depleting them. The text and luminous illustrations make the science concepts accessible even to young children. In Geoff Waring's *Oscar and Bat: A Book about Sound* (2008), Bat teaches Oscar, the kitten, to hear and identify the sounds around him. Boxed inserts with factual information are on some pages to emphasize key points such as how male grasshoppers rub their wings together to communicate with female grasshoppers.

Procedural Texts

Procedural texts provide readers with the information necessary to do or to make something. They may begin by listing the materials needed to complete a project, and many include illustrations that help readers follow the directions (Young & Ward, 2012a, 2012b). Common procedural texts for children include recipes, experiments, and directions for games. For example, Dinah Bucholz's (2010) *The Unofficial Harry Potter Cookbook: From Cauldron Cakes to Knickerbocker Glory* contains over 150 recipes mentioned in the *Harry Potter* series. Similarly, *Super Science: Matter Matters!* by Tom Adams (2012) provides students with seven chemistry experiments that they can try with adult supervision. The experiments help students to better understand chemical reactions, density, radioactivity, and even chemistry's role in baking a cake.

Argument Texts

Argument or persuasive texts are written to convince readers that they should change their beliefs or actions (Young & Ward, 2012a, 2012b). Authors of persuasive texts provide evidence to support their claims. In the case of Melissa Stewart's (2014) *A Place for Butterflies*, each two-page spread introduces a butterfly species, its habitat, and how changes made to their environment are challenging their survival. Stewart also provides steps humans (even children) can take to help the butterflies. Michele Miché's *Nature's Patchwork Quilts: Understanding Habitats* (2012) serves an introduction to earth's diverse ecosystems, food chains, and food webs. The author writes persuasively to convince readers that if people work together the earth's rich biodiversity can be saved. The illustrations make use of traditional pieced quilt themes to illustrate the diverse plants and animals of each habitat.

Locating Texts for the Classroom

Some professionals express concern about where they can find the right texts for their classrooms. However, today there is a wide range of resources available that can help professionals find the perfect text. From trade books to multimedia and online texts there is a whole scope of resources available. Teachers are encouraged to contact their local librarian or library media specialist to find what is available locally. Here are offered several resources for locating and exploring texts the authors have found particularly useful. These resources, including trade book award lists, publishers' websites, and book review websites, are among the favorites. Additionally, a list of great websites where free multimedia and online texts can be found is offered. By combining trade books, textbooks, magazine and newspaper articles, Internet resources, and primary source documents teachers can create text sets of materials for students to read and synthesize for any topic or standard.

Trade Book Awards

AAAS/Subaru SB&F Prizes for Excellence in Science Books: http://www.sbfonline.com/Subaru/Pages/PrizesHome.aspx

Association for Library Service to Children Book and Media Awards (includes the Newbery, Caldecott, Sibert, Geisel, and other medals): http://www.ala.org/alsc/awardsgrants/bookmedia

Association for Library Service to Children Notable Lists: http://www.ala.org/alsc/awardsgrants/notalists

International Reading Association—Children's Choices (includes fiction and nonfiction): http://www.reading.org/resources/booklists/childrenschoices.aspx

National Book Award for Young People's Literature: http://nationalbook.org/

National Council for the Social Studies—Carter G. Woodson Book Award: http://www.socialstudies.org/awards/woodson

National Council for the Social Studies—Notable Trade Books for Young People: http://www.socialstudies.org/resources/notable

National Council of Teachers of English Award for Excellence in Poetry for Children: http://www.ncte.org/awards/poetry

National Council of Teachers of English Orbis Pictus Award: http://www.ncte.org/awards/orbispictus

National Science Teachers Association Outstanding Science Trade Books for Students K–12: http://www.nsta.org/publications/ostb/

Texas Library Association TAYSHAS Award (includes fiction and nonfiction): http://www.txla.org/groups/tayshas

United States Board on Books for Young People Outstanding International Books http://www.usbby.org/list_oibl.html

Utah's Beehive Book Award: http://www.clau.org

Publishers' Websites

Traditional Trade Book Publishers

Abrams: http://www.abramsbooks.com/

Bloomsbury Publishing: http://www.bloomsbury.com/us/childrens/

Candlewick Press: http://www.candlewick.com/

Disney Book Group: http://disney.go.com/books/index

DK: http://us.dk.com/

HarperCollins: http://www.harpercollinschildrens.com/

Hachette Book Group/Little Brown: http://www.hachettebookgroup.com/; http://www.hachettebookgroup.com/kids/

Holiday House: http://www.holidayhouse.com/

Houghton Mifflin Harcourt: http://www.hmhco.com/

Lee and Low Books: http://www.leeandlow.com/

Macmillan: http://us.macmillan.com/

Penguin Young Readers: http://www.us.penguingroup.com/static/pages/youngreaders/

Random House Publishing: http://www.randomhousekids.com/

Scholastic: http://www.scholastic.com

Simon & Schuster: http://teen.simonandschuster.com/

School and Library Market Publishers

ABDO Publishing Company (Imprints: Magic Wagon, Spotlight): http://www.abdopub.com/

Bearport Publishing: http://www.bearportpublishing.com/

Bellwether Media, Inc.: http://www.bellwethermedia.com/

Capstone Press (Imprints: Capstone Press, Compass Point Books, Heineman-Raintree, Picture Window Books, Stone Arch Books): http://www.capstonepub.com/

Charlesbridge Publishing: http://www.charlesbridge.com/

Cherry Lake Publishing: http://cherrylakepublishing.com/

The Child's World: http://childsworld.com/
Enslow Publishers: http://www.enslow.com/
Gareth Stevens Publishing: http://www.garethstevens.com/
Lerner Publishing Group (Imprints: Lerner Publications Co; Millbrook Press; Twenty-First Century Books):
    http://www.lernerbooks.com/
Mitchell Lane Publishers: http://www.mitchelllane.com/
Morgan Reynolds Publishing: http://www.morganreynolds.com/
National Geographic School Publishing: http://www.ngsp.com/
ReferencePoint Press: http://www.referencepointpress.com/
Rosen Publishing (Imprints: PowerKids Press, Rosen Central, Rosen Young Adult, Britannica Educational Publishing, Windmill Books): http://www.rosenpublishing.com
Sylvan Dell Publishing: http://www.sylvandellpublishing.com/

Review Websites

Booklist and *Book Links*: http://booklistonline.com/Default.aspx
Children's Book and Play Review: http://ojs.lib.byu.edu/spc/index.php/CBPR/index
The Children's Book Review: http://www.thechildrensbookreview.com/
Great Common Core Nonfiction: http://www.greatcommoncorenonfiction.com/
KidsReads: http://www.kidsreads.com/
Kirkus Reviews: http://www.kirkusreviews.com/
The Nonfiction Detectives: http://www.nonfictiondetectives.com/
Nonfiction Monday: http://nonfictionmonday.wordpress.com/
Publishers Weekly: http://www.publishersweekly.com/
TeenReads: http://www.teenreads.com/

Freely Available Texts

250+ Killer Digital Libraries and Archives: http://oedb.org/library/features/250-plus-killer-digital-libraries-and-archives/
Artstor Digital Library: http://library.artstor.org/library/welcome.html#1
Digital Public Library of America: http://dp.la/
Federal Registry for Educational Excellence: http://free.ed.gov/
The Getty Research Institute—Digital Collections: http://www.getty.edu/research/tools/digital_collections/
Library of Congress—Digital Collections: http://www.loc.gov/library/libarch-digital.html
OpenDOAR: Directory of Open Access Repositories: http://www.opendoar.org/
Project Gutenberg: http://www.gutenberg.org/
Smithsonian Libraries—Digital Library: http://library.si.edu/digital-library/
Wikipedia: List of digital library projects: http://en.wikipedia.org/wiki/List_of_digital_library_projects
Wikipedia: List of online newspaper archives: http://en.wikipedia.org/wiki/Wikipedia:List_of_online_newspaper_archives

Applying the Text Complexity Model to Children's Literature

In the previous chapter, one example of how the three-tiered model of text complexity can be applied to a text was offered. Here are offered four more examples of this analysis. Each example represents a different format, genre, and reading level. The intent here is to further extend readers' understanding of the model now that the basics of the field of children's literature have been covered. Additionally, here several examples of tasks connected to these texts will be offered. These tasks will connect to the remaining chapters where pedagogy, research, and other practical applications are discussed.

Xander's Panda Party by Linda Sue Park, illustrated by Matt Phelan. Clarion Books, 2013

Fiction; format: picture book; genre: modern fantasy

Quantitative Assessment

Flesch–Kincaid grade level: 3.9 (fourth grade)
SMOG: 3.9 (fourth grade)
Coleman–Liau index: 7 (seventh grade)
Gunning fog index: 5.5 (text scale, fairly easy to read)
Dale–Chall readability index: 7.85 (ninth to tenth grade)
ATOS/Accelerated Reader: interest level: lower grades, grade level: 2.7
Lexile: AD380L (K–1st grade CCSS equivalent)

Qualitative Assessment

	Commentary	Assessment
Detail	Setting has the least amount of detail, as the zoo setting is familiar. Plot and characters have more detail. Limited figurative language. The book has a steady rhythm and there are some bigger words (like jubilation) that add detail. The details connect the plot and characters together and make the text clearer. The illustrations are integral to the text and reiterate many details of the plot.	Beginning complexity
Development	The development of all the elements (plot and character especially) are direct and move from one point to the next very logically. The illustrations provide support for the development of all the elements, especially the setting, which is only developed in the illustrations. All the structures provide support for all the other structures.	Beginning complexity
Didacticism	The main purpose is for entertainment, but there is a subtle instructional purpose talking about the different classifications of animals connected to a theme of inclusion. The instructional purpose is very hidden and will not be obvious to children. The structures are typical and will be expected by most children who have experience with picture books.	Beginning complexity
Depth	The text does not address overly profound themes, but the playful style and tone adds a larger level of complexity to the text. The text's connections are basic, but reflect important parts of children's lives which will connect to readers. The approach and characters are fresh and fun, even if the plot will be somewhat expected by more mature readers. The illustrations add depth to the characters and the plot.	Beginning complexity
Design	Text is constructed like a typical picture book. The text is in short dense text blocks but the font is larger. The text is grouped together and is placed at varying parts of the pages to support the illustrations. The illustrations support and add to the text in expected ways. There are several pages where the illustrations tell the story on their own. These parts require a greater visual literacy and raise the complexity.	Beginning complexity

	Commentary	Assessment
Dialogue	The text requires very little knowledge from the reader. Only a very basic knowledge of zoos may be required. The text provides all the information needed. The text will connect easily to many readers' experience and may help them to see their own experiences in a new light. Text is very similar to other texts that connect with the same theme and animal characters. There could be some strong dialogue with other texts that are similar in character or theme. There are significant connections that can be made to science instruction since animal species classifications are outlined.	Beginning complexity

Overall the text's characteristics all come out at a beginning level of complexity although some aspects like language, illustrations, and dialogue raise the complexity slightly. Because of this the text rates at about a second-grade level for reading, but could easily be read-aloud with a much younger audience.

Reader Assessment

Development and cognitive ability	The cognitive level of the text is more complex than some picture books. The rhythm the text uses and the use of some complex vocabulary raises the complexity of the text. The context of the text offers a lot of information through which the language can be defined and interpreted. However, for younger audiences some of the vocabulary may need to be covered in advance. The text is very developmentally appropriate for a read-aloud for very young audiences and very accessible for students up to second grade.
Emotional and social needs	The theme of the text addresses inclusion, a typical concern for many children. Children of many ages and situations will connect at a healthy emotional level with this text because of the use of personified animal characters. The text's characters deal with the social elements very well and will provide connections to many children's social experience with being invited to a birthday party. Emotionally and socially approachable for a wide range of ages and types of children.
Motivation	Animals are a loved character type of many children. The panda on the cover alone may provide motivation for students to read the text. The playful rhythm of the text will also engage readers' motivation. The illustrations are clear and interesting and will motivate readers to pick up the text.
Interest	Again students who love animals, especially pandas, will be interested in the text. The bright watercolor illustrations are attractive and will draw many readers in with their movement and action. Some older readers may be familiar with the author who is a Newbery Award winner, a fact that may increase interest.
Experience	Text expresses typical experiences. Most children will have been to a zoo, will have been invited to a party, and will have felt the need to be included; all typical experiences which are addressed in the book. These experiences will not be out of the ordinary so most children will easily have the experiences needed to engage with this text.

The text is appropriate and very accessible to a wide range of readers. The experiences are typical and character types will provide interest and motivation. Overall the reader level will be anywhere from kindergarten to second grade, although older readers will have connections to the themes and characters that could also engage this level of readers.

Task Assessment

Because this text has a widely accessible age range there is a number of tasks that could be connected at many grade levels. Also many standards could be addressed. For example, Anchor Standard for Reading 3, which asks students to analyze how and why individuals, events, and ideas develop and interact in the text, is easily addressed by this text.

A.R.3 Analyze how and why individuals, events, and ideas develop and interact

K–3rd-Grade Standards Connection

Have the students draw or create masks or puppets that represent two of the animal characters in
  the book.
Some basic templates are found here: http://www.firstpalette.com/Craft_themes/Animals/
  animalmasks/animalmask.html or http://www.first-school.ws/theme/crafts/paper_bag_puppets.htm
Have the students put on the masks or use the puppets to reenact a portion of the book when those two
  characters interacted. Have the students focus their recreation on the responses to challenges, feelings, sequence, and depth of the character interactions as indicated by the grade-level standard.

Fourth–Sixth-Grade Standards Connection

Have the students read the text and identify sections where different types of animals interact with one another. Have the students describe how the illustrations and text portray the characters. Have them answer the following questions: What do we know about the characters from the text? What do we know about the characters from the illustrations? What does the text tell us that the illustrations don't? What do the illustrations tell us that the text does not? What inferences can we make about the personalities and character-istics of the characters given the information in the text and the illustrations? How would these inferences change if we only had information from the text or the illustrations? Have the students write another story where two characters from the text would interact with one another at the party. Using the details offered in the text have the students build off what is offered there to extend the characters into a plot structure.

Bink and Gollie by Kate DiCamillo, illustrated by Alison McGhee and Tony Fucile. Candlewick Press, 2010

Fiction; format: beginning chapter book; genre: realistic fiction

Quantitative Assessment

Flesch–Kincaid grade level: 3.4 (third grade)
SMOG: 4.4 (fourth grade)
Coleman–Liau index: 5 (fifth grade)
Gunning fog index: 5.3 (text scale, easy to read)
Dale–Chall readability index: 7.54 (ninth or tenth grade)
ATOS/Accelerated Reader: interest level: lower grade, grade level: 2.5
Lexile: 420L (second–third grade CCSS equivalent)

Qualitative Assessment

	Commentary	Assessment
Detail	Of all the structures the characters are the most detailed. The text is entirely dialogue so the details that reveal the characters are given through their conversations and in their illustrated depictions. Setting is very basic. Each of the three chapters has a different plot line so there is a higher level of complexity in that the stories are different even though the same characters appear throughout. The language used in the dialogue is very sophisticated. There is extensive vocabulary and use of idioms. The grammar used also has a higher level of complexity. The illustrations have a lot of details. Emotions are often conveyed only in the faces of the characters. Several pages have no text and only the illustrations carry the story. Point of view comes from both the main characters through their dialogue. Each is equally presented, but having two points of view raises complexity.	Midrange complexity
Development	Two main characters are highly developed and complex. The style and tone of the dialogue used develop a unique personality for each character. There are just a few other characters that speak and interact only rarely with the main characters. They have little development. The point of view of each of the characters is developed sequentially through the dialogue and in the illustrations. The focus of the entire text is on the characters' development, so the plots and setting are less developed. Because there are three stories there are gaps in the plot development. It does not progress in a linear way but is just a snapshot of events. This raises complexity.	Midrange complexity
Didacticism	The text is entertaining and carries no other explicit purpose. The conflict, which is between the two characters as they navigate the ups and downs of their friendship, is obliquely instructive, but the intent is only to show the characters not to instruct through those interactions. The text is divided into chapters; the division of the chapters helps readers to navigate the different episodes of the plot. These structures provide support so readers understand that the story is going to change.	Beginning complexity
Depth	The text in regards to the relationship of the characters is very deep. The interaction of the two characters is interesting and provides a profound look at their friendship. The characters and their interactions are fresh and fun. The ideas the text addresses are basic since the intent of the characters and their conflicts is not to address a deep theme. Even though the theme is typical of lots of friendship texts and other realistic fiction, the characters unique depth give the text an unexpected level of complexity. The situations the characters encounter in the plot are also unique again raising complexity.	Midrange complexity
Design	Text is designed and constructed as a typical beginning reader. The text is in bold, large font that is easy to read. The text is organized into three chapters, an organization that is typical and expected. The illustrations are complex and must be read to get the whole story. The illustrations give lots of information, especially about character emotions, and so they extend the text. The illustrations alone raise the complexity of the text slightly.	Beginning complexity

	Commentary	Assessment
Dialogue	The text requires very little background knowledge of the reader. Some experience with a format like a graphic novel or with texts that rely solely on dialogue and illustrations could be helpful. The text will speak to a majority of children's experiences interacting with their own friends. There will be connections to other texts thematically addressing friendship or other realistic fiction. Addresses some more general social issues of developing and extending friendships.	Beginning complexity

The extensive character development through the exclusive use of dialogue, the detailed use of idioms and other interesting langue structures, as well as the designs heavy reliance on illustrations make this text more complex than other texts meant for beginning readers. Overall this text has a midrange complexity level that ranks it at about a third- or fourth-grade level.

Reader Assessment

Development and cognitive ability	There is little text overall in this book so the reading demands are lower. However, the complexity of some of the vocabulary and the idioms raise this level of complexity. Readers will need to have some basic understanding of the conventions of dialogue and how it is constructed to convey information. Readers will also need a level of visual literacy in order to read the pictures for essential information on character development. For most readers these things will most likely not create too much cognitive load so as to prevent them from navigating and understanding the text. The characters interactions are portrayed in a developmentally appropriate way and will connect to the developmental needs of a wide range of children.
Emotional and social needs	The text deals with the theme of friendship with humor and imagination. Children will have had their own experiences with best friends so the experiences of these characters will be familiar. The emotions that characters deal with are very typical of many real friendships and are appropriate for the age group that is being targeted (second–fourth grade approximately). The social interactions between the characters are a main focus of the text and many readers will connect to these interactions as they will have had some of the same ones themselves.
Motivation	The characters' personalities will engage readers and provide motivation to continue through the text. Once readers get to know Bink and Gollie they will be interested in their further adventures. There are also other texts about these characters that extend into a series and these additional texts may also extend motivation. The humor and playfulness of the text and illustrations will also be motivational for a wide range of readers.
Interest	The characters are unique and will prove interesting to many children. The child-like nature of the character's interactions and the imaginative lens through which both characters view the world will interest children. The humor of the text and illustrations will strengthen interest.
Experience	The experiences conveyed in the text are typical and will not put too much of a demand on any reader. Experience with idioms could prove helpful for some students. Also experience with reading illustrations and understanding of how pictures build a story could also be helpful. But any of these requirements will be minimal and not prevent most readers from experiencing the text.

The text is appropriate and matched very well to the needs of mature beginning readers. The experiences of the characters and focus on friendship themes will reach a wide range of readers. Overall the reader level will be anywhere from third to fourth grade, although older readers will have connections to the themes and characters that could also engage this level of readers.

Task Assessment

With an overall assessment of appropriateness for third or fourth grade this text fits best at that level. Because of its use of dialogue and illustrations it does not make a good read-aloud so has limited use at younger grade levels. However, from second or third grade and up there are a number of tasks that could be connected. For example, Anchor Standard for Reading 4, which asks students to determine word meanings and to analyze specific word choices, could be addressed.

> ## A.R.4   Interpret words and phrases, determine technical, connotative, and figurative meaning, analyze specific word choices

Third-Grade Standards Connection

Have the students identify vocabulary from the text. Have them focus on words they don't know or ones that they find interesting. Have students look up the words in a dictionary to define them. With the words and definitions have the students create a standard memory card matching game.
Blank card templates can be found here: http://donnayoung.org/homeschooling/games/game-cards. htm
Have the students play the game to match the word with the correct definition.

Sixth-Grade Standards Connection

Have students identify phrases that the author uses in a unique way in the text. Have students address why they think the author used the phrase in that way. Have them rewrite the section of dialogue with another phrase that means the same thing. Have the students discuss why their phrase changes the meaning and tone of the text. Have the students write a piece of dialogue for one of the pages that has illustrations only. Have the students defend why they selected the words they did and how their word choices maintain or extend the tone and style that the author uses.

When Stravinsky Met Nijinsky: Two Artists, Their Ballet, and One Extraordinary Riot by Lauren Stringer. Harcourt Children's Books, 2013

Nonfiction; format: picture book; category: narrative nonfiction

Quantitative Assessment

Flesch–Kincaid grade level: 7.1 (seventh grade)
SMOG: 8.1 (eighth grade)
Coleman–Liau index: 10 (10th grade)
Gunning fog index: 9.2 (text scale, fairly easy to read)
Dale–Chall readability index: 8.29 (11th or 12th grade)
ATOS/Accelerated Reader: interest level: lower grades, grade level: 3.4
Lexile: 760L (second/third grade CCSS equivalent)

Qualitative Assessment

	Commentary	Assessment
Detail	The characters and conflict are presented with sufficient detail. The details used here are repetitive and connected to the figurative language the author uses to convey the essence of sound and movement. Many complex onomatopoeias, metaphors, and similes are used to show in great detail how the composer and choreographer engaged with their music and dance. These details make the text clearer and bring the sounds and movement to life for the reader while raising the complexity. All the details convey a tone and style that connects well to the story being told. The setting and plot are less detailed but sufficient detail is given for understanding which gives these structures less complexity. Much of the setting is conveyed through the illustrations that are detailed and bold. The pictures support the text so they do not have much complexity.	Midrange complexity
Development	The author goes from start to finish describing one collaboration between the two artists. The plot progression is straightforward and linear showing a lower level of complexity. The focus is on character development and the theme of collaboration, so most of the development is given to these elements however they all remain at a lower level of complexity. The other elements (plot, setting, point of view) are sufficiently developed and integrate well with the other elements. No unique features are used to convey development.	Beginning complexity
Didacticism	As a nonfiction text some of the intent is instructional allowing readers to learn about these two men and their work together. However, the intent is not overt and the way the story is constructed makes any instructional intent not obvious. The text is designed as a typical picture book so there are no additional structures that add support or complexity to the text.	Beginning complexity
Depth	The theme and conflict of the text are not profound nor do they express many layers of meaning. However, the approach that is used is fresh and intriguing. The use of figurative language that is repeated and connected throughout makes the tone and style unexpected and interesting, all of which raises complexity slightly.	Beginning complexity
Design	Design is typical of a picture book. Text is bold and solid black in an easy-to-read font. However, at times the size and location of the text blocks are manipulated to convey different meanings. For example, when the music is "loud" the text gets bigger. This use of text to convey meaning raises complexity. The text is fully integrated into the illustrations and they support one another. The illustrations are bold, colorful, and unique. They are placed at varying points on the page; sometimes they take up whole pages other times they don't. This variation makes the illustrations more complex. Additional information at the end of the text (in a small font) gives additional biographical and event information that builds on the basic information given in the text.	Midrange complexity

	Commentary	Assessment
Dialogue	The text gives the reader all the information necessary to understand this one event and the character's collaboration. There are certainly other biographies about these or other composers or choreographers that could be connected to this text. Because the text recounts information about real people and events there are many connections to real-world events. These extended connections raise the complexity of the text. Additionally, the illustrator used as the basis for his style the work of painters who were contemporary to the time period of the text (in particular Mattise and Picasso). These connections make the illustrations more complex.	Midrange complexity

The format, language, and colorful illustrations give this text a complexity level suitable for even a younger audience from kindergarten to second grade, especially if it is read aloud. However, the complexity of the figurative language and the connections to other texts and events make this text complex enough for third grade and up. Overall the text complexity is about at a midrange from second to fourth grade.

Reader Assessment

Development and cognitive ability	With the exception of the character names, which could be challenging for some who struggle with pronunciation, the language used in the text is simple and straightforward. So the majority of the text should not be too demanding for even younger readers. However, the use of figurative language makes the text more complex and even though the comparisons used are mostly common they could be a stumbling block for some readers who have not yet mastered a level of cognitive processing for this kind of language. The added information at the end is complex and will be best suited for readers at a higher developmental level who will be able to understand the broader connections.
Emotional and social needs	The emotions addressed are appropriate for even younger children. The use of language to express the ideas of music and dance will connect to emotions especially for those children who already connect to those things at a personal level. The theme of collaboration is not as directly related to children's social needs but working together to create something is certainly something that many children will understand and connect to.
Motivation	Readers with personal connections to music or dance will certainly be motivated to engage with this text. However for general audiences the topic of the text alone may not provide motivation to many children, especially since most will be unfamiliar with these characters and events. However, the bold illustrations are sure to draw some readers in and the bold and playful language is sure to keep them motivated to finish. The unexpected reaction that many people have to the piece could also serve to motivate readers to find out more about the events in the text, by first reading the extended information and then possibly reading additional texts.
Interest	Many children have a special affinity toward music and dance. The way the author approaches these concepts and the use of great figurative language to bring them to life will especially appeal to those children with interests in these areas. Additionally, the illustrations with their sweeping movement and unexpected placement throughout the text will interest many children who are connected to art and artistic forms.

Experience	The text provides all the background necessary for readers to understand the text. Some experience with music and dance may be helpful but not specifically necessary. However, the text has great potential to expand the experience of readers beyond the text. Some additional information on the characters both before and after reading could be useful to add to the text, especially for older readers.

The text is accessible to readers at a wide range of complexity levels. Since it does not require large amounts of background information and the language and illustrations are approachable this text can connect to even younger readers. However, the context that can be extended beyond the text and the complex use of language makes the text suitable for third and fourth graders as well. Professionals can match this text to a broad range of readers depending on their classroom makeup.

Task Assessment

Despite its appropriateness for younger grades, the extended connections this text makes are most suitable for tasks from grades 3 to 6. For example, Anchor Standard for Reading 7 that asks students to integrate content from visual media and other formats works well with this text.

A.R.7   Integrate and evaluate content from textual, visual, and quantitative media and other formats

Third to Sixth-Grade Standards Connection

Have students identify words or phrases in the text that describe music or movement in a way that helps the reader understand these forms. Explore why the author chooses these words to express these concepts.

Have the students listen to "The Rite of Spring."

BBC Proms 2013 version with conductor François-Xavier Roth can be found here: https://www.youtube.com/watch?v=rq1q6u3mLSM

Have the students select one passage of the music and then come up with other words or phrases that express how that passage sounds or feels.

Have students identify ways that the illustrator uses pictures to express music or dance in a way that helps readers understand these forms. Explore why the illustrator chooses these images to express these concepts.

Have the students watch versions of "The Right of Spring."

Joffrey Ballet 1987 version can be found here: https://www.youtube.com/watch?v=jF1OQkHybEQ

Another version that provides an animated graphical score can be found here: https://www.youtube.com/watch?v=O2tkp6eeh40

Explore how these images change or enhance understanding of the music. How do the different versions differ? What does each offer that other versions may not? Have the students select a passage from the music and create a picture or movement that captures how the passage sounds or feels.

Stronger Than Steel: Spider Silk DNA and the Quest for Better Bulletproof Vests, Sutures, and Parachute Rope by Bridget Heos, illustrated by Andy Comins. Houghton Mifflin Company, 2013

Nonfiction; format: chapter book; category: expository texts

Quantitative Assessment

Flesch–Kincaid grade level: 6.7 (seventh grade)
SMOG: 7 (seventh grade)
Coleman–Liau index: 8 (eighth grade)
Gunning fog index: 9.4 (text scale, fairly easy to read)
Dale–Chall readability index: 7.15 (ninth to tenth grade)
ATOS/Accelerated Reader: interest level: middle grade, grade level: 6.2
Lexile: 860L (fourth/fifth grade CCSS equivalent)

Qualitative Assessment

	Commentary	Assessment
Detail	All the text structures are highly detailed and complex. The plot, setting, and characters are described with concrete details that engage readers with the complexity of the scientific topics being addressed. In addition to the main text there are sidebars that extend the detail offered in the text by expanding on concepts and issues already discussed. The purpose of the details is to make the text clear and interesting. The concepts of DNA and genetic engineering can be complex and the details serve to engage readers and clarify concepts. The details are conveyed through a style that maintains the scientific integrity of the text but makes it clear for readers who don't have experience with these issues. The text uses a wide range of complex scientific vocabulary. Much of it is defined or made clear from the context of the text. The author uses interesting language to describe the ideas presented. The photographs are detailed and raise the complexity by offering in-depth, detailed views of the processes and ideas described in the text.	Higher complexity
Development	The text is structured to model the process of scientific inquiry. Because of this the development is not truly linear since this process is often recursive in nature. This raises the complexity of the text. The text is divided so it flows well even though it is not direct from beginning to end. Headings that divide the text and photograph captions are features that guide the reader throughout the text. These guides tend to lower complexity somewhat. Sidebars and pages of additional information break up the main text and interrupt the development with additional information. These features not only support the text but also break it up in a way that makes it more complex. The illustrations both support and extend the development of the ideas covered in the text giving them a midrange level of complexity.	Higher complexity
Didacticism	The informational nature of the text connects to an instructional purpose. However, the text is designed to be more narrative in style and tone so the instruction is not overt. The text uses a few structures that help guide the reader in such a way that the higher complexity level is supported for readers who may need that help. The addition of photograph captions and sidebars helps support the texts information but because of the amount and their placement they can interrupt the flow of the text and make it more complex to navigate.	Higher complexity

	Commentary	Assessment
Depth	The text goes into great depth with its theme of scientific discovery by covering a wide range of processes the scientists used to address one problem. The text connects and raises all sorts of scientific questions that can be connected to the topic addressed in this and other texts. The text uses interesting language and photographs to make the process of scientific discovery interesting. Also the focus on the people behind the discovery, which is the typical approach of this series (*Scientists in the Field*), makes the text interesting and brings what could be a dry topic to life at a very high complexity level.	Higher complexity
Design	The text is designed in a longer picture book format. The text is very small and densely packed making this part of the design very complex. Full color photographs are included on each page. Some photographs cover a full page with only a small caption of text. Sidebars and boxes break up the text and add additional information. These additions break up the expected organization, so that each page is unusual making the text flow in a scattered manner. This scattering makes the text much more complex. Overall the design of the text is bold and eye catching. The photographs support and extend the text by illustrating the issues discussed and giving new information.	Higher complexity
Dialogue	The complex level of scientific ideas and vocabulary presented in the text expect a certain level of background from the reader with scientific discussion. However, the load is not extensive and readers who do not have this background should not be overly burdened with the text. The text is similar to other informational texts including the others in the series. This text has the potential to connect with other texts about scientific discovery or even scientist biographies.. The focus of the text on real people and real discoveries connects with the broader scientific community. All of these connections raise the complexity of the text.	Higher complexity

This text engages all the text characteristics and structures at a very high level making it a very complex text. While sections of the text could easily be used with students in the lower grades overall the text complexity rates as appropriate for the higher grades especially for fifth and sixth graders.

Reader Assessment

Development and cognitive ability	The scientific concepts and vocabulary require a higher level of cognitive ability from the reader. Readers should be at a developmental level where information about the scientific method and discovery would be covered. The density of the text and the small font size will require readers with a higher level of reading development.
Emotional and social needs	The text approaches the topic from an emotional level that is very approachable for older students. The text focuses on the interaction between the scientists and it models some good social interactions allowing readers to extend their social understanding. The context of the text extends readers' emotional and social experience in a positive way that could encourage them to engage in their own scientific discovery.
Motivation	Readers with high interest in science will automatically have high motivation with this text. Readers who have read other texts in this series may also show a higher level of motivation. The eye-catching photographs will motivate some readers to engage with the text. Additionally, those who have an interest in animals or who have read other texts about spiders may show higher levels of motivation to engage with this text.

Interest	Those who are bent toward science and animals will be interested in this text. The eye-catching spider on the front cover will engage the interest of many readers. The photographs in the body of the text will continue to engage reader's interest. Some sidebars also offer an experiment and questions for readers. These sections will interest those readers who prefer more active forms of learning.
Experience	The level of scientific knowledge and vocabulary in this text will require a basic of background knowledge that readers will need to have experienced previously. However, the text does support the needs of readers without this experience so a large amount of experience will not be necessary for readers to engage with the text. The text will build and extend readers' experience in ways that will allow them to engage with other scientific texts and vocabulary.

The text is complex, making it appropriate and very accessible for the oldest readers. With a high range of vocabulary and concepts that need to engage scientific understanding older readers will make the best connections to the themes and characters.

Task Assessment

This text's complexity level makes it most suitable for the upper grades, 4 and up. It can connect to a wide range of standards, for example, Anchor Standard for Reading 5, which asks students to analyze structure and how it relates to the whole.

A.R.5   Analyze structure including sentence, paragraph, section, chapter, scene, stanza, and how they relate to the whole

Fourth- and Fifth-Grade Standards Connection

Have students identify one process through which the scientists were expecting to produce new sources of spider silk. Have students create a thinking map that outlines the sequence and order the scientists went through to develop the process.

Examples of thinking maps can be found here: http://thinkingmaps.com/thinking_maps_common_core.php

Focus on the scientific method and determine how the process described in the book and outlined in the chart follows the method. Determine what questions the scientists asked and how they determined what might work. Focus on how they determined what caused the results and what effect those results had on their inquiry.

Other Core Connections

Additional information for this text can be found in the discussion and activity guide given at the following site: http://www.sciencemeetsadventure.com/pdfs/scientistinthefieldguide_strongerthansteel.pdf

Bibliography

Adams, T. (2012). *Super science: Matter matters*. Watertown, MA: Candlewick Press.

Alcott, L. M. (1868). *Little women*. Boston, MA: Roberts Brothers.

Alden, K. C., Lindquist, J. M., & Lubkeman, C. A. (2003). *Using literature to increase reading motivation* (unpublished master's thesis). Saint Xavier University, Chicago, IL.

Allington, R.L. (2012). *What really matters for struggling readers: Designing research-based programs*. Boston, MA: Pearson.

Auxier, J. (2014). *The night gardener*. New York: Abrams/Amulet.

Avi. (2002). *Crispin: The cross of lead*. New York: Hyperion Books for Children.

Bang, M., & Chisholm, P. (2014). *Buried sunlight: How fossil fuels have changed the earth*. New York: Blue Sky/Scholastic.

Bartoletti, S.C. (2005) *Hitler Youth: Growing up in Hitler's shadow*. New York: Scholastic.

Baum, L.F. (1900). *The wonderful wizard of Oz*. Chicago, IL: George M. Hill Co.

Baumann, J.F., Hooten, H., & White, P. (1999). Teaching comprehension through literature: A teacher-research project to develop fifth graders' reading strategies and motivation. *Reading Teacher, 53*(1), 38–51.

Baumann, J.F., & Ivey, G. (1997). Delicate balances: Striving for curricular and instructional equilibrium in a second-grade, literature/strategy-based classroom. *Reading Research Quarterly, 32*(3), 244–275.

Benson, K. (2015). *Draw what you see: The life and art of Benny Andrews*. New York: Clarion.

Blakemore, M.F. (2013). *The water castle*. New York: Bloomsbury.

Blume, J. (1970). *Are you there God? It's me, Margaret*. New York: Yearling.

Bucholz, D. (2010). *The unofficial Harry Potter cookbook: From cauldron cakes to knickerbocker glory*. Avon, MA: Adams Media.

Calkins, L., Ehrenworth, M., & Lehman, C. (2012). *Pathways to the Common Core: Accelerating achievement*. Portsmouth, NH: Heinemann.

Cambourne, B. (1995). Toward an educationally relevant theory of literacy learning: Twenty years of inquiry. *The Reading Teacher, 49*(3), 182–190.

Cantrell, S.C. (1999). The effects of literacy instruction on primary students' reading and writing achievement. *Reading Research and Instruction, 39*(1), 3–26.

Carroll, L. (1865). *Alice's adventures in wonderland*. London: Macmillan.

Cohen, D. (1968). The effect of literature on vocabulary and reading achievement. *Elementary English, 45*(2), 209–213.

Cole, J. (2010). *The magic school bus and the climate challenge*. New York: Scholastic.

Collodi, C. (n.d.). *The adventures of Pinocchio* (C. Della Chiesa, Trans.). Retrieved from http://www.gutenberg.org/ebooks/500

Collins, S. (2008). *The hunger games*. New York: Scholastic.

Collins, S. (2009). *Catching fire*. New York: Scholastic.

Collins, S. (2010). *The mocking jay*. New York: Scholastic.

Comenius, J.A. (1887). *The Orbis Pictus of John Amos Comenius*. Syracuse, NY: C.W. Bardeen. Retrieved from http://www.gutenberg.org/files/28299/28299-h/28299-h.htm

Cox, L. (2014). *Elizabeth, queen of the seas*. New York: Random House.

Curtis, C.P. (1999). *Bud, not buddy*. New York: Delacorte Books for Young Readers.

Cushman, K. (1995). *The midwife's apprentice*. New York: Clarion Books.

Donovan, G. (2013). *The waffler*. New York: Dial Books for Young Readers.

Dr. Seuss. (1957). *The cat in the hat*. New York: Random House.

Durkin, D. (1961). Children who read before grade one. *The Reading Teacher, 14*(3), 163–166.

Ehlert, L. (1989). *Color zoo*. New York: Lippincott.

Fader, D., & McNeil, E. (1976). *The new hooked on books*. New York: Berkley.

Fitzgerald, L.M. (2014). *Under the egg*. New York: Dial Books for Young Readers.

Fitzhugh, L. (1964). *Harriet the spy*. New York: Harper and Row.

Fleischman, P. (1988). *Joyful noise: Poems for two voices*. New York: Harper and Row.

Floca, B. (2013). *Locomotive*. New York: Atheneum Books for Young Readers.

Foxlee, K. (2014). *Ophelia and the marvelous boy*. New York: Random House.

Freedman, R. (1987). *Lincoln: A photobiography*. New York: Clarion Books.

Gág, W. (1928). *Millions of cats*. New York: Coward-McCann.

Gaiman, N. (2008). *The Graveyard Book*. New York: Harper Collins.

Ghiso, M.P., Campano, G., & Hall, T. (2012). Braided histories and experiences in literature for children and adolescents. *Journal of Children's Literature, 38*(2), 14–22.

Greaney, V. (1980). Factors related to amount and type of leisure reading. *Reading Research Quarterly, 15*(3), 337–357.

Guzzetti, B.J., Kowalinski, B.J., & McGowan, T. (1992). Using a literature-based approach to teaching social studies. *Journal of Reading, 36*(2), 114–122.

Henkes, K. (2004). *Kitten's first full moon*. New York: Greenwillow.

Hepler, S.I. (1982). *Patterns of response to literature: A one-year study of a fifth and sixth grade classroom* (doctoral dissertation). Retrieved from dissertations and thesis (Proquest) (ProQuest document ID 303075290).

Hesse, K. (1997). *Out of the dust*. New York: Scholastic Press.

Hoban, T. (1972). *Push-pull, empty-full: A book of opposites*. New York: Macmillan.

Holm, J.L. (2014). *The fourteenth goldfish*. New York: Random House.

Holmes, K., Powell, S., Holmes, S., & Witt, E. (2007). Readers and book characters: Does race matter? *Journal of Educational Research, 100*(5), 276–282.

Jarrow, G. (2014). *Red madness: How a medical mystery changed what we eat*. Honesdale, PA: Calkins Creek.

Jenkins, S. (2014). *Eye to eye: How animals see the world*. New York: Houghton Mifflin Books for Children.

Jennings, C. (1998). *Theatre for young audiences: 20 great plays for children*. New York: St. Martin's Press.

Judge, L. (2014). *Born in the wild: Baby mammals and their parents*. New York: Roaring Brook Press.

Kadohata, C., & Kuo, J. (Illustrator). (2013). *The thing about luck*. New York: Atheneum Books for Young Readers.

Keats, E.J. (1962). *The snowy day*. New York: Puffin Books.

Kipling, R. (1894). *The jungle book*. London: Macmillan.

Konigsburg, E.L. (1985). *A proud taste for scarlet and miniver*. New York: Dell.

Lancia, P.J. (1997). Literary borrowing: The effects of literature on children's writing. *Reading Teacher, 50*(6), 470–475.

Larrick, N. (1987). Illiteracy starts too soon. *Phi Delta Kappan, 69*(3), 184–189.

Lasky, K., & Knight, C. (Illustrator). (1983). *Sugaring Time*. New York: Macmillan.

Lee, H. (1995). *To kill a mockingbird*. New York: HarperCollins.

Levine, K. (2012). *The lions of little rock*. New York: G.P. Putnam's Sons.

Lobel, A. (1970). *Frog and toad are friends*. New York: Harper & Row.

Lohfink, G., & Loya, J. (2010). The nature of Mexican American third graders' engagement with culturally relevant picture books. *Bilingual Research Journal, 33*(3), 346–363.

Lukens, R.J., Smith, J.J., & Coffel, C.M. (2012). *A critical handbook of children's literature* (9th ed.). Oxford, OH: Scott Foresman.

MacLachlan, P. (1985). *Sarah, plain and tall*. New York: Harper & Row.

McTaggart, J. (2008). Graphic novels: The good, the bad, and the ugly. In N. Frey & D.B. Fisher (Eds.), *Teaching visual literacy: Using comic books, graphic novels, anime, cartoons, and more to develop comprehension and thinking skills* (pp. 27–46). Thousand Oaks, CA: Corwin Press.

Miché, M. (2012). *Nature's patchwork quilts: Understanding habitats*. Nevada City, CA: Dawn Publications.

Minarik, E. H., & Sendak, M. (Illustrator). (1957). *Little bear*. New York: Harper and Brothers.

Morrow, L. M., Pressley, M., Smith, J. K., & Smith, M. (1997). The effect of a literature-based program integrated into literacy and science instruction with children from diverse backgrounds. *Reading Research Quarterly*, *32*(1), 54–76.

Ness, M. (2009). Laughing through rereadings: Using joke books to build fluency. *Reading Teacher*, *62*(8), 691–694.

O'Sullivan, O., & McGonigle, S. (2010). Transforming readers: Teachers and children in the Center for Literacy in Primary Education Power of Reading Project. *Literacy*, *44*(2), 51–59.

Ottaviani, J., & Wicks, M. (Illustrator). (2013). *Primates: The fearless science of Jane Goodall, Dian Fossey, and Birute Galdikas*. New York: First Second.

Pachtman, A. B., & Wilson, K. A. (2006). What do the kids think? *Reading Teacher*, *59*(7), 680–684.

Park, L. S. (2001). *A single shard*. New York: Clarion Books.

Pate, G. S. (1988). Research on reducing prejudice. *Social Education*, *52*(4), 287–289.

Paulsen, G. (1988). *Hatchet*. New York: Puffin Books.

Perrault, C. (1901). *The tales of mother goose* (C. Welsh, trans.). Boston, MA: D.C. Heath. Retrieved from http://www.gutenberg.org/files/17208/17208-h/17208-h.htm

Phelan, M. (2011). *Around the world*. Somerville, MA: Candlewick Press.

Pinkney, A., & Pinkney, B. (2010). *Sit-in, how four friends stood up by sitting down*. New York: Little Brown.

Ponti, C. (2012). *Chick and Chickie play all day!* Somerville, MA: Toon Books.

Pratchett, T., & Beech, M. (Illustrator). (2015). *Dragons at crumbling castle and other tales*. New York: Clarion Books.

A Pretty Little Pocket Book (1st Worcester ed.) (1787). Worcester, MA: Isaiah Tomas. Retrieved from http://lcweb2.loc.gov/cgi-bin/ampage?collId=rbc3&fileName=rbc0001_2003juv05880page.db&recNum=0

Reis, S., Eckert, R., McCoach, D. B., Jacobs, J. K., & Coyne, M. (2008). Using enrichment reading practices to increase reading fluency, comprehension, and attitudes. *Journal of Educational Research*, *101*(5), 299–315.

Richards, J. (2010). *Three rivers rising: A novel of the Jamestown Flood*. New York: Alfred A. Knopf.

Roy, K. (2014). *Neighborhood sharks: Hunting with the great whites of California's Farallon Islands*. New York: David Macaulay Studio/Roaring Brook Press.

Russell, P. C., & Scott, S. B. (Illustrator). (2014). *The graveyard book graphic novel*. Moosic, PA: Harper-Collins.

Salinger, J. D. (1951). *Catcher in the Rye*. New York: Little, Brown and Co.

Selznick, B. (2007). *The invention of Hugo Cabret*. New York: Scholastic Press.

Sendak, M. (1963). *Where the wild things are*. New York: Harper and Row.

Shurtliff, L. (2013). *Rump: The true story of Rumpelstiltskin*. New York: Random House.

Shurtliff, L. (2015). *Jack: The true story of Jack in the beanstalk*. New York: Random House.

Singer, M. (2010). *Mirror, mirror: A book of reversible verse*. New York: Dutton Children's Books.

Smith, J., Monson, J., & Dobson, D. (1992). A case study on integrating history and reading instruction. *Social Education*, *56*(7), 370–375.

Stevenson, R. L. (1916). *A child's garden of verses*. Chicago, IL: M.A. Donohue and Co. Retrieved from http://www.gutenberg.org/ebooks/19722

Stewart, M. (2014). *A place for butterflies*. Atlanta, GA: Peachtree.

Stone, P. (2012). *The boy on Cinnamon Street*. New York: Arthur A. Levine Books.

Szymusiak, K., Sibberson, F., & Koch, L. (2008). Beyond leveled books: Supporting early and transitional readers in grades K–5 (2nd ed.). Portland, ME: Stenhouse.

Tan, S. (2007). *The arrival*. New York: A.A. Levine.

Trelease, J. (1985). *The read-aloud handbook*. New York: Viking/Penguin.

Tunnell, M.O. (1986). The natural act of reading: An affective approach. *The Advocate, 5*, 156–164.

Tunnell, M.O., Jacobs, J. S., Young, T. A., & Bryan, G. (2012). *Children's literature briefly* (5th ed.). Boston, MA: Pearson.

Twain, M. (1884). *The adventures of Tom Sawyer*. Hartford, CT: The American Publishing Co. Retrieved from http://www.gutenberg.org/files/74/74-h/74-h.htm

Van den Heuvel-Panhuizen, M., & Van den Boogaard, S. (2008). Picture books as an impetus for kindergartners' mathematical thinking. *Mathematical Thinking and Learning: An International Journal, 10*(4), 341–373.

VanSledright, B.A., & Kelly, C. (1998). Reading American history: The influence of multiple sources on six fifth graders. *The Elementary School Journal, 98*(3), 239–265.

Waring, G. (2008). *Oscar and bat: A book about sound*. Cambridge, MA: Candlewick Press.

Wiesner, D. (2013). *Mr. Wuffles*. New York: Clarion Books.

Wiles, D. (2010). *Countdown*. New York: Scholastic Press.

Willard, N., Provensen, A., & Provensen, M. (Illustrators). (1981). *A visit to William Blake's inn: Poems for innocent and experienced travelers*. New York: Harcourt Brace Jovanovich.

Williams, M. (1998). *Tales from Shakespeare*. Cambridge, MA: Candlewick Press.

Wilson, G.P., Martens, P., Arya, P., & Altwerger, B. (2004). Readers, instruction, and the NRP. *Phi Delta Kappan, 86*(3), 242–246.

Young, T.A., & Ward, B.A. (2012a). Common Core and informational text. *Book Links, 22*(1), 31–36.

Young, T.A., & Ward, B.A. (2012b). Learning science content and skills: Informational text within the Common Core. *Book Links, 22*(3), 30–35.

Zusak, M. (2006). *The book thief*. New York: Knopf Books for Young Readers.

5 The Teaching Principles behind the Core

Despite common misconceptions, the Core dictates neither curriculum nor pedagogy. The Core outlines only standards and then leaves the rest up to teachers, administrators, and districts to determine how to implement them. However the research base the Core draws from makes implied connections to some important teaching principles that can certainly impact how individuals will implement the standards. These principles are not explicitly outlined in the Core; however, they are an important part of the overall philosophy of the Core. With a research base that shows how dynamic and important these approaches can be in classrooms in preparing students to be college and workplace ready, inquiry learning, 21st-century skills, and close reading will be important parts of any Core implementation.

Inquiry Learning

There are a great variety of ways to approach instruction. From explicit direct instruction models to more openly progressive ones, there are many ways to design and implement instructional environments that will engender learning. However, despite the many possibilities, there is one model that connects directly with the Core and that is the model of inquiry learning. Inquiry learning at its base is focused on teaching students how to learn. An environment based in inquiry is not about reciting facts and figures, nor is it about checking off boxes on a standardized form. The inquiry model focuses on the cognitive dispositions necessary to learn any discipline or to successfully approach and complete new tasks. This approach involves more than just rote memorizing or regurgitation. The dispositions necessary for inquiry revolve around discovery, innovation, creation, reflection, self-assessment, and inferential and inductive thinking (Stripling, 2008). Because these are the same dispositions that the Core requires students to have in order to be college and workplace ready, the Core and inquiry learning go hand in hand.

Many mistake inquiry learning models to be representative of excessively progressive models where students take all the responsibility and are left free to learn whatever they can in whatever way they can. However, inquiry is not about letting students discover on their own. In fact it is a model that is highly direct and structured. There are many specific ways in which inquiry learning can be broken down for implementation; however, each approach applies the basic philosophies that separate inquiry approaches from other techniques. Inquiry learning at its basis is student centered, collaborative, and active.

Inquiry Learning Is Student Centered

One of the greatest benefits of inquiry learning is that it is student centered. Using this model, students are asked to be an integral part of the learning process. No longer will students only sit and absorb what the instructor tells them. In an inquiry learning environment they will be engaged both as learners and oftentimes as teachers. Ultimately, inquiry puts the onus on the student in the process of creating meaning. It is no longer the obligation of the teacher to give the students what they require, but it will be the duty of the leaner to be fully engaged. When using inquiry learning models, teachers must design learning experiences that allow students to examine, investigate, question, and reflect so that they can become aware of their own learning styles, processes, and strategies. Professional expertise is essential in this environment, since the ability to draw out students' natural learning instincts requires the implementation of complex processes that are purposefully designed to be approachable and widely accessible.

Inquiry Learning Is Collaborative

Everyone is involved in inquiry learning because students are an integral part of the process. Both teachers and learners are required to participate as they engage in tasks and then reflect upon how and what they have learned. Since everyone is involved in inquiry the process becomes highly collabora-tive. Even though everyone works together in inquiry, each does have his or her own role. In inquiry the teacher's role is to serve as a mentor and guide. Teachers design instruction to ensure that everyone can participate and then it is the job of the teacher to guide students through the process. Teachers are no longer the sage on the stage doling out instruction to students. Teachers guide students through the process both from the forefront and from the side as they mold the instruction to reach the learn-ing outcomes. The students' role is to engage with the content in order to make meaning. To engage, students work with the teacher and all the students work with other students so that everyone both teaches and learns together.

Inquiry Learning Is Active

Inquiry is not a passive endeavor. For inquiry to work all participants must actively engage in it. As noted, inquiry is not about rote learning or memorization. The whole process becomes an active one because inquiry focuses on dispositions such as discovery and creation that by their very nature require active questioning and engagement. Additionally, the collaborative nature of inquiry also adds an active element. Collaboration requires that everyone be involved, and this involvement means that all participants must be active. Active learning engages students in all the process of learning by ask-ing them not only to engage with learning activities but also to think about and analyze the processes of learning itself. Because it is active, inquiry then becomes the process of learning how to learn.

Each of these elements creates the conditions that make inquiry learning possible. From this basic foundation, inquiry learning exhibits many important benefits. Research has shown that inquiry learn-ing has the ability to directly improve student learning while at the same time increasing engagement and motivation (Tuan, Chin, & Tsai, 2005; Wilhelm & Wilhlem, 2010). The most obvious reason inquiry improves student learning is because inquiry is a natural state for learning. Human beings naturally question, and it is a natural inclination to work to find the answers to these questions. Think about almost any great invention or scientific discovery and there will almost certainly be a problem behind it. Great inventors and scientists confronted these problems by asking questions and then used a variety of methods to discover a solution. This process used for centuries to create the modern world is basically the process of inquiry. Not only do these connections to real experience verify the natural-ness of inquiry, but cognitive scientists also articulate additional support. Scientists from a field known as constructivism argue that knowledge is constructed within the mind of the learner. Because of this, they conclude that learning must be an active process where learners are engaged in making sense of their own experience. For constructivists, learners are not passive beings waiting to be filled with knowledge, but they are meaning seekers who need to be engaged in the learning process (Driscoll, 2000). Thus constructivism shows that learning happens best when learners are actively engaged in analyzing, questioning, and exploring (Applefield, Huber, & Moallem, 2001).

Not only does inquiry match the basic nature of the human learning process, it has also been shown to increase motivation. As has been discussed, motivation is a complex issue and even the extensive research on the subject by psychologists like Mihaly Csikszentmihalyi (1990) and journalists like Daniel Pink (2009) gives us a wide variety of answers about what motivates humans. However, despite the diversity, we do know some basics about what is motivational. The research has shown that human beings are motivated, among other things, when they feel in control, when they feel competent, and when they are appropriately challenged. The process of inquiry learning offers a natural connection to these known motivators. Inquiry learning allows learners to feel in control since inquiry naturally affords multiple branches of exploration, and this allows learners to control the path of their own learn-ing to a great extent. The student-centered focus of inquiry allows learners to feel competence since they are fully a part of the investigation. Inquiry learning also places a premium on proper scaffolding, the process by which learning is supported and tailored to a student's individual needs. Scaffolding, by using more intervention at beginning stages and then limiting support when mastery is reached, allows teachers to ensure that each student is given the appropriate level of challenge. By meeting this challenge, learners are able to have success and feel validated in their ideas, thus they are also able to build their self-efficacy and competence. The overall process and characteristics of inquiry connect to these proven motivators in a way that allows professionals to create environments that are motivational in just the right ways to nurture the independent, actively engaged learners who will ultimately be college and workplace ready.

As noted earlier, the process of inquiry builds on the natural learning patterns that have been applied by many of the world's great scientists from Galileo to Einstein in their own explorations. All of these great thinkers build off the natural pattern of inquiry, but each certainly approached it in his or her own way. Inquiry in the classroom also can take many forms, and overall specific implementations of inquiry can all look a little different. However, the way inquiry learning is structured in the classroom has its foundation in the exploration of meaningful questions. These questions serve as the focus for the remainder of the method and provide teachers with the scope needed to select the tools and tasks they will ultimately use. All inquiry starts with a challenging problem or question that is meaningful and worthy of exploration. These questions must be complex in that they have multiple dimensions or attributes. Grant Wiggins and Jay McTighe (1998) contend that the best questions to structure inquiry should address important aspects of a discipline, resurface time and again, bring to light other questions, have the ability to be answered in many different ways, and be connected to the interests of humanity. Another way to state these ideas is that good inquiry questions will transfer across time and place, representing universal issues or problems that are important to all civilizations. Very often these questions will never have one "right" answer. If a question can be answered "yes" or "no" or "true" or "false" then it will not be a question that suits inquiry. Since inquiry questions will inherently ask learners to develop new ideas, analyze positions, and create new knowledge, during the process learners will be required to take lots of data points into consideration to come to a conclusion. Along the way learners may get data from lots of other questions that have "yes" or "no" answers, such as when they use a mathematical equation or scientific test to gather evidence; however, these questions are only smaller parts of the larger issue they will be exploring. As Wiggins and McTighe (1998) note, asking more questions during inquiry is a natural state because the kinds of intriguing and authentic questions asked in inquiry often lead to other questions. In the process, all questions, whether they are used to build background in outlying areas or to develop deep understanding of a problem or issue, are connected and lead learners along the path of discovery that is inquiry learning.

From the foundation built by important universal questions, other structures that engage students in the inquiry process can vary. Teachers can look at a wide range of sources to find the specific process of inquiry that works well for them. One example of the implementation of inquiry breaks down the process into six concrete steps (Chu, Chow, Tse, & Kuhlthau, 2008; Littleton, Scanlon, & Sharples, 2012; Wilhelm, 2007).

1. Generate an intriguing question or find an interesting problem: This step as noted earlier provides the foundation for all inquiry learning. The work of generating questions and problems for inquiry can be done by a teacher alone or depending on the class environment it can be done as a group with both the teacher and the learners.
2. Articulate a plan: The next step is to decide how to go about answering the question at hand. This process most often starts with building on prior knowledge to determine what students do and don't know. However, it then quickly moves on to deciding what other information and data are needed. Once it is understood what information is needed, it is time to articulate a plan of how to find or gather the necessary resources.

3. Gather needed resources: Knowing what is needed leads to the next step, which is to gather the resources. This may entail gathering data from a scientific experiment, reading a book, or doing an interview. No matter what type of data is gathered, this step is the application of the plan that was articulated in the previous step.
4. Synthesize the resources: After all the resources have been gathered, the next step is to synthesize them into a whole picture that answers the question and creates new meaning. This step will require several actions or activities which ensure that students can engage with important skills including selection, analysis, evaluation, and reading. Once the synthesis is complete, students should then be able to apply the totality of information they have found to determine the answer or solution.
5. Communicate new understanding: Once students have determined an answer or solution, they then need to communicate their new understanding. This step can take many forms from reports to videos, to oral presentations or dramatic readings. Most often in classrooms the communication portion takes the form of the assessment that the teacher will use to evaluate the students' learning.
6. Reflect on the outcome: The last step is to reflect on what has been learned in order to determine if the question has been answered. This step is also part of the natural assessment process used in classrooms. Reflection also gives students time to see what new questions their inquiry brought to light, and this then returns them to the first step in the inquiry process so they can begin their exploration anew.

Another example of how the inquiry process might be articulated is offered by Claudia Cornett (2015). Cornett's process for creative inquiry also consists of six stages:

1. Challenge—in this stage questions are developed.
2. Collect—in this stage information and data are collected.
3. Connect—in this stage students explore the information collected and test it to see how it works.
4. Conclude—in this stage students synthesize the information and make conclusions based on their findings.
5. Critique—in this stage students look at all the information and evaluate what has been found, making revisions as necessary.
6. Communicate—in this stage students share the information that was found.

Each of these examples conceptualizes in similar but distinct ways the exact steps that inquiry might take. Overall, these examples are pretty indicative of what a process of inquiry learning will look like. However, it would be remiss to not note that inquiry can and does take many forms. Sometimes the steps outlined will come in a different order. Sometimes it is necessary to abandon a step at a certain point and return to earlier steps to reevaluate or recompose the direction. The unpredictable and recursive nature of this process is what makes it interesting, but at the same time it can make it very difficult. Despite any difficulties the implementation of inquiry methods can be very empowering. The practice of discovery that allows for changes along the way is a natural part of the process of teaching, and many professionals, the authors included, find it to be the most exciting part. However, for many other professionals this free-flowing process makes them feel a lack of control, which can be frightening. But by sticking to the basics and connecting to the standards, it is possible to learn how to be comfortable with this type of instruction.

Another great way to address any challenges inherent in inquiry learning within an already established comfort zone is to use children's literature. Children's books are something that most teachers already use, and utilizing these familiar tools can also make the transition to inquiry more comfortable. The great thing is that children's literature is a perfect match for inquiry learning for several reasons. First, since students are at the center of inquiry learning, having texts that meet the developmental and emotional needs of the students is paramount. Children's books are the perfect type of texts to address these needs at levels of complexity and interest that are perfect for a wide range of students. Having texts that perfectly connect to children's developmental needs create just the right kind of environment for inquiry to happen. Secondly, part of the inquiry process is to gather and synthesize a wide range of information. To do this, teachers and students will need to draw from a wide range of texts. A variety of texts is needed because no one source will be able to answer the kinds of complex questions that inquiry is based on. Additionally, textbooks and other classroom texts often only offer just one point of view. However, inquiry is about gathering a wide range of viewpoints. In order to access these viewpoints it is necessary to draw on other texts. The genre of children's literature encompasses the widest possible range of viewpoints which is one way children's books makes it possible for students to engage in real inquiry. Lastly, the end outcome of all inquiry is for students to communicate their findings. To support this outcome students need good models to show them how communication should happen. Quality children's literature offers great models for students to drawn on. Authors of children's books present their own outcomes of inquiry in their texts. As students engage with these books they will have at hand the perfect models of what the ending of an inquiry process might look like. Emulating these great examples is a good place for students to start building the communication skills they need to complete the inquiry process.

Inquiry is an exciting and dynamic process. Here it has been possible to only provide the broadest strokes for the process. In the remaining chapters additional connections between the inquiry processes and children's literature will be drawn. Beyond what is yet to be offered, professionals are encouraged to look to their colleagues for support. The implementation of the Core represents a new environment for all involved. Working together is a great way to help build and learn the skills that are lacking, and together teachers can help fill in areas where others may not feel comfortable. Additionally, there are a great many professional resources available to help expand understanding of inquiry learning. A few author recommended resources are offered below.

Resources on Inquiry Learning

Dana, N.F., Burns, J.B., Wolkenhauer, R.M. (2013). *Inquiring into the Common Core*. Thousand Oaks, CA: Corwin.

Harada, V.H., & Coatney, S. (Eds.) (2013). *Inquiry and the Common Core: Librarians and teachers designing teaching for learning*. Santa Barbara, CA: Libraries Unlimited.

Littleton, K., Scanlon, E., & Sharples, M. (Eds.) (2012). *Orchestrating inquiry learning*. New York: Routledge.

McTighe, J., & Wiggins, G. (2013). *Essential questions: Opening doors to student understanding*. Alexandria, VA: Association for Supervision and Curriculum Development.

Pagliaro, M.M. (2011). *Exemplary classroom questioning: Practices to promote thinking and learning*. Lanham, MD: Rowman & Littlefield Education.

Ratzer, M.B., & Jaeger, P. (2014). *Rx for the Common Core*. Santa Barbara, CA: Libraries Unlimited.

Alberta Inquiry Model: http://education.alberta.ca/media/313361/focusoninquiry.pdf

Concept to Classroom Workshop, Inquiry-based learning: http://www.thirteen.org/edonline/concept2class/inquiry/

Essential Questions, Scholastic Instructor: http://www.scholastic.com/teachers/article/essential-questions

Inquiry-Based Learning, EduTechWiki: http://edutechwiki.unige.ch/en/Inquiry-based_learning

The Keys to Inquiry by Tina Grotzer, Project Zero Harvard Graduate School of Education: http://hea-www.harvard.edu/ECT/Inquiry/inquiry1text.html

21st-Century Skills

In its overview of the research, the authors of the Core state that evidence has shown that current educational approaches have not done enough to build college- and workplace-ready students who are independently able to apply the skills needed for success in these venues. The overall intent of the Core is to ensure that students have learning environments that will give them those skills. For the ELA standards, college and career readiness means that students have mastered important skills related to reading, writing, speaking and listening. While these groups of skills have and will always be important, the Core places its emphasis on how these standard abilities should be applied in the 21st century. The Core's focus is on the patterns of thinking and communication that students will be expected to engage with, both in school and throughout their lives. So the skill sets the Core wants students to build are the essential 21st-century skills that students will need for their future. Fisch and McLeod (2007) extrapolate from U.S. Department of Labor statistics that today we are educating students for jobs that don't even exist. In preparing students for a future that is still developing, the only way to succeed is to teach them how to engage skills that they can implement in any number of situations. Because of this, the Core puts less emphasis on mastery and restatement and instead looks at the processes and applications of fundamental skills. For example, the Core asks that students be involved in building the skills for creative thinking and synthesis instead of focusing on rote comprehension and fluency. The Core changes the focus from reading, writing, and math, but also adds in communication, collaboration, creativity, problem solving, critical thinking, technology, citizenship, information literacy, and life skills.

These skills encompass the more complex aspects of education. Many of the current educational approaches used in classrooms tend to focus more on what could be considered lower levels of thinking. Considering Bloom's taxonomy (Bloom, 1956) as a hierarchy of learning processes, current approaches might be found at the very lowest levels of knowledge and comprehension. However, these lower level skills are not the only ones that are necessary to compete in 21st-century environments. Skills that are vital for the conditions found in modern colleges and workplaces revolve around the higher order skills that Bloom outlines, such as application, analysis, synthesis, and evaluation. With the implementation of the Core teachers are being asked to focus on these more complex skills. This does not mean teachers will abandon lower order skills in any way. Comprehension and knowledge skills are still fundamental; however, the Core asks that professionals diversify their practice to ensure that they are teaching and assessing all levels of skills.

Teaching and learning under these expectations has the potential to be very different than it was in the past. The challenge will be to assess practice and discern the best way to teach these complex 21st-century skills at the level the Core expects. The language used in the Core expresses the types of 21st-century skills students are expected to learn. Verbs such as analyze, summarize, interpret, integrate, evaluate, delineate, build, and comprehend, all used in the Anchor Standards, show teachers what types of 21st-century skills the Core focuses on. In addition to the Core's documentation, other educational organizations have also been working to express the importance of these skills. For example, as early as 2000 with the creation of the Association of College and Research Libraries Information Literacy Competency Standards for Higher Education (ACRL, 2000) and in 2007 with the American Association of School Librarians Standards for the 21st-century learner (AASL, 2007), other professionals have been advocating for the exact same skills the Core is now requiring. Here verbs like *inquire, think, create, apply, share, participate, determine, access, use, incorporate, understand,* and *draw* express what these organizations see as essential 21st-century skills. An examination of the Core along with these standards shows that their intent and application are highly connected. In fact, the American Association of School Librarians makes this connection even clearer in their crosswalk from the 21st-century standards to the Core that they have provided on their website (http://www.ala.org/aasl/standards-guidelines/crosswalk). The Core's increased emphasis on important 21st century and higher order thinking skills is directly connected to the fundamental skills that many professionals have long been advocating, but now is the time to incorporate them more fully into the teaching and learning processes.

It is important to note that when 21st-century skills are mentioned, many automatically make direct connections to technology. While technology is an important component of these skills, they are not only applicable in that environment. For example, one can summarize a text with or without technology. When considering the 21st-century skills the Core requires, it is best to look at what verbs the Core uses to express the skills students need to have. These verbs should be the focus of instruction. From there, technology serves as only one of many tools with which these skills can be taught, learned, and assessed. When considering 21st-century skills, the widest possible range for when and how these skills can be used should be considered. The intent after all is to prepare students to use these skills in contexts that have yet to be invented, so engaging students in a variety of contexts will help students to transfer these skills into other areas.

In addition to technology as a supportive tool for building students' 21st-century skills, children's literature also serves as another way to engage students. The complex skills the Core is asking students to have require some form of input. For you cannot think, for example, if you have nothing to think about. Texts serve as the basic form of input for all the Core skills, and this is one reason that the Core puts so much emphasis on text complexity. There are a great number of texts that could serve to structure the learning of Core skills. In fact, the Core advocates for the widest range of texts when it asks students in Anchor Standard 7 to use content presented in diverse media and formats, including textual and visual ones. However, along with the wide range of texts that should be used, children's literature can serve as an important foundation. This is because, as noted with inquiry, children's literature is the perfect match between complexity requirements and the developmental and emotional needs of students. When asking students to learn complex skills, having a text that meets developmental needs makes a lot of sense. If a text is far too complex or emotionally taxing, then a student's focus will be on just trying to navigate the text with very little focus left for learning a skill. The perfect balance here is between a reader's needs and the task requirements. When this balance is found students can focus on what the learning outcome is instead of letting the text get in the way. Children's literature is also one of the most innovative genres out there, and its creativity offers a great connection for instructing 21st-century skills. Creators of children's books today are engaged in making some of the most pioneering texts. They are breaking the bounds of traditional texts to offer interesting postmodern takes on texts. Picture books like David Wiesner's *The Three Pigs* (2001), where the characters seemingly break out of the confines of the page are exciting examples of how authors are redefining the traditional text. Other authors have completely broken the confines of a text by adding online components to their stories, like James Dashner in the *Infinity Ring* series where readers can play out the story themselves as part of a game. Children's books are no longer the stogy, didactic works of yesteryear. Today they offer great examples of multimodal communication and show an expanse of creative processes that fit directly with the Core's emphasis on 21st-century skills.

Creating instruction that uses supportive tools like technology and children's literature to teach and assess complex 21st-century skills will be a new process for many. Standard pedagogical approaches may no longer work in such an environment. The best place to start, however, is with inquiry learning. This pedagogical technique, which we have already discussed, is the perfect fit for building 21st-century skills. In fact, a great many of the skills inquiry uses are the exact same kinds of skills outlined by the Core and the other associations. Inquiry and 21st-century skills go hand-in-hand and one can certainly be used to build the other. The remainder of this text will also reveal some more connections between classroom activities, children's literature, and 21st-century skills. Additionally, there are a great many professional resources available to help expand understanding of 21st-century skills. A few author recommended resources are offered below.

Resources on 21st-Century Skills

Brookhart, S. M. (2010). *How to assess higher-order thinking skills in your classroom*. Alexandria, VA: Association for Supervision & Curriculum Development.

Greenstein, L. M. (2012). *Assessing 21st century skills: A guide to evaluating mastery and authentic leaning*. Thousand Oaks, CA: Corwin.

Pellegrino, J. W., & Hilton, M. L. (Eds.). (2012). *Education for life and work: Developing transferable knowledge and skills in the 21st century*. Atlanta, GA: The National Academies Press. Retrieved from http://www.nap.edu/catalog.php?record_id=13398

Ritchhart, R. (2011). *Making thinking visible: How to promote engagement, understanding, and independence for all learners*. San Francisco, CA: Jossey-Bass.

Trilling, B., & Fadel, C. (2012). *21st century skills: Learning for life in our times*. San Francisco, CA: Jossey-Bass.

AASL Standards for the 21st-Century Learner: http://www.ala.org/aasl/standards-guidelines/learning-standards

AASL Learning Standards & Common Core State Standards Crosswalk: http://www.ala.org/aasl/standards-guidelines/crosswalk

AASL Standards for the 21st-Century Learner Lesson Plan Database: http://www.ala.org/aasl/standards-guidelines/lesson-plan

Association of College and Research Libraries Information Literacy Competency Standards for Higher Education: http://www.ala.org/acrl/standards/informationliteracycompetency

Assessment & Teaching of 21st Century Skills: http://atc21s.org/

Partnership for 21st Century Skills: http://www.p21.org/

Close and Critical Reading

Fundamental to the Core is the understanding that in order to be college and workplace ready, students will need to be able to independently and proficiently read and understand complex texts. This essential philosophy is fully expressed in Anchor Standard 10, but the expectation of how independent and proficient reading should look is characterized by all the other standards. The type of reading students are asked to do under the Core delves to a much deeper level than may have been considered before. The Core wants students to be critical and analytical readers who engage with texts at a very close level in order to extract meaning. This type of deep engagement then goes beyond a surface or quick reading and becomes a task devoted to gaining deep comprehension. What the Core wants from readers is close reading. In fact, it even goes so far as to state in Anchor Standard 1 that students should "read closely." The concept of close reading was first introduced by literary theorist Ivor Armstrong Richards (1942) and was later developed into a foundational theory of the New Criticism movement that enveloped American literary criticism during the mid-20th century. This theory advocated for the reading and rereading of very short passages of text. The hope was that a sustained look at the individual words and grammar of a passage would reveal meaning. Even though the movement of New Criticism was supplanted by other literary theories in the late 20th century, today many still connect the idea of close reading to the deep study of very small selections of text (Lehman & Roberts, 2014).

However, close reading has also exploded from the confines of its new critical roots to encompass a much broader definition and scope. Fisher and Frey (2014) define close reading very broadly when they consider it to be the practice of analyzing a text to find deep meaning. Like the Core, Fisher and Frey see close reading as a process that is connected to critical thinking in that it allows students to make connections between texts and the world at large. Here the abilities for close reading include being able to identify key themes and details, to inspect word usage and text structures, and to synthesize understanding to create new knowledge. These key abilities should look very familiar as they are the exact same ones the Core outlines. Also these skills connect directly to the concepts of inquiry learning and the 21st-century skills that have been discussed. In inquiry and in the application of 21st-century skills, the overall purpose is to learn how to create new understanding and knowledge and then to learn how to communicate that learning to others. In order to achieve this level of deep understanding, a closer, more critical type of reading is needed than if one were reading to learn just basic facts. Close reading is the way readers need to engage with texts in order to uncover layers of meaning. This process of discovering what texts have to say then allows students to be prepared for the activities that require them to integrate and share the knowledge they have gained.

Close reading is a term that is repeated throughout the standards. Close reading involves guiding students to return to a portion of challenging text to "probe more thoroughly for deeper comprehension" (Boyles, 2014, p. 1). While close reading helps students develop strategies, its ultimate purpose is to develop knowledge (Pearson & Hiebert, 2013). Close reading is most successful when teachers develop text-dependent questions related to the standards that require students to use evidence from the text in their answers. Teachers may return to the same portion of the text more than once with new text-dependent questions guiding students to carefully examine the text for multiple purposes (Frey & Fisher, 2013). Close reading as articulated by the Core tends to focus on the analysis of the text structures, since the exploration of text structures lies at the heart of the Core. From the focus on themes in Anchor Standard 2 to the focus on point of view in Anchor Standard 6, the Core covers all the main text structures from character to language. This strong connection to text structures is one reason why teachers are encouraged to conduct an analysis of them as part of the qualitative dimension. By looking closely at the structures, teachers will be able to find just the right texts to connect to each standard. In order for students to closely analyze the words, ideas, and content of a text, they must have a text that is the best exemplar for that structure. Through the qualitative analysis, teachers will have done the assessment necessary to find just the right text for each standard.

The teaching of text structures has always been a fundamental task in ELA classrooms. However, the Core expects that through close and critical reading students will go beyond the understanding that may have previously been expected to strengthen overall content understanding (Sinatra, 2000). In this way the Core then connects the analysis of a text's purpose and structure to the larger concept of understanding and meaning making. Close reading in the Core is not about understanding the structure of individual texts per se, but expanding that context to compare, integrate, and evaluate all texts. So the close reading the Core requires asks that students understand the text as a whole and also how a text converses with other texts. In applying the Anchor Standards, close reading is necessary, but depending on the situation the act of close reading can look very different. From breaking apart a very short passage to assess the figurative meaning of words used in a text (Anchor Standard 5) to reading a whole text with a critical eye in order to determine how the author develops characters over the course of the text (Anchor Standard 3), close and critical reading can be structured in many ways. In the end, however, the purpose of close reading should be to get students to read like a writer (Robb, 2004) so they can think about and critically analyze what texts are doing and saying.

As with the principles of inquiry learning and 21st-century skills espoused by the Core, children's literature is a perfect fit when applying close and critical reading strategies. Once again, children's literature makes good connections here because it is developmentally and emotionally appropriate for elementary school students. Close reading requires focused and sustained effort over a period of time, which requires a lot of motivation and interest on the part of the reader to sustain. Because developmentally appropriate works tend to be of more interest to readers, and interest increases motivation, children's literature will be a good choice for the effort that needs to be expended with close reading. Beyond this, children's literature is motivational in and of itself. With lots of interesting topics and imaginative presentations to draw from, children's books offer the widest possible range of texts that will motivate their readers. With such scope at their fingertips, teachers are sure to find just the right kind of text that will engage readers during the sustained effort close reading requires.

Children's literature also proves to be a good fit for close reading because there is a great variety of text lengths. As has been noted, close reading can focus on a small portion of a text or a larger one depending upon the circumstances. However, there are times that a whole text is needed but at the same time it needs to be short in order for students to engage in necessary tasks. Children's books offer just these kinds of texts. Complex picture books or easy readers are of a perfect short length so that a whole text can be used for analysis without taking too much time. For the Anchor Standards that look at text cohesion, like number 3 that looks at development over the course of a text or number 5 that looks at both parts and the whole text, having shorter texts that are complete provides a less time-intensive way to address these requirements. This perspective may mean that teachers need to look at text formats in bold new ways. Picture books are not just for kindergartens anymore; with the right connections to a task these books can certainly be raised to the level of complexity for even a sixth grader. Herein lies another important reason that children's literature connects to close reading. Within this genre there is the widest possible range of complexity levels. Not only are myriad complexity levels needed when addressing readers' needs, they are also essential when addressing tasks. When a task or skill that teachers are asking students to learn is very complex, the text used to teach that task will likely need to be of lesser complexity. When a task or strategy is first learned the focus should be on the task, not on the text. Then as mastery is gained the level of complexity of the text can be raised. This approach at scaffolding tasks and texts at the right level of complexity for optimal learning is an important part of close reading. Students cannot, for example, focus on close reading to determine how specific words shape the tone of a text (Anchor Standard 4) if the text is too complex for them. In the case of an overly complex text, students most likely will focus on the text and their frustrations with it instead of on the skill to be taught. Scaffolding up from less complex texts allows students to focus on the skill, and then after finding success there they can apply the skill to other sources. Children's literature provides just the right range and scope of texts needed to achieve proper scaffolding. Teachers have so many texts to drawn on in this genre that they are certain to find just the right connections for all their readers and tasks.

Many teachers will already have been trained in the processes of close reading as part of the pre-service education or professional development. This understanding will transfer well to expectations of the Core. Working together with other professionals is also a great way to help build and learn the skills that are lacking. Together all professionals can help fill in areas where others may not feel comfortable. The remainder of this text will also reveal some more connections between close reading and children's literature that will help support professional inquiry into this strategy. Additionally, there are a great many professional resources available to help expand understanding of close reading. A few author recommended resources are offered below.

Resources on Close and Critical Reading

Beers, K., & Probst, R. E. (2012). *Notice and note: Strategies for close reading*. Portsmouth, NH: Heinemann.

Boyles, N. (2012). Closing in on close reading. *Educational Leadership, 70*(4), 36–41.

Buckley, E. M. (2011). *360 Degrees of text: Using poetry to teach close reading and powerful writing*. Urbana, IL: National Council of Teachers of English.

Cummins, S. (2012). *Close reading of informational texts: Assessment-driven instruction in grades 3–8*. New York: Guilford Press.

Fisher, D., & Frey, N. (2014). *Close reading and writing from sources*. Newark, DE: International Reading Association.

Fisher, D., & Frey, N. (2012). Close reading in elementary schools. *Reading Teacher, 66*(3), 179–188.

Lehman, C., & Roberts, K. (2014). *Falling in love with close reading: Lessons for analyzing texts—and life*. Portsmouth, NH: Heinemann.

Lewin, L. (2010). Teaching critical reading with questioning strategies. *Educational Leadership 67*(6), n.p. Retrieved from http://www.ascd.org/publications/educational-leadership/mar10/vol67/num06/Teaching-Critical-Reading-with-Questioning-Strategies.aspx

Close Reading of Literary Texts: A Strategy Guide from ReadWriteThink: http://www.readwritethink.org/professional-development/strategy-guides/close-reading-literary-texts-31012.html

The Art of Close Reading from the Critical Thinking Community: http://www.criticalthinking.org/pages/the-art-of-close-reading-part-one/509

Reading Critically, Harvard Library Research Guides: http://guides.library.harvard.edu/sixreadinghabits

"Understanding Critical Reading and Thinking": http://www.pearsonhighered.com/showcase/anderson1e/assets/ch3.pdf

Bibliography

American Association of School Librarians (AASL). (2007). *Standards for the 21st-century learner.* Retrieved from http://www.ala.org/aasl/standards-guidelines/learning-standards

Applefield, J.M., Huber, H., & Moallem, M. (2001). Constructivism in theory and practice: Toward a better understanding. *The High School Journal, 84*(2), 35–53.

Association of College and Research Libraries (ACRL). (2000). *Information literacy competency standards for higher education.* Retrieved from http://www.ala.org/acrl/standards/informationliteracy-competency

Bloom, B.S. (1956). *Taxonomy of educational objectives, handbook I: The cognitive domain.* New York: David McKay Co Inc.

Boyles, N. (2014). *Closer reading grades 3–6: Better prep, smarter lessons, deeper comprehension.* Thousand Oaks, CA: Corwin.

Chu, S., Chow, K., Tse, S.-k., & Kuhlthau, C.C. (2008). Grade 4 students' development of research skills through inquiry-based learning projects. *School Libraries Worldwide, 14*(1), 10–37.

Cornett, C.E. (2015). *Creating meaning through literature and the arts: Arts integration for classroom teachers* (5th ed.). Boston, MA: Pearson.

Csikszentmihalyi, M. (1990). *Flow: The psychology of optimal experience.* New York: HarperCollins.

Driscoll, M. (2000). *Psychology of learning for instruction* (2nd ed.). Needham Heights, MA: Allyn & Bacon.

Fisch, K., & McLeod, S. (2007, February 8). Did you know; shift happens—globalization; information age [video file]. Retrieved from https://www.youtube.com/watch?v=ljbI-363A2Q

Fisher, D.B., & Frey, N. (2014). *Close reading and writing from sources.* Newark, DE: International Reading Association.

Frey, N., & Fisher, D.B. (2013). *Rigorous reading: 5 Access points for comprehending complex texts.* Thousand Oaks, CA: Corwin.

Lehman, C., & Roberts, K. (2014). *Falling in love with close reading: Lessons for analyzing texts—and life.* Portsmouth, NH: Heinemann.

Littleton, K., Scanlon, E., & Sharples, M. (2012). *Orchestrating inquiry learning.* New York: Routledge.

Pearson, P.D., & Hiebert, E.H. (2013). Understanding the Common Core State Standards. In L. Mandel Morrow, K.K. Wixson, & T. Shanahan (Eds.), *Teaching with the Common Core Standards for English language arts, grades 3–5.* New York: Guilford.

Pink, D. (2009). *Drive: The surprising truth about what motivates us.* New York: Riverhead Books.

Richards, I.A. (1942). *How to read a page: A course in effective reading, with an introduction to a hundred great words.* New York: W.W. Norton & Co.

Robb, L. (2004). *Nonfiction writing: From the inside out.* New York: Scholastic.

Sinatra, R.C. (2000). Teaching learners to think, read, and write more effectively in content subjects. *Clearing House*, 73(5), 266–273.

Stripling, B. (2008). Inquiry: Inquiring minds want to know. *School Library Media Activities*, 25(1), 50–52.

Tuan, H.-L. Chin, C.-C., & Tsai, C.-C. (2005). Investigating the effectiveness of inquiry instruction on the motivation of different learning styles students. *International Journal of Science and Mathematics Education*, 3(4), 541–566.

Wiesner, D. (2001). *The three pigs*. New York: Clarion Books.

Wiggins, G., & McTighe, J. (1998). *Understanding by design*. Alexandria, VA: Association for Supervision and Curriculum Development.

Wilhelm, J.D. (2007). *Engaging readers and writers with inquiry*. Jefferson City, MO: Scholastic Teaching Resources.

Wilhelm, J.D., & Wilhlem, P.J. (2010). Inquiring minds learn to read, write and think: Reaching "all" learners through inquiry. *Middle School Journal*, 41(5), 39–46.

6 Core Skills and Strategies for a Love of Reading

Everyone—parents, administrators, teachers, legislators, and community members—wants to see high levels of literacy for students. This is certainly the very aim the Core is trying to achieve as well. However, what meets the requirements for literacy success differs among educators. For some people, high achievement test scores will suffice. But these individuals probably fail to consider the fact that even while some students receive high scores on tests they rarely choose to read and write. To others, standardized test scores contribute only a small part of what they consider highly literate behavior. Instead, they seek literacy engagement for students. According to Guthrie (2004), there are two aspects of engagement: First, students are actively involved in reading and writing. Second, engaged reading and writing involve deep thinking and strategy use when writing to communicate and reading to learn with text rather than merely completing assignments. The standards of the Core fall most clearly under the vision of this second stance since its focus on skill building and depth are more directly connected to Guthrie's idea of engagement. While there is little doubt that Core implementations can lead to such engagement, the Core documentation does not directly address these issues to such an extent that many believe that engagement is the missing link in the Core Standards (Guthrie & McPeake, 2013). The goal of every teacher, particularly those who are trying to build the kind of independent readers and writers who will be college and workplace ready, should be to build literacy engagement. Since this goal is wholly compatible with the Core, but not directly addressed there, let's look to the research to see what kinds of skills and strategies teachers can use to achieve this goal.

To build independent, engaged readers, teachers must address both the will and the skill—the will to read and the skills and strategies necessary to do so. To engage their students' will teachers must help their students develop a love of reading. To address their skills teachers will need to help their students develop the skills and strategies necessary to read at high levels. The CCSS addresses skills and strategies that students must develop in order to be college and career ready. However, they only briefly address the issues of will. Despite the lack of information from the Core on this issue most professionals strongly believe that teachers who work as hard helping kids love reading as they do teaching kids skills and strategies are the ones who see lasting gains in literacy achievement. The Core was never designed to address every issue in regards to reading instruction and teaching, so its cursory address of reading engagement is not surprising. However, to gain the kind of achievement that the Core requires there is little doubt that building a love of reading will be an essential part of its implementation. To build the will, teachers will need to look to other research to discover the best ways they can help their students learn to love reading while at the same time facilitating the development of skills and strategies.

Developing Classrooms Where a Love of Reading Flourishes

Gambrell (2011) cited research from the 2010 Program for International Student Assessment (PISA) that students who enjoyed reading the most performed significantly better than students who did not enjoy reading as much. This study of students from 64 countries illustrates the link between liking to read and reading achievement. An alarming finding in the study was that 37 percent of the students reported that they do not read for enjoyment at all. Since as Gambrell notes that the most important goal of reading instruction is helping students fall in love with reading; teachers must design their instruction in such a way that it engages their students will to read. Research shows that there are seven main components that have been proven to create the kinds of classrooms where the love of reading flourishes. These components include the teacher, time to read, reading aloud, classroom libraries, student choice, interesting texts, and structured classroom pedagogies.

The Teacher

The teacher's role in helping students fall in love with reading is paramount. The first step for teachers who wish to give their students a love of reading is to be readers themselves. A number of research studies have found that teachers who are readers have students who are both engaged readers and high achievers. Teachers' reading habits significantly affect student achievement, motivation, and engagement (Applegate & Applegate, 2004). Morrison, Jacobs, and Swinyard (1999) conducted a study in which they found that teachers who are enthusiastic readers are more likely to use recommended innovations in their teaching than their peers who are not passionate readers. McKool and Gespass (2009) had similar findings. In particular their study noted that teachers who are avid readers are more likely to incorporate the best practices that promote a love of reading such as reading aloud, providing time to read, book discussion, and literature circles. Additionally, Burgess, Sargent, and Smith (2011) found that teachers with higher knowledge of children's books employed more reading best practices than did teachers with less knowledge of children's books. Trelease (2013) notes that when teachers know both their children and books they are better able to serve as "matchmakers" who are able to find the right books to keep their students reading. This is important because such teachers can recommend books that their students will more likely read and enjoy.

Time to Read

A second important aspect for classrooms where students love to read is that they are given the time they need to read. Most students need more time to read in school. Hiebert and Martin (2009) have summarized research that suggests elementary children may read only 7–18 minutes per a day in school, even when the school dedicates 90 minutes to literacy instruction. However, the reality is that it takes time and practice for children to become readers, so in order to be readers they need to take the time to read.

One way by which teachers can give students more time to read is by using pedagogies and strategies that allow students to do all kinds of independent reading. Researchers have found a number of benefits associated with independent reading. In summarizing this research, Moss and Young (2010) found five noteworthy outcomes:

1. increased vocabulary development;
2. greater background and domain knowledge;
3. better fluency and comprehension;
4. improved reading achievement; and
5. greater interested in books and motivation to read.

These outcomes illustrate how some activities result in both affective and cognitive benefits. Additionally, Cunningham and Allington (2011) note that students need (1) instruction, (2) practice on the skills, and (3) practice with the whole act of reading. They recommend that students need a minimum of 20 minutes of daily independent reading. There are many strategies that teachers can use to implement independent reading in their classroom; sadly a discussion on these is outside the scope of this work. For teachers who want more information about how to make independent reading work in their classrooms, the following are recommend: *The Daily 5: Fostering Literacy Independence in the Elementary Grades* (Boushey & Moser, 2014) and *The Book Whisperer: Awakening the Inner Reader in Every Child* (Miller, 2009).

Reading Aloud

The third component of a classroom where a love of reading flourishes is reading aloud. Reading aloud enables teachers to model reading to their students. At the same time, they share their passion for reading and demonstrate reading's many benefits including finding pleasure, gaining information, meeting personal needs, solving problems, taking an escape, and providing writing road maps. Reading aloud to students is essentially an invitation to them to become readers (Fisher, Flood, Lapp, & Frey, 2004). Research has shown that there are many benefits of reading aloud to students. For instance, reading aloud:

- provides a model of expressive, fluent reading (Mooney, 2004);
- plays a fundamental role in "inviting listeners to be readers" (Fisher et al., 2004);
- offers a pleasurable experience to listeners (Young, 2006a);
- introduces students to new titles, authors, illustrators, genres, and text structures (Miller & Kelley, 2014; Young, 2006a);
- builds a sense of community (Serafini & Giorgis, 2003);
- provides students with support in choosing books for their own reading (Miller & Kelley, 2014);
- increases both listening and reading vocabulary (Stahl, 1999);
- provides students with access to books they may not be able to experience on their own (Serafini & Giorgis, 2003); and
- when teachers read aloud and discuss texts, their students tend to read more and experience literacy growth (Fox, 2013; Heath, 1983; Trelease, 2013).

There are other reasons for reading to students. Today's students need to be introduced to the many cultures in our society and world. Reading to students is often the best approach to meet this goal. Moreover, the approach makes it possible to encourage an understanding of the diverse nature of our society, and, at the same time, to see commonalities across cultures and nationalities. It is critical for today's students to have opportunities to think about and discuss issues related to gender, class, power, and other issues and roles.

Many teachers have learned that reading daily to their students is a sound investment of their time. The daily reading aloud of a poem, a picture book, a chapter from a chapter book, and some nonfiction excerpt from a book, magazine, newspaper, or digital text both enriches students' lives and provides them with a full range of reading in different genres and text forms (Young, 2006a). While such reading takes time in the busy instructional day, it is a sound investment in students' reading lives. Indeed, students need daily opportunities to hear books read aloud even if it is only for 20 or 25 minutes.

It is important for teachers to keep track of what they read aloud to their students. Teachers often note the books they read aloud to their students in some type of log. This log enables them to note which genres their students have experienced, the balance between male and female protagonists, balance in cultures, which nonfiction text features and structures were presented, and which authors and illustrators were introduced (Young, 2006a). Some teachers create charts to remind students of what has been read aloud, or put the books read aloud in a special section of the classroom library (Cunningham & Allington, 2011; Miller & Kelley, 2014). Teachers often notice that the recently read read-aloud books are in high demand by students who want to re-experience the book.

Sadly, researchers have noted that there is a negative correlation with grade level and read-aloud experiences in elementary school. That is, the higher the grade level, the less likely teachers are to read aloud to their students (Duke & Young, 1993). Cunningham and Allington (2011) note that this is unfortunate since most children become readers between the ages of 8 and 11, and reading aloud to older students provides them the motivation to read when they have the skills to take advantage of the motivation. So even in the upper grades reading aloud will be a significant part of any classroom that is designed to build a love of reading.

Classroom Libraries

One essential factor in getting students to read independently is access to books. Students are likely to spend more time reading when they are in classrooms with adequate classroom libraries. Thus, classrooms that are packed with books are a fourth component of classrooms where students love to read. Interviews with avid readers have found that children who love to read almost always have access to books at home. Since many students today do not have that access, it is paramount that all children are provided with books in the classroom (Fractor, Woodruff, Martinez, & Teale, 1993; Moss & Young, 2010).

Classroom libraries provide students with immediate access to books. Students who have ready access to books in their classrooms have better attitudes about reading, reading achievement, and comprehension than their peers with less access to books in their classrooms. Moreover, students are likely to spend more time reading when they are in classrooms with adequate classroom libraries (Allington & Cunningham, 2006; Krashen, 1998; Moss & Young, 2010; Routman, 2003). For example, Morrow (2003) and Neuman (1999) both report that students read 50–60 percent more in classrooms with libraries than in classrooms without them.

More books in the classroom lead to more voluntary reading, which in turn results in higher achievement (Krashen, 2004). In a study of 32 schools in Maryland, Guthrie, Schafer, Von Secker, and Alban (2000) found that an abundance of trade books in the classroom predicted gains on statewide reading, writing, and science tests. Another study by Gambrell asked students in grades 1, 3, 5, and 8 where they found their favorite books to read, and the overwhelming responses were the classroom library as opposed to in the home, or the school, or public libraries (Moss & Young, 2010).

It is not enough to have books in the classroom. Teachers must be intentional about the books they put in their classrooms and about how they promote the books to their students. To build useful classroom libraries it is suggested that teachers should work toward the following matters:

- about half of the classroom library should be nonfiction since many students prefer nonfiction to fiction (Moss & Young, 2010);
- of the nonfiction in the classroom library, two-thirds should be expository since the ability to read expository text correlates with school success (Kletzien & Dreher, 2004);
- fiction books in the classroom library should include all of the literary genres (contemporary realistic fiction, folk literature, historical fiction, modern fantasy, and science fiction) (Moss & Young, 2010; Tunnell, Jacobs, Young, & Bryan, 2012);
- a classroom library should include an assortment of poetry ranging from the funny light verse to the more serious poems for children (Tunnell et al., 2012);
- a classroom library should include some books for English learners in their native language so they can maintain their language and have easier reading experiences (Hadaway & Young, 2010);
- a classroom library should have a balance of books with boy and girl protagonists so all students can find books to which they can relate (Moss & Young, 2010);
- well-stocked classroom libraries should have at least seven books per child (International Reading Association, 1999);
- classroom libraries should include comics, graphic novels, magazines, funny books, scary books, and series books (Cunningham & Allington, 2011; Young, 2006b);
- classroom libraries should have books representing many cultures (Moss & Young, 2010), and include some international books (Hadaway & Young, 2010);
- classroom libraries should include books that will appeal to gifted readers (Moss & Young, 2010); and
- at least one-third of the books should be below grade level so all children can find easy books to read (Moss & Young, 2010).

Likewise, having books on the classroom shelves is not enough. Teachers can increase student reading of classroom library books by better organization of the books. It is important to organize the classroom collections to support student book choice and engagement by:

- regularly adding new books to the collection (Kletzien & Dreher, 2004);
- rotating books according to what is being taught across the curriculum (Young, 2006b);
- posting a map that shows the layout of the classroom library (Moss & Young, 2010);
- shelving some of the books so students can see their covers (Kletzien & Dreher, 2004);
- introducing students to books through book talks, displays, reading aloud, and other classroom routines (Moss & Young, 2010; Young, 2006a);
- organizing the books so they are easily located (Kletzien & Dreher, 2004);
- placing books at students' eye level and below (Moss & Young, 2010); and
- including carpet, chairs, or pillows to make the area warm and welcoming (Kletzien & Dreher, 2004).

While the entire discussion here has been focused on classroom libraries, it is important to note that libraries of all types play an important role with reading engagement in children. Like the research that shows that classroom libraries lead to gains in achievement and engagement, there are also complementary studies that show that school libraries provide the same types of benefits. In fact studies from all over the country have shown that having a school library that is properly staffed and having adequate resources leads to higher achievement even when other factors like socioeconomic status are taken into account (*School Libraries Work!*, 2008). Additional information and an overview of the extensive studies that have been done showing the positive impact of school libraries can be found at http://www.iasl-online.org/advocacy/make-a-difference.html. The resources provided in school libraries, including knowledgeable staff and extensive text resources, will no doubt prove essential to any implementation of the Core. School librarians have the knowledge to help connect teachers to resources they may not be aware of. Librarians can also provide important instructional support and collaboration for teaching especially when it comes to addressing the standards that focus on 21st-century skills and the research skills required in the Writing Standards. School libraries can also serve as repositories for all types of textual resources. From a wide range of children's literature to other texts like articles from databases, school libraries can provide teachers with texts in a way that classroom libraries will never be able to. The authors often tell their preservice teachers that beyond the principal the two people in their schools they should get to know will be the janitors and the librarians. This advice seems to be even more applicable in the age of the Core since libraries have much to offer that will impact the standards. Additionally, like teachers school librarians have the same capacity to help readers discover the will to read. Savvy teachers would do well to utilize this capacity as they collaborate with librarians to implement the Core in ways that will engage their students.

Student Choice

The fifth component in building classrooms focused on reading engagement is to allow student choice. Some issues of choice have already been discussed; however, let's take a closer look at the research on this issue. Providing students with choice is one way of motivating students to read. When teachers provide choices during learning, both students' engagement and comprehension of texts are increased when compared to students in control groups without the element of choice (Guthrie & McPeake, 2013). Providing choice in reading results in increased interest in reading and time spent reading (Guthrie & Humenick, 2004). Such choices may include which book to read; whether to read independently or with a partner; where to do the reading within the classroom; how to respond to the book; which concept to become an expert on; which genre and authors to read; how to demonstrate understanding of a text by drawing, summarizing, or mapping; or even reading from a particular character's perspective (Guthrie & Humenick, 2004; Guthrie & McPeake, 2013). Guthrie and his colleagues caution teachers to give students a small number of choices so they are not overwhelmed. One important reason to give students choices is that choice in reading materials encourages students to become the kind of lifelong, independent readers the Core is wanting to achieve (Johnson & Blair, 2003). As students select their own books to read and enjoy their chosen books, they develop confidence in their abilities to choose books for themselves (Miller & Kelley, 2014).

Some students know how to make wise book choices, and others require more support in choosing books because they lack background knowledge about books and authors. Miller and Kelley (2014) suggest that teachers help students learn how to choose books for themselves by

- providing book recommendations;
- increasing student access to interesting and engaging books, and
- taking opportunities to promote books in the classroom and especially when conferring with individual students.

However, they stress that students cannot depend on their teachers' help forever. Students must learn to choose their own books to meet their personal and academic goals.

Effective teachers provide a balance of literature choices, depending upon the type of pedagogy they are using:

Teacher Choice	Managed Choice	Student Choice
• Community books • Read-alouds • Guided reading • Shared reading	• Literature circles • Independent reading • Text sets (related to thematic or disciplinary units)	• Sustained silent reading • Reading workshop

For activities like read-alouds and guided and shared reading where the entire class will be engaging with the same books, teachers will have to exercise full control over the choice of texts. Managed choice is when teachers provide students a range of texts to choose from. By doing so, the teacher is providing students with a few choices that they can successfully read with teacher guidance and support. For activities like sustained silent reading and reading workshop, children can choose whatever they want. Giving this range of choices will enable those students who have keen interest and deep background knowledge to read the widest range of texts including those that are within and well beyond their instructional abilities. Beyond their instructional needs this range of choices will make it possible for students to have books they can enjoy.

Interesting Texts

Teachers in classrooms where reading flourishes understand that for students to love reading they need interesting texts. Students typically are intrinsically motivated to read, read more, and comprehend better if they read texts they find interesting (Guthrie & McPeake, 2013). Guthrie and Humenick (2004) note that *interest* refers to the text attributes that help students comprehend and learn from books. "Interesting" can be a relative term, as what may interest one child may not interest another. Thus, it is important for teachers to learn about their students' interests and then apply the aspects of the reader dimension to match readers with texts at both the perfect interest and complexity level.

The role of student interest is powerful. Student interest in a book can be the difference between one who persists in completing the book and one who gives up easily. While there is no one magic formula that can connect a book to a reader, Moss and Young (2010) have synthesized some of the research that gives some important clues for teachers about what makes books appealing to young readers:

- content or topic is typically regarded as the most important criterion students use in selecting books;
- physical appearance of a book is also important as well;
- students often enjoy characters who have similar experiences to their own; and
- students are not attracted to books with small fonts and dense text.

Structured Classroom Pedagogies

This is the last component that has proven to create the kinds of classrooms where the love of reading flourishes connects with the pedagogies and strategies that teachers use in their instruction. While there are many strategies that can empower students with their reading, research has shown that three of the most useful are collaboration, responses to reading activities, and innovative uses of technology.

Collaboration

Collaboration is a perfect technique to empower students in their reading since opportunities to work with other students are highly motivating and energize classrooms. Researchers note that collaborations can result in increased engagement, deeper comprehension, and greater learning (Guthrie & McPeake, 2013). Providing students with opportunities to work in pairs or small groups can foster intrinsic motivation for reading and learning (Guthrie & Humenick, 2004). Building relationships with other readers fosters students' interest in reading because it presents reading as a desirable activity (Miller & Kelley, 2014). Beyond the research, however, collaboration is also an important strategy because of its direct connection to the Core. The third Anchor Standard for speaking and listening directly asks students to participate in a range of collaborations with diverse partners. Collaboration then not only allows students to build reading motivation but also to directly address an important component of the Core.

Response to Reading Activities

All teachers will need to build some type of assessment into their instruction. So having students respond to their reading is a natural component of teaching. However, there are two other purposes for students to respond to reading. First, response activities often deepen students' understanding and appreciation of the book read. Second, students are often motivated to read a book after observing one of their peer's responses to reading (Moss & Young, 2010). Although there is value and power in students' response to reading, teachers must be intentional in how response activities are used in the classroom. First and foremost, students need to spend most of their time reading. Responses cannot overwhelm reading such as one instance the authors experienced where students created elaborate models or detailed paintings that required more time than reading the book. As Routman (2003) notes a response activity should never take more than 20 percent of the time required to read the book. Another important consideration is to remember not to force students to submit a formal response to every book they read independently. Stead (2009) notes that responses should be fueled by students' natural curiosity and wonder. Requiring students to respond to every book becomes tedious and removes any possible joy the students may have experienced.

One way by which response activities can be made pleasurable for students is by giving them some choice in books they respond to and how they respond. Moss and Young (2010) suggest that students may respond to books through many activities. For instance, art is a tool for sharing illustrator studies, collage, paintings, or comics. They can also respond through drama with puppetry, choral reading, readers theatre, or student written plays. Writing offers a host of response activities such as writing book reviews, poetry, or letters from one character.

Innovative Uses of Technology

While technology and reading may not seem to be natural partners, the two really support each other to engage students with texts. This is true because, especially today, students are motivated to use technology (Moss & Young, 2010). Many teachers have found ways to use technology to enhance their students' comprehension and response to reading. One such teacher is Kelly Killorn, a sixth-grade teacher from Bloomington, Minnesota, and the recipient of the 2009 IRA Award for Technology and Reading. She found that technology has both great appeal to and benefits for her students (Killorn, n.d.). When one of the authors interviewed her, Ms. Killorn reported that technology is not only fun but also especially motivating to reluctant readers (K. Killorn, personal communication, 2010). Moreover, technology aids all her students in their attempts to comprehend text, helps them organize their thinking, and enhances their learning. She reports that the major benefit to using technology is that it provides students with an authentic audience beyond their teacher and classmates. Ms. Killorn uses technology in particular ways to support her struggling readers and to allow her students to respond to their reading.

Students who are struggling readers especially benefit from using technology while reading. To help these readers Ms. Killorn uses audio books. She loads the popular books that more advanced students are reading onto MP3 players and lets the students listen to the text while following along in the book. This allows struggling students to experience the texts their more capable peers are reading, which enables them to discuss and respond to the books that they otherwise would not be able to read. Their responses indicate that they are just as capable of thinking about the books as their peers.

Additionally, Ms. Killorn uses technology to allow students to respond to their reading. Ms. Killorn believes that many of her students feel more comfortable in discussing books online than they do in class discussions. They often feel a sense of security being in front of a computer monitor instead of in face-to-face discussions. The online forum gives students more time to think through and edit their responses, and it provides them with opportunities to interact with students in other classes about the books they are reading. She feels the quality of her students' written online responses is much more thoughtful and deeper than what students might share orally in class. These benefits alone would be sufficient reason to use technology. However, the implementation of the Core offers even more. The Core Anchor Standards for Writing include the call to use technology to produce and publish writing. Additionally, the writing standards ask students to produce clear and coherent writing that they have planned, revised, edited, and rewritten. Each of these Core requirements connect directly to the types of outcomes that Ms. Killorn found while using technology with her students. While there are many ways to incorporate technology into student responses Ms. Killorn has found that book advertisements, wikis, message boards, and blogs are particularly useful.

Book Advertisements. Book advertisements, or book trailers, are like commercials for a book created by students. These responses can easily be made into cooperative projects since each student can take a role in these projects. The roles include script writing, designing a backdrop, selecting music to accompany the production, finding an appropriate video clip to include, and editing the video in the computer lab. Ms. Killorn's students take great pride in their work, and few people would guess that sixth graders actually do all the work themselves. Ms. Killorn notes that she is amazed by what her students can do with technology and that oftentimes her students exceed her expectations on a project or an assignment because they enjoy the work so much.

Wikis. A wiki provides students with a space where they can respond to questions regarding the books they are reading. As part of a genre study unit, Ms. Killorn's students blog entries as book characters and post video diaries (like those seen on reality television shows) on the wiki. The video diaries are made using small handheld cameras. Her students note that the video diaries help them visualize the book characters and to focus on those characters' problems and goals. Ms. Killorn observes that the student wiki postings and video diaries are a great way to motivate other students to read the books that their classmates have chosen.

Message Boards. Ms. Killorn also uses message boards to allow students to respond to their reading. In her classes she uses ning (www.ning.com) to create a secure message board that is much like the popular social networking site Facebook. She notes that she never requires her students to use technology at home because not all students have access to the Internet. Yet she and other teachers find that, even at home, there are always some kids logged in and having fun with things directly related to the school and the books they are reading. This extension of their reading experiences outside the wall of the classroom can only be a good thing, she notes, since it engages her students more deeply in their texts.

Teacher Blog. Gambrell (2009) notes that today's teachers should talk about what they are reading, and this talk becomes an important model of reading purposes and behaviors. Ms. Killorn accomplishes this through the blog she keeps for her own reading of children's and young adult books. Her students, in turn, can earn extra credit for reading books on her blog and then posting reviews of the books read for their peers.

Developing Classrooms Where Skills Flourish

There is little doubt that the use of techniques that will build a love of reading will go a long way toward achieving the kind of college- and workplace-ready readers the Core requires. But beyond a love of reading, building skills will also be an essential part of Core implementation. Research also shows teachers as the essential components of classrooms designed to facilitate students in their development of skills and strategies. Among the most significant of these are the teacher and an environment that allow for the learning of important reading abilities.

The Teacher

Teachers are really what make the difference in terms of student achievement. This fact was clearly shown in the now-classic *First Grade Studies* of the 1960s which concluded regardless of the quality of a program, resource, or strategy; it is the teacher and learning situation that make a difference (Bond & Dykstra, 1997). Other researchers have also repeatedly noted that teacher quality and expertise consistently and accurately predict student achievement (Darling-Hammond, 2000; Reutzel, 2013).

Teachers can take quite a bit of credit for their students' learning. Ferguson (1991) determined that only 48 percent of the variance in student achievement could be attributed to home and family factors that are largely out of the school's control. So it is possible for teachers to claim credit for 52 percent of student learning. While this amount is impressive, New Zealand educators suggest that a teacher's influence can be even greater. This research suggests that quality teaching and the learning environments generated by the teacher and students are the key variables in explaining 59 percent or more of the variance in student achievement (Alton-Lee, 2003). It is important to remember that what teachers do and how they teach their students matter most; it is teachers, not programs, curriculum, or tools, that make a difference. A case in point, Reutzel (2013) noted that effective teachers get three times the grade-level growth of their students than what their less effective colleagues' students gain.

To achieve these kinds of gains in achievement there are certain characteristics and attitudes that teachers can cultivate. Allington and Johnston (2002) outline many of these qualities that they have gleaned from their research on teachers whose students were considered to be highly literate. These students' literacy was assessed by more than achievement; they also exhibited characteristics that showed that they had developed an individual identity as a reader and that had established a relationship with reading that helped them to cultivate values and beliefs. The teachers' qualities that contributed to their students' high level of literacy included the following personality traits and characteristics:

- warm, caring, supportive, encouraging, friendly, genuinely likes people, trusting, respectful, and nonjudgmental;
- enthusiastic, enjoys work;
- accurate self-assessment, and
- demonstrate a sense of agency through their firm understanding of literacy and realization that their intentional selection of strategies and approaches has an impact on their students' learning.

According to Allington and Johnston, these traits manifest themselves in teachers who draw attention to the positive aspects of their interactions with students. They expressed interest in the students' lives and ways of thinking. They also organized instruction to engage students and to encourage student self-management.

Likewise, these teachers possessed certain beliefs, attitudes, and expectations that enhanced their interactions with students and contributed to the classroom environment, they:

- expect diversity in their students;
- always assume their students have the potential to learn and progress;
- believe that learning is social;
- understand that learning requires ownership, relevance, and choice;
- recognize that mistakes are a part of learning and a sign of growth and potential; and
- know that teacher modeling is key to student learning.

These characteristics, beliefs, attitudes, and expectations greatly influence all forms of classroom interaction and create the underpinnings of both the physical and emotional classroom environments. Moreover, the teacher's beliefs determine the role literature will play in students' reading and learning. With the premium that the Core places on professional judgment, teachers will continue to play a strong role in creating the kinds of classrooms where students can master the skills they need to be college and career ready.

Reading Abilities

In order for students to build the skills they need to become engaged with the Core Standards they will need to develop important reading abilities. A classroom environment that helps students to build the essential skills that make reading possible is an important part of creating a classroom where skills can flourish. Professionals should strive to use instructional techniques that help their students build reading stamina.

Stamina

Helping students develop stamina is critical to their success as learners. Reading stamina can be defined as the student's ability to read independently for long periods of time without giving up, getting too tired, or becoming distracted by their environment (Reading Rockets, 2012). Stamina develops over time and requires consistent teacher effort and monitoring. Some ways of increasing students' stamina include (Boushey & Moser, 2014) the following:

- teaching and modeling what is expected during independent reading time (i.e., students read the entire time and remain in their seats);
- sharing with students the benefits of increasing their reading stamina;

- using stamina charts to help the class and individuals see how long they have read and attended to relevant tasks to show student progress;
- making sure that students have "just right" books immediately available for them to read during independent reading time; and
- setting reasonable, age-appropriate goals for how long students should read independently.

In addition to these tips, Boushey and Moser's (2014) *The Daily 5* serves as an excellent teacher resource that is filled with suggestions for how to increase students' reading stamina.

Comprehension

Engaged readers need instruction that helps them develop literacy and enables them to think deeply about their reading and writing. Skilled readers typically use a variety of strategies to become deeply engaged in the text they are reading (Malloy & Gambrell, 2013). The comprehension strategies students need to develop include the following: building background knowledge, constructing mental images, inferring, determining importance, predicting, summarizing and synthesizing, as well as monitoring and evaluating their understanding of text (Allington, 2006; Harvey & Goudvis, 2007; Keene & Zimmerman, 2007). Teachers are most effective when their instruction includes modeling, explanation, and demonstration of how and why to use strategies along with scaffold student practice that enables them to apply the strategies independently in real reading situations. Often the guided practice and scaffolding take place in small groups or with partners (Pressley, 2002). The teaching strategies and activities to be offered in Chapter 7 will prove to connect the standards to all the ways teachers can structure learning to develop comprehension.

Vocabulary

Implicit in the Common Core Standards is that vocabulary is critical to comprehension. Students need to be taught how to determine the meanings of words through the use of a variety of word-learning activities and strategies in both the literacy block and across the curriculum (Blachowicz & Baumann, 2013). As Blachowicz and Baumann synthesized the research related to vocabulary instruction they found that teachers need to accomplish four important things:

1. provide rich and varied language experiences;
2. teach individual words;
3. teach word-learning strategies; and
4. foster word consciousness.

Providing rich and varied language experiences requires that students be immersed in language-rich environments that lead to the development of both oral and written vocabulary. Reading aloud to students, independent reading, drama, literature circles, conversations about books and words, and instructional language related to strategy instruction all contribute to the rich and varied language experiences needed for children to develop broad vocabularies.

Teaching individual words prior to reading has long been a tradition of teachers across the grades. However, Blachowicz and Baumann (2013) note that in order to enhance reading comprehension, such instruction needs to include defining, context, repeated exposure, and deep levels of processing. Word-learning strategies teach students to use a variety of sources of information to infer word meanings of new words and known words used in new contexts. Word-learning strategies include teaching context clues, structural or morphemic analysis (root words, prefixes, and suffixes), and word derivation.

Fostering word consciousness involves creating a sense of word wonder where students appreciate the amazing words used in oral and written language (Blachowicz & Baumann, 2013). Cunningham and Allington (2011) recommend that teachers make time to promote a sense of word wonder by displaying words in various ways in the classroom, reading books about words such as *Double Trouble in Walla Walla* by Andrew Clements, 1997; *Nellie May Has Her Say* by Cynthia DeFelice, 2013; and *Exclamation Mark!* by Amy Krouse Rosenthal to the class, and holding a special "Words Are Wonderful Day" where students celebrate wonderful words through a variety of activities such as discussing word play, choosing a "wonderful word" of the week, and playing word-related games. Chapter 7 will feature additional books about word play, poetry, and other activities that will contribute to a word-conscious environment.

As the Common Core Standards are explicit about the development of disciplinary knowledge and skills, when considering vocabulary it is important to make science and social studies a part of instructional plans. If not as separate subjects, science and social studies topics should at least be integrated into the reading and language arts time. Children who do not have access to science and social studies content often have serious vocabulary deficits that affect their learning and achievement (Cunningham & Allington, 2011). Moreover, the informational passages on standardized tests often reflect science and/or social studies content. Because of this teachers may find that they will need to pay attention to building discipline-specific vocabulary skills in addition to those required for general reading ability.

Foundational Skills

In the No Child Left Behind and Reading First era, phonics, phonemic awareness, and fluency played a prominent role in reading instruction. The Common Core focuses almost exclusively on comprehension and vocabulary yet recognizes the importance of print concepts, phonemic awareness, phonics, and fluency to reading comprehension. The standards articulate this important connection as it articulates the Reading Foundational Skills standards for kindergarten through fifth grade. These standards engage with the type of scaffolding necessary to build solid reading skills. To become a skilled reader students must develop reading comprehension abilities. However, comprehension is dependent upon fluency. Fluency is dependent on a readers' ability to decode or recognize words in the text. Thus in order to reach high levels of comprehension students must first master word recognition and other basic print concepts related to phonological or speech sound awareness (Rasinski, Kuhn, & Nageldinger, 2013).

To help students understand *print concepts* such as letters, words, beginning of sentence, and top of page, Taberski and Burke (2014) recommend the following for young students:

- provide shared reading with big books and enlarged text so students can easily see the text and learn about how text works;
- encourage emergent readers to point to words as they read aloud;
- utilize the language experience approach and interactive writing; and
- write lines from a poem on sentence strips and have students put them in proper order.

Additionally, Tricia Zucker, Allison Ward, and Laura Justice's (2009) article "Print Referencing during Read-Alouds" is an excellent resource for helping young learners increase their understanding of print concepts while reading aloud.

Phonics and word recognition are generally thought of as the domain for the lower grades. Yet, Adams (2013) notes that nearly half of the struggling readers in the middle and upper grades have word recognition problems. Here are some practical recommendations to help students develop phonics and word recognition skills:

- use authentic text to introduce phonics elements (Taberski & Burke, 2014);
- show students how to use phonics along with semantics and syntax to figure out unknown words (Taberski & Burke, 2014);
- utilize the close procedure frequently (Taberski & Burke, 2014);
- encourage students to highlight prefixes and suffixes to determine the meaning of unknown words (Blauman & Burke, 2014);
- focus on patterns in words with word families (Rasinski et al., 2013);
- teach morphemic analysis and word building (Rasinski et al., 2013); and
- utilize adaptive, computer-assisted instruction with older children struggling with phonics and word recognition (Adams, 2013).

Fluency

Fluency in reading is the ability to read words in context quickly, accurately, and with proper expression. Rasinski et al. (2013) note that the development of fluency is dependent upon both wide reading and deep reading.

Wide reading involves the silent independent reading discussed earlier in this chapter. Researchers note that independent reading is most successful at improving fluency and reading achievement when teachers help their students make appropriate book choices and hold students accountable for the time spent reading (Reutzel, Jones, Fawson, & Smith, 2008). Independent reading need not take a large amount of time since small batches of time add up. For example, daily independent reading for 20 minutes over the 180-day school year adds up to 60 hours of engaged reading (Rasinski et al., 2013).

Deep reading, or repeated reading, involves students in reading a somewhat challenging text multiple times. Students rehearse the text so it can be read with high levels of accuracy, automaticity, and expression (Rasinski et al., 2013). Readers' theatre and choral reading are popular practices that involve repeated reading.

Here are some practical recommendations to help students increase their reading fluency:

- model fluent, expressive reading when reading aloud and shared reading (Cunningham & Allington, 2011);
- teach students how to attend to text cues such as exclamation points, question marks, quotation marks, words in bold, and words printed larger or smaller than the others since these cues signal how a text should be read (Taberski & Burke, 2014);
- provide audio books for students to listen to and follow along (Taberski & Burke, 2014). Consider recording yourself while reading aloud picture books and poetry to your students (Cunningham & Allington, 2011);
- encourage students to prepare for and present poetry podcasts (Blauman & Burke, 2014); and
- have students recite portions of famous speeches and documents (Blauman & Burke, 2014).

Combining Love and Skills for a Balanced Classroom

To develop the kinds of independent, engaged readers that will be college and workplace ready, professionals will need to address both the will and the skill of reading. Helping students develop the will to read and the skills and strategies necessary to do so will be essential to any Core implementation. The research and strategies outline here will help professionals to build the kind of balanced classrooms where love and skills both flourish. Teachers are encouraged to seek out a balance between skill development and creating a life-long love of reading. Too often teachers feel overwhelmed with all that is expected of them, and their dominant emphasis becomes skills development. Thus, they do not take the time to read aloud or to model the other activities that emphasize the joy of reading. Yet researchers have noted that students who enjoy reading read more and those who read more have higher achievement. Achieving balance is challenging, but it is ultimately worth the effort.

Bibliography

Adams, M. J. (2013). Common Core State Standards: Productivity is the key. In S. B. Neuman & L. B. Gambrell (Eds.), *Quality reading instruction in the age of Common Core Standards* (pp. 204–218). Newark, DE: International Reading Association.

Allington, R. L. (2006). *What really matters for struggling readers: Designing research-based programs. Second edition.* Boston, MA: Allyn & Bacon.

Allington, R. L., & Cunningham, P. M. (2006). *Schools that work: Where all children read and write.* Boston, MA: Pearson/Allyn & Bacon.

Allington, R. L., & Johnston, P. (2002). *Reading to learn: Lessons from exemplary 4th grade classrooms.* New York: Guilford.

Alton-Lee, A. (2003). Quality teaching for diverse students in schooling: Best evidence synthesis iteration (BES). Retrieved from http://www.educationcounts.govt.nz/publications/series/2515/5959

Applegate, A. J., & Applegate, M. D. (2004). The Peter effect: Reading habits and attitudes of preservice teachers. *The Reading Teacher, 57,* 554–563.

Blachowicz, C. L. Z., & Baumann, J. F. (2013). Language standards for vocabulary. In L. Mandel Morrow, K. K. Wixson, & T. Shanahan (Eds.), *Teaching with the Common Core Standards for English language arts, grades 3–5* (pp. 131–151). New York: Guilford.

Blauman, L., & Burke, J. (2014). *The Common Core companion: The standards decoded, grades 3–5.* Thousand Oaks, CA: Corwin.

Bond, G. L., & Dykstra, R. (1997). The cooperative research program in first-grade reading instruction. *Reading Research Quarterly, 32,* 348–428.

Boushey, G., & Moser, J. (2014). *The daily 5: Fostering literacy independence in the elementary grades.* Portland, ME: Stenhouse.

Burgess, S. R., Sargent, S., & Smith, M. (2011). Teachers' leisure reading habits and knowledge of children's books: Do they relate to the teaching practices of elementary school teachers? *Reading Improvement, 42,* 88–102.

Clements, A. (1997). *Double trouble in Walla Walla.* Minneapolis, MN: Millbrook Press.

Cunningham, P. M., & Allington, R. L. (2011). *Classrooms that work: They can all read and write.* Boston, MA: Pearson.

Darling-Hammond, L. (2000). Teacher quality and student achievement: A review of state policy evidence. *Educational Policy Analysis Archives, 8*(1). Retrieved from http://epaa.asu.edu/ojs/article/view/392

DeFelice, C. C. (2013). *Nellie Ma has her say.* New York: Farrar, Straus and Giroux.

Dole, J. A., Donaldson, B. E., & Donaldson, R. S. (2014). *Reading across multiple texts in the Common Core classroom.* New York: Teachers College Press.

Duke, C. L., & Young, T. A. (1993, March). Promoting interest in reading: Teacher priorities and practices. Paper presented at the Reading Research Conference of the Washington Organization for Reading Development, Tacoma, WA.

Ferguson, R. F. (1991). Paying for public education: New evidence on how and why money matters. *Harvard Journal on Legislation, 28*(2), 465–498.

Fisher, D., Flood, J., Lapp, D., & Frey, N. (2004). Interactive read-alouds: Is there a common set of implementation practices? *The Reading Teacher, 58,* 8–17.

Fox, M. (2013). What is next in the read-aloud battle? Win or lose? *The Reading Teacher, 67,* 4–8.

Fractor, J.S., Woodruff, M.C., Martinez, M., & Teale, W.H. (1993). Let's not miss the opportunities to promote voluntary reading: Classroom libraries in the elementary school. *The Reading Teacher, 46,* 476–484.

Gambrell, L. (2009). Creating opportunities to read more so that students read better. In E.H. Hiebert (Ed.) *Read more, read better* (pp. 251–266). New York: Guilford.

Gambrell, L. (2011). Seven rules of engagement: What's most important to know about motivation to read. *The Reading Teacher, 65*(3), 172–178.

Guthrie, J.T. (2004). Teaching for literacy engagement. *Journal of Literacy Research, 36*(1), 1–29.

Guthrie, J.T., & Humenick, N.M. (2004). Motivating students to read: Evidence for classroom practices that increase reading motivation and achievement. In P. McCardle & V. Chhabra (Eds.) *The voice of evidence in reading research* (pp. 329–354). Baltimore, MD: Paul H. Brookes.

Guthrie J.T., & McPeake, J. (2013). Literacy engagement: The missing link. In S.B. Neuman & L.B. Gambrell (Eds.), *Quality reading instruction in the age of Common Core Standards* (pp. 162–175). Newark, DE: International Reading Association.

Guthrie, J.T., Schafer, W.D., Von Secker, C., & Alban, T. (2000). Contributions of integrated reading instruction and text resources to achievement and engagement in a statewide school improvement program. *Journal of Educational Research, 93,* 211–226.

Hadaway, N.L., & Young, T.A. (2010). *Matching books and readers: Helping English learners in grades K–6.* New York: Guilford Press.

Harvey, S., & Goudvis, A. (2007). *Strategies that work: Teaching comprehension for understanding and engagement.* Portland, ME: Stenhouse.

Heath, S.B. (1983). *Ways with words: Language, life, and work in communities and classrooms.* New York: Cambridge University Press.

Hiebert, E.H., & Martin, L.A. (2009). Opportunity to read: A critical but neglected construct in reading instruction. In E.H. Hiebert (Ed.), *Reading more, reading better* (pp. 3–29). New York: Guilford.

International Reading Association. (1999). *Providing books and other print materials for classroom and school libraries.* Newark, DE: Author.

Johnson, D., & Blair, A. (2003). The importance and use of student self-selected literature to reading engagement in an elementary reading curriculum. *Reading Horizons, 43,* 181–202.

Keene, E.O., & Zimmerman, S. (2007). *Mosaic of thought: The power of comprehension strategy instruction.* Portsmouth, NH: Heinemann.

Killorn, K. (n.d.). *Reading and technology.* Retrieved from https://sites.google.com/site/huslireadtech/profile

Kletzien, S.B., & Dreher, M.J. (2004). *Informational text in K–3 classrooms: Helping children read and write.* Newark, DE: International Reading Association.

Krashen, S.D. (1998). Every person a reader: An alternative to the California Task Force report on reading. In C. Weaver (Ed.), *Reconsidering a balanced approach to reading* (pp. 425–452). Urbana, IL: National Council of Teachers of English.

Krashen, S.D. (2004). *The power of reading: Insights from the research.* Westport, CT: Libraries Unlimited.

Malloy, J.A., & Gambrell, L.B. (2013). Reading standards for literature. In L. Mandel Morrow, K.K. Wixson, & T. Shanahan (Eds.), *Teaching with the Common Core Standards for English language arts, grades 3–5* (pp. 22–49). New York: Guilford.

McKool, S., & Gespass, S. (2009). Does Johnny's reading teacher love to read? How teachers' personal reading habits affect instructional practices. *Literacy Research and Instruction, 48,* 264–276.

Miller, D. (2009). *The book whisperer: Awakening the inner reader in every child.* San Francisco, CA: Jossey-Bass.

Miller, D., & Kelley, S. (2014). *Reading in the wild: The book whisperer's keys to cultivating lifelong reading habits*. San Francisco, CA: Jossey-Bass.

Mooney, M. E. (2004). *A book is a present: Selecting text for intentional teaching*. Katonah, NY: Richard C. Owens Publishers, Inc.

Morrison, T. G., Jacobs, J. S., & Swinyard, W. R. (1999). Do teachers who read personally use recommended literacy practices in their classrooms? *Reading Research and Instruction, 38*, 81–100.

Morrow, L. M. (2003). Motivating lifelong voluntary reading. In J. Flood, D. Lapp, J. R. Squires, & J. M. Jensen (Eds.), *Handbook of research on teaching the English language arts* (pp. 857–867). Mahwah, NJ: Lawrence Erlbaum.

Moss, B., & Young, T. A. (2010). *Creating lifelong readers through independent reading*. Newark, DE: International Reading Association.

Neuman, S. B. (1999). Books make a difference: A study of access to literacy. *Reading Research Quarterly, 34*, 286–311.

Pressley, M. (2002). *Reading instruction that works: The case for balanced teaching*. New York: Guilford.

Rasinski, T., Kuhn, M., & Nageldinger, J. (2013). Reading standards: Foundational skills. In L. Mandel Morrow, K. K. Wixson, & T. Shanahan (Eds.), *Teaching with the Common Core Standards for English language arts, grades 3–5* (pp. 67–87). New York: Guilford.

Reading Rockets (2012). *Building reading stamina*. Retrieved from http://www.readingrockets.org/article/building-reading-stamina

Reutzel, D. R. (2013). Implementation of the Common Core State Standards and the practitioner: Pitfalls and possibilities. In S. B. Neuman & L. B. Gambrell (Eds.), *Quality reading instruction in the age of Common Core Standards* (pp. 59–74). Newark, DE: International Reading Association.

Reutzel, D. R., Jones, C. D., Fawson, P. C., & Smith, J. A. (2008). Scaffolded silent reading: A complement to guided repeated oral reading that works. *The Reading Teacher, 62*, 194–207.

Rosenthal, A. K. (2013). *Exclamation mark*! New York: Scholastic.

Routman, R. (2003). *Reading essentials: The specifics you need to teach reading well*. Portsmouth, NH: Heinemann.

School Libraries Work! (2008). New York: Scholastic Library Publishing. Retrieved from http://www.scholastic.com/content/collateral_resources/pdf/s/slw3_2008.pdf

Serafini, F., & Giorgis, C. (2003). *Reading aloud and beyond: Fostering an intellectual life with older readers*. Portsmouth, NH: Heinemann.

Stahl, S. A. (1999). *Vocabulary development*. Cambridge, MA: Brookline.

Stead, T. (2009). *Good choice!: Supporting independent reading and response K–6*. Portland, ME. Stenhouse.

Taberski, S., & Burke, J. (2014). *The Common Core companion: The standards decoded, grades k–2*. Thousand Oaks, CA: Corwin.

Trelease, J. (2013). *The read-aloud handbook* (7th ed.). New York: Penguin Books.

Tunnell, M. O., Jacobs, J. S., Young, T. A., & Bryan, G. W. (2012). *Children's literature, briefly* (5th ed.). Boston, MA: Pearson.

Young, T. A. (2006a). Reading to students. In M. E. Mooney & T. A. Young (Eds.), *Caught in the spell of writing and reading: Grade 3 and beyond* (pp. 3–19). Katonah, NY: Richard C. Owens Publishers, Inc.

Young, T. A. (2006b). Weaving the magic together: Threads of student success and engagement. In M. E. Mooney & T. A. Young (Eds.), *Caught in the spell of writing and reading: Grade 3 and beyond* (pp. 175–189). Katonah, NY: Richard C. Owens Publishers, Inc.

Zucker, T. A., Ward, A. E., & Justice, L. M. (2009). Print referencing during read-alouds: A technique for increasing emergent readers print knowledge. *The Reading Teacher, 63*, 62–72.

7 Children's Literature and the Core in Practice

Thus far the Core, its connections to children's literature, and a research base has been outlined. Having made the case for the power of the Core to connect with children's literature, now it is time to take all these pieces and put them into practice. Because the Core will rightly look very different in every classroom the purpose here is not to be prescriptive about practice or curriculum. The authors believe that professional judgment plays the highest role in connecting standards, texts, pedagogies, and activities into lessons and units. To encourage professionals to engage with the types of approaches that are best for their students, only the building blocks from which teachers can create their own learning opportunities are offered here. Drawing upon what has already been discussed it is hoped that with these final resources teachers will have all the pieces they need to creatively implement the Core.

Extending on previous discussion this chapter will provide a variety of options of texts and activities. From these teachers can pick those that work for them in order to create their own lessons and units. Ideas for each of the nine standards will be outlined. Note that while the authors have selected to place texts and activities under one specific standard, the Core is very recursive, and many standards can be addressed through more than one approach. The placement of texts and ideas under one standard should not limit teachers. Understand that all these texts and ideas will meet several standards at once, so all the structures here can address many areas of the Core even though here they have been relegated to one area. First, a table which summarizes the Reading Standards is given. This table summarizes the Anchor and Grade-Level Standards. In these tables the major ideas from the standards are outlined. Note that quotation marks indicate that the standard follows the format of the previous standard. Additional information that is added to that specific standard is given after the slash. The focus here is on the Reading Standards; however, as tasks are addressed the Writing, Speaking and Listening, and Language Standards will also be addressed. Throughout the standards will be referred to by the short hand references used in the Core documentation.

A = Anchor Standard
RL = Reading Literature Standard
RI = Reading Informational Text Standard
W = Writing Standard
SL = Speaking and Listening Standard
L = Language Standard

Also note that the first number/letter after the standard indicator represents the grade level. The second number indicates the standard number.

For each of the nine standards three building blocks are offered. First is a list of texts that particularly connect to that standard. These lists can serve as a basis for teachers to build their instruction. In these lists a wide range of texts is offered so as to make sure that both teachers and students have the widest possible range of texts from which to choose. Many of these texts will be readily available to teachers through libraries or other sources. When these texts are not available, teachers may wish to select some to procure for their own classroom libraries. However, these need not be the only texts that teachers can use. The structures and outlines offered can certainly guide teachers to other texts that share characteristics to the ones offered. A wide range of texts is available so teachers are encouraged to find the best ones to use, even if they are not the ones offered here.

Second, four specific texts or text sets with an associated task are given. These texts and activity sets are designed to assist teachers in visualizing how works of children's literature can be directly connected to the skills the Core asks students to master. Again, the texts offered here can be interchangeable with a wide range of other texts, and the activities also can be used with different standards or texts as needed. Lastly, an overview of an integrated inquiry unit will be given. This unit again will offer only the building blocks that teachers can use to build their own full lessons. Based in essential questions these units are perfectly primed for inquiry learning and can be easily extended to fit any other format or pedagogy that teachers wish to use. Primary texts, secondary texts, and multimedia texts are all included in the outlines. This wide range of texts is given because it is through this range that important 21st-century skills can be addressed. Also this range allows teachers to connect to students' interest and abilities, provides great opportunities for close reading, and allows teachers to build in more reading during the school day. The unit outlines end with a number of ideas for classroom activities. The combination of essential questions, engaging texts, and exciting activities can all serve to let teachers build the kinds of classrooms outlined in Chapter 6 where both reading will and skills flourish. As teachers create their own lesson plans from these building blocks the strategies and structures discussed in the last chapters will also serve as a type of glue that can hold all the pieces together. Professionals are encouraged to use all the strategies that have been discussed and those they have experienced previously to create lessons and units that implement the Core. There are so many options that can be selected from and rearranged to meet the needs of any classroom. Professionals should use their own creative approaches when engaging with these ideas. There is no one right or wrong way to use these elements to create interesting lessons and units. The Core opens the widest possible range of potential to teachers. It is hoped that what is offered here will only serve as a beginning of what is sure to be just the start of how teachers will use children's literature to implement the Core.

Standards 1–3: Key Ideas and Details: What the Text Says
Standard 1

A.R.1	Read closely, show what text says explicitly and make inferences, cite textual evidence
RL.K.1; RI.K.1.; RL.1.1; RI.1.1	Ask and answer questions from key details
RL.2.1; RI.2.1	"" / who, what, when, where, why, how
RL.3.1; RI.3.1	"" / demonstrate understanding, text-based answers
RL.4.1; RI.4.1	Details and examples show what text says explicitly and make inferences
RL.5.1; RI.5.1	"" / quote accurately
RL.6.1; RI.6.1	"" / cite evidence

Texts

Questioning and inferencing are essential skills associated with Standard 1. While a great many texts can be used to teach these skills, mysteries and graphic novels are particularly useful. At their base mysteries are about answering questions that may at the outset seem unanswerable. This focus allows this genre to connect well to the types of basic and in-depth questioning skills Standard 1 addresses. Graphic novels offer great opportunities for students to learn how to make inferences. This is because they combine both textual and visual literacy skills to the interpretation of the text, and it is necessary to read both the text and the pictures to engage with the whole text. Here are some suggestions of the authors' favorite texts for this genre and format.

Mysteries

K–2 Texts

The Composer Is Dead by Lemony Snicket, illustrated by Carson Ellis. HarperCollins, 2008.

Detective Blue by Steve Metzger, illustrated by Tedd Arnold. Orchard Books, 2011.

Hermelin the Detective Mouse by Mini Grey. Alfred A. Knopf, 2014.

January Joker (Calendar Mysteries #1) by Ron Roy. Random House, 2009.

The Mystery of the Gold Coin (Greetings from Somewhere #1) by Harper Paris, illustrated by Marcos Calo. Little Simon, 2014.

Nate the Great (Nate the Great #1) by Marjorie Weinman Sharmat, illustrated by Marc Simont. Coward, McCann & Geoghegan, 1972.

Who Pushed Humpty Dumpty?: And Other Notorious Nursery Tale Mysteries by David Levinthal, illustrated by John Nickle. Schwartz & Wade Books, 2012.

3–6 Texts

The Absent Author (A to Z mysteries #1) by Ron Roy, illustrated by John Steven Gurney. Random House, 1997.

Absolutely Truly (Pumpkin Falls Mysteries #1) by Heather Vogel Frederick. Simon & Schuster Books for Young Readers, 2014.

The Book of Lost Things (Mister Max #1) by Cynthia Voigt, illustrated by Iacopo Bruno. Alfred A. Knopf, 2013.

The Case of the Deadly Desperados (Western Mysteries #1) by Caroline Lawrence. G. P. Putnam's Sons, 2012.

The Case of the Missing Marquess (Enola Holmes Mysteries #1) by Nancy Springer. Philomel Books, 2006.

The Chameleon Wore Chartreuse (Chet Gecko Mystery #1) by Bruce Hale. Harcourt Brace, 2001.

Chasing Vermeer (Chasing Vermeer #1) by Blue Balliett, illustrated by Brett Helquist. Scholastic Press, 2004.

The Ghosts of Tupelo Landing by Sheila Turnage. Kathy Dawson Books, 2014.

Greenglass House by Kate Milford. Clarion Books, 2014.

Knightley and Son (Knightley and Son #1) by Rohan Gavin. Bloomsbury, 2014.

Masterpiece by Elise Broach, illustrated by Kelly Murphy. Henry Holt and Co., 2008.

Missing on Superstition Mountain (Superstition Mountain Mysteries #1) by Elise Broach, illustrated by Antonio Javier Caparo. Henry Holt, 2011.

Moxie and the Art of Rule Breaking: A 14 Day Mystery by Erin Dionne. Dial, 2013.

The Ring of Rocamadour (Red Blazer Girls #1) by Michael D. Beil. Alfred A. Knopf, 2009.

Sammy Keyes and the Hotel Thief (Sammy Keyes Mysteries #1) by Wendelin Van Draanen. Alfred A. Knopf, 1998.

The Westing Game by Ellen Raskin. Dutton, 1978.

Graphic Novels

K–2 Texts

Andy Also by Maxwell Eaton. Blue Apple Books, 2014.

Awesome Dawson by Chris Gall. Little, Brown and Company, 2013.

Benjamin Bear in Bright Ideas! by Philippe Coudray. Toon Books, 2013.

Benjamin Bear in Fuzzy Thinking by Philippe Coudray. Toon Books, 2011.

Benny and Penny in Lights Out! by Geoffrey Hayes. Toon Books, 2012.

Best Friends Forever (Bink & Gollie #3) by Kate DiCamillo and Alison McGhee, illustrated by Tony Fucile. Candlewick Press, 2013.

Binky the Space Cat (Binky #1) by Ashley Spires. Kids Can Press, 2009.

Binky to the Rescue (Binky #2) by Ashley Spires. Kids Can Press, 2010.

BirdCatDog: A Graphic Novel by Lee Nordling. Graphic Universe, 2014.

Laundry Day by Maurie Manning. Houghton Mifflin Harcourt, 2012.

Maya Makes a Mess by Rutu Modan. Toon Books, 2012.

Okay, Andy! by Maxwell Eaton. Blue Apple Books, 2014.

Pinocchio (Cartoon Classics) by Kate McMullan, illustrated by Pascal Lemaitre. Henry Hold and Company, 2014.

The Shark King by R. Kikuo Johnson. Toon Books, 2012.

Silly Lilly and the Four Seasons by Agnes Rosenstiehl. Toon Books, 2008.

A Trip to the Bottom of the World by Frank Viva. Toon Books, 2012.

Two for One (Bink & Gollie #2) by Kate DiCamillo and Alison McGhee, illustrated by Tony Fucile. Candlewick Press, 2012.

Zig and Wikki in Something Ate My Homework by Nadja Spiegelman, illustrated by Trade Loeffler. Toon Books, 2010.

The Zoo Box by Ariel Cohn, illustrated by Aron Nels Steinke. First Second, 2014.

3–6 Texts

Amulet: The Stonekeeper (The Amulet #1) by Kazu Kibuishi. GRAPHIX, 2008.

Dragonbreath (Dragonbreath #1) by Ursula Vernon. Dial Books, 2009.

Calamity Jack (Rapunzel's Revenge #2) by Shannon Hale and Dean Hale, illustrated by Nathan Hale. Bloomsbury, 2010.

Cardboard by Doug TenNapel. GRAPHIX, 2012.

El Deafo by Cece Bell, illustrated by David Lasky. Abrams Books, 2014.

Foiled (Foiled #1) by Jane Yolen, illustrated by Mike Cavallaro. First Second, 2010.

Ghostopolis by Doug TenNapel. GRAPHIX, 2010.

Into the Volcano by Don Wood. Blue Sky Press, 2008.

Jellaby (Jellaby #1) by Kean Soo. Hyperion Books, 2008.

Lunch Lady and the Cyborg Substitute (Lunch Lady #1) by Jarrett J. Krosoczka. Knopf Books for Young Readers, 2009.

Nathan Hale's Hazardous Tales: One Dead Spy (Nathan Hale's Hazardous Tales #1) by Nathan Hale. Harry N. Abrams, 2012.

Nathan Hale's Hazardous Tales: Big Bad Ironclad! (Nathan Hale's Hazardous Tales #2) by Nathan Hale. Harry N. Abrams, 2012.

Rapunzel's Revenge (Rapunzel's Revenge #1) by Shannon Hale and Dean Hale, illustrated by Nathan Hale. Bloomsbury, 2008.

Smile by Raina Telgemeier. GRAPHIX, 2010.

Zeus: King of the God (Olympians #1) by George O'Connor. First Second, 2010.

Text Activities

1. *Whales* by Seymour Simon. HarperCollins, 2006—The semantic feature analysis technique helps students categorize and recognize the relationships of interrelated terms (Hadaway, Vardell, & Young, 2002). An example can be found in Appendix 1.1. This teaching strategy can be used prior to reading, during reading, or after reading. It is especially helpful as a culminating activity to synthesize information from the text reading. To create a Semantic Feature Analysis, first create a grid of rows and columns. Place the book title or the topic above the grid as a title. Down the first column on the left, place members of your topic (e.g., whale types). Across the top row, place the features or attributes of the members of the topic (e.g., have teeth). It is always good to leave spaces for students to add other topics or attributes. Then have students determine which characteristics belong to each member of the topic under study and place Xs in those boxes. Follow up with a discussion, and encourage students to add any other members of the topic to their grids. The Semantic

Feature Analysis can also be used with fiction to illustrate character traits. In doing so, list the character names down the left column and the character traits or attributes across the top of the grid.

2. *Oh Rats!: The Story of Rats and People* by Albert Marrin, illustrated by C.B. Mordan. Dutton Juvenile, 2006—An anticipation/reaction guide presents a series of statements to tap into what students already know or believe about the upcoming reading selection (Hadaway et al., 2002; Stead, 2009). An example is found in Appendix 1.2. These guides serve as a motivational technique to get students interested in reading a text by arousing their curiosity about the topic prior to reading so they read to satisfy the curiosity. Whisler and Williams (1991) recommend using controversial statements that address common preconceptions, create conceptual conflict, or challenge commonly held beliefs when creating the guides. When using the guides in the classroom, it is best to follow these steps:

   a) Students complete the guides independently and then meet with their groups of around four students to share their responses.
   b) Emphasize that students are making predictions and their responses are not right or wrong.
   c) Then discuss the students' responses with the entire group asking students to share their rationale for their choices. (This step often increases students' curiosity and interest in reading the selection.)
   d) Assign the text selection and ask students to complete the "After" portion of the guide.
   e) Then students meet again with their groups to share their responses. These discussions often prompt further discussion.

   Some tips for creating the guides:

   a) Generally include five statements on the guide, but guides can include more for a chapter book or for older students.
   b) For longer books, the guide can be for only a portion or cover the entire book.
   c) With fiction texts, focus on attitudes, values, and issues related to the story content when creating the statements.
   d) With nonfiction texts, create some statements that students will assume are false but the text will show that they are true.
   e) Include at least one statement that will require the students to make an inference.

3. *The Yellow Star: The Legend of King Christian X of Denmark* by Carmen Agra Deedy, illustrated by Henri Sorensen. Peachtree, 2000—We'd Rather is a cooperative strategy that invites students to hypothesize a solution to a problem in forthcoming reading selection (Whisler & Williams, 1991). The strategy gives the students the opportunity to explore the story problem before encountering it in the text. This is an effective prereading strategy that builds students' anticipation to read the text. An example is found in Appendix 1.3. Create the We'd Rather by writing a brief synopsis of the story's problem. The synopsis ends with a key question or phrase that invites the students to insert themselves in the story. Then write around eight sentences or phrases that are possible solutions to the problem with one of them being the actual solution from the selection. Make sure this all fits easily on a single page. Use the following steps to implement We'd Rather in the classroom:

   a) Present the We'd Rather to students on an overhead projector or document camera.
   b) Working in groups students copy the phrases each onto separate strips of paper, or even provide preprinted strips to young children.
   c) Using the strips the groups rank the items from 1 to 8 with 1 being what they would most likely do and 8 being what they believe would be the worst possible situation.

d) Groups share their seventh and eighth choices and tell why. Then they share their second and finally, first choices and explain why.

e) Students then read the selection to see which solution was used in the text and discuss how their decisions matched or differed from the text.

4. *The Big Blue Thing on the Hill* by Yuval Zommer. Templar, 2015—In question answer relationships (QAR), students learn to both answer and generate questions in relation to the source of the answer. The answers can come from within the book or within the students' background knowledge and experience. Raphael and Au (2005) note that QAR provide students with language to talk about comprehension thought processes that are essentially invisible to the eye. Thus, students and teachers have a common instructional language for discussing sources of information and how to learn to use the strategies. For common question types and sources of information in addition for instructional strategies to apply to QAR see the charts in Appendix 1.4. Typically the instruction takes place by teachers modeling the questions, answers, classifying the question according to its QAR type, and then explaining why. Students gradually take on more and more of the responsibility until they can generate and answer the various types of QAR questions. Reading aloud picture books to students is an excellent way for introducing the QAR strategy. Yuvall Zommer's *The Big Blue Thing on the Hill* (2015) fantasy story is about how the local wildlife responds when a camper van arrives on Howling Hill. Here are some sample QAR questions (and answers) about *The Big Blue Thing on the Hill*:

- *Right There*: Where was Howling Hill? (In the middle of the forest far from the city.)
- *Think and Search*: What did the animals do to frighten the Big Blue Thing away? (Describe the actions of the foxes, bears, boars, wolves, and insects.)
- *Author and You*: What term describes the type of animals that made the forest and hill come alive? (Nocturnal.)
- *On My Own*: How do you respond to something strange that frightens you? (Answers will vary.)

Integrated Unit Overview

Theme: Internment of Japanese Americans During World War II (WWII)
Potential Essential Questions • Why did the U.S. Government relocate Japanese Americans to internment camps during WWII? • How did those who were sent to the camps feel about it? • How did the American public at large feel about the action? • What was life like in the internment camps? What did the Japanese Americans do as they lived in these camps? • Were the internment camps justified? • What role did things like prejudice and bigotry play in the decision to relocate Japanese Americans? • Could this happen again? • Is a government responsible to care for its citizens? In what way? • What are human rights? What responsibility does governments have to protect them?
Primary Texts **Fiction:**w *K–2*: *Baseball Saved Us* by Ken Mochizuki, illustrated by Dom Lee. Lee & Low, 1993.

(Continued)

Fish for Jimmy: Inspired by One Family's Experience in a Japanese American Internment Camp by Katie Yamasaki. Holiday House, 2013.
So Far From The Sea by Eve Bunting. Clarion Books, 1998.
Under One Flag: A Year at Rohwer by Liz Smith Parkhurst, illustrated by Tom Clifton. August House, 2005.
3–6:
Dash by Kirby Larson. Scholastic Press, 2014.
A Diamond in the Desert by Kathryn Kitzmaurice. Viking Children's Books, 2012.
Gaijin: American Prisoner of War by Matt Faulkner. Disney Hyperion Books, 2014.
Missing In Action by Dean Hughes. Atheneum Books for Young Readers, 2010.
Weedflower by Cynthia Kadohata. Atheneum Books for Young Readers, 2006.

Nonfiction:
K–2:
Barbed Wire Baseball by Marissa Moss, illustrated by Yuko Shimizu. Harry N. Abrams, 2013.
3–6:
The Children of Topaz: The Story of a Japanese-American Internment Camp, Based on a Classroom Diary by Michael O. Tunnell. Holiday House, 1996.
Farewell to Manzanar: A True Story of Japanese American Experience During and After the World War II Internment by Jeanne Wakatsuki Houston. Houghton Mifflin, 1973.
In America's Shadow by Kimberly Komatsu and Kaleigh Komatsu. Thomas George Books, 2002.
Remembering Manzanar: Life in a Japanese Relocation Camp by Michael L. Cooper. Clarion Books, 2002.

Supporting Texts	Multimedia Texts
Children of the Camps Internment History: http://www.pbs.org/childofcamp/history/ Internment of San Francisco Japanese at Virtual Museum of the City of San Francisco: http://www.sfmuseum.org/war/evactxt.html Japanese-American Interment: http://www.ushistory.org/us/51e.asp Japanese-American Internment Camps During WWII at J. Willard Marriott Library, the University of Utah: http://www.lib.utah.edu/collections/photo-exhibits/japanese-American-Internment.php Japanese Relocation and Internment during World War II at the National Archives: http://www.archives.gov/research/alic/reference/military/japanese-internment.html Letters from the Japanese American Internment from Smithsonian Education: http://www.smithsonianeducation.org/educators/lesson_plans/japanese_internment/index.html	Conditions at Japanese Internment Camps: http://www.history.com/speeches/conditions-at-japanese-internment-camps#conditions-at-japanese-internment-camps George Takei On the Japanese Internment Camps During WWII: https://www.youtube.com/watch?v=yogXJl9H9z0 Japanese-American Relocation: http://www.history.com/topics/world-war-ii/japanese-american-relocation Japanese Internment Camp: http://www.c-span.org/video/?305111–1/japanese-internment-camp Pat Morita On Being Held in A Japanese Internment Camp: https://www.youtube.com/watch?v=2XpPb-BoxBME

Potential Assessments (Unit Projects)
- Have students create quiz questions that can be answered from the text. Have students take the quiz written by other students or make it into a game and conduct a quiz show where students compete to answer the questions.
- Have students act as reporters. Identify an important question or issue that readers in a newspaper at the time might want to know about. Using one or more of the texts for their sources, have the students write a newspaper article (A.W.2) answering the who, what, when, where, and why questions.
- Using one or more characters from one of the texts have the students write an imagined dialogue (A.W.3) between themselves and that character. Use details and quote accurately from the text for the characters portion of the dialogue.
- Conduct a sustained research project (A.W.7) on one of the internment camps. Students should focus on the conditions, people, and experiences. Have students use what the texts say explicitly to glean quotes and other details from the texts to create oral presentations (A.SL.4) that makes use of digital media (A.SL.5) as part of the presentation.

- Have students select a photograph or event from one of the nonfiction texts. Have the students write a narrative about the picture or event (A.W.3). Ensure that the students use details from the text to enhance the accuracy of their story. Use the fictional texts as models where needed for the students to base their stories on.

Standard 2

A.R.2	Determine central idea or theme, analyze development, summarize key details and ideas
RL.K.2	Retell familiar stories using key details
RL.1.2	"" / understand central message
RL.2.2	"" / fables, folktales, diverse cultures
RL.3.2	Recount fables, folktales, myths, diverse cultures, central message/lesson/moral
RL.4.2	Determine theme (story, drama, poetry); summarize text
RL.5.2	"" / determine how characters respond to challenges
RL.6.2; RI.6.2	Describe theme or central idea; summarize text without personal opinions
RI.K.2; RI.1.2	Identify main topic with key details
RI.2.2	"" / topic of specific paragraphs
RI.3.2	"" / recount key details to support main idea
RI.4.2	"" / summarize
RI.5.2	Determine two or more main ideas with key details / summarize

Texts

Standard 2 calls directly for the use of fables, folktales, myths, and stories from diverse cultures. Here are some suggestions of favorites in each of these genres.

Fables

Ackamarackus: Julius Lester's Sumptuously Silly Fantastically Funny Fables by Julius Lester, illustrated by Emilie Chollat. Scholastic Press, 2001.
Aesop's Fables retold and illustrated by Jerry Pinkney. SeaStar Books, 2000.
The Crocodile and the Scorpion by Rebecca and Ed Emberley. Roaring Brook Press, 2013.
Fables by Arnold Lobel. Harper & Row, 1980.
Feathers and Fools by Mem Fox, illustrated by Nicholas Wilton. Harcourt Brace, 1996.
Flossie and the Fox by Patricia C. McKissack, illustrated by Rachel Isadora. Dial Books, 1986.
Lion and the Mouse by Jerry Pinkney. Little, Brown Books, 2009.
Mouse and Lion by Aesop, retold by Rand Burkert, illustrated by Nancy Ekholm Burkert. Michael Di Capua Books, 2011.
The Rabbit and the Turtle: Aesops Fables retold and illustrated by Eric Carle. Orchard Books, 2008.
Squids Will Be Squids: Fresh Morals, Beastly Fables by Jon Scieszka, illustrated by Lane Smith. Viking, 1998.

Folk and Fairy Tales

The Blue Fairy Book by Andrew Lang. Dover, 1880. Free e-book edition available here: http://gutenberg.org/ebooks/503
The Brave Little Seamstress by Mary Pope Osborne, illustrated by Giselle Potter. Atheneum Books for Young Readers, 2002.

The Bunyans by Audrey Wood, illustrated by David Shannon. Blue Sky Press, 1996.

Coyote: A Trickster Tale from the American Southwest by Gerald McDermott. Houghton Mifflin Harcourt, 1999.

From Sea to Shining Sea: A Treasury of American Folklore and Folk Songs edited by Amy L. Cohn, illustrated by Molly G. Bang. Scholastic, 1993.

The Goblin and the Empty Chair by Mem Fox, illustrated by Leo and Diane Dillon. Beach Lane Books, 2009.

Goldilocks and the Three Bears by Lauren Child, illustrated by Polly Borland and Emily L. Jenkins. Disney-Hyperion, 2009.

Heckedy Peg by Audrey Wood, illustrated by Don Wood. Harcourt Brace Jovanovich, 1987.

How the Rooster Got His Crown retold and illustrated by Amy Lowry Poole. Holiday House, 1999.

Paul Bunyan's Sweetheart by Marybeth Lorbiecki, illustrated by Renee Graef. Sleeping Bear Press, 2007.

The Pied Piper of Hamelin by Robert Holden, illustrated by Drahos Zak. Houghton Mifflin, 1997.

Sleeping Beauty illustrated by K.Y. Craft. Chronicle Books, 2002.

Snow White translated from the Brothers Grimm by Paul Heins, illustrated by Trina Schart Hyman. Little, Brown Books for Young Readers, 1974.

The Talking Eggs by Robert D. San Souci, illustrated by Jerry Pinkney. Dial Books, 1989.

Tops and Bottoms by Janet Stevens. Harcourt Brace, 1995.

Myths

Black Ships before Troy: The Story of The Iliad by Rosemary Sutcliff, illustrated by Alan Lee. Delacorte Press, 1993.

D'Aulaires' Book of Greek Myths by Ingri and Edgar Parin D'Aulaire. Doubleday, 1962.

D'Aulaires' Book of Norse Myths by Ingri and Edgar Parin D'Aulaire. New York Review of Books, 2005.

Favorite Norse Myths by Mary Pope Osborne, illustrated by Troy Howell. Scholastic, 1996.

The Gods and Goddesses of Ancient Egypt by Leonard Everett Fisher. Holiday House, 1997.

The Gods and Goddesses of Olympus written and illustrated by Aliki. HarperCollins, 1994.

Gods and Goddesses of the Ancient Maya by Leonard Everett Fisher. Holiday House, 1999.

Gods and Goddesses of the Ancient Norse by Leonard Everett Fisher. Holiday House, 2001.

Greek Gods and Goddesses by Geraldine McCaughrean, illustrated by Emma Chichester Clark. Margaret K. McElderry Books, 1998.

The Illustrated Book of Myths: Tales and Legends of the World by Neil Philip, illustrated by Nilesh Mistry. Dorling Kindersley, 1995.

In the Beginning: Creation Stories from around the World by Virginia Hamilton, illustrated by Barry Moser. Harcourt Brace Jovanovich, 1988.

Musicians of the Sun by Gerald McDermott. Simon & Schuster Books for Young Readers, 1997.

The Names Upon the Harp: Irish Myth and Legend by Marie Heaney, illustrated by Patrick James Lynch. Arthur A. Levine Books, 2000.

The Odyssey by Gillian Cross, illustrated by Neil Packer. Candlewick Press, 2012.

Treasury of Egyptian Mythology: Classic Stories of Gods, Goddesses, Monsters, and Mortals by Donna Jo Napoli, illustrated by Christian Balit. National Geographic Society Children's Books, 2013.

Folktales and Other Stories Representing Diverse Cultures

The Elephant's Friend and Other Tales from Ancient India by Marcia Williams. Candlewick Press, 2012.

Fa Mulan: The Story of a Woman Warrior by Robert D. San Souci, illustrated by Jean and Mou-Sien Tseng. Hyperion, 1998.

Fin M'Coul: The Giant of Knockmany Hill retold and illustrated by Tomie de Paola. Holiday House, 1981.

Grandma and the Great Gourd: A Bengali Folktale by Chitra Banerjee Divakaruni, illustrated by Susy Pilgrim Waters. Roaring Brook Press, 2013.

Her Stories: African American Folk Tales, Fairy Tales, and True Tales told by Virginia Hamilton, illustrated by Leo and Diane Dillon. Blue Sky Press, 1995.

Hosni the Dreamer: An Arabian Tale by Ehud Ben-Ezer, illustrated by Uri Shulevitz. Farrar, Straus and Giroux, 1997.

Mouse Match: A Chinese Folktale by Ed Young. Harcourt Brace, 1997.

The Polar Bear Son: An Inuit Tale retold and illustrated by Lydia Dabcovich. Clarion Books, 1997.

The Seven Chinese Sisters by Kathy Tucker, illustrated by Grace Lin. A. Whitman, 2003.

Seven Daughters and Seven Sons by Barbara Cohen and Bahija Lovejoy. Atheneum, 1982.

A Story, a Story: An African Tale retold and illustrated by Gail E. Haley. Atheneum, 1970.

Tim O'Toole and the Wee Folk: An Irish Tale retold and illustrated by Gerald McDermott. Viking, 1990.

The Way Meat Loves Salt: A Cinderella Tale from the Jewish Tradition by Nina Jaffe, illustrated by Louise August. Henry Holt, 1998.

White Tiger, Blue Serpent retold by Grace Tseng, illustrated by Jean and Mou-sien Tseng. Lothrop, Lee & Shepard, 1999.

Why the Sky Is Far Away: A Nigerian Folktale by Mary-Joan Gerson, illustrated by Carla Golembe. Little, Brown Books for Young Readers, 1995.

Text Activities

1. *Zomo the Rabbit: A Trickster Tale from West Africa* by Gerald McDermott. Harcourt Brace Jovanovich, 1992—Use a retelling guide as a scaffold for students to use when retelling a story, an example is found in Appendix 2.1. Use of the story guide helps students understand what to include in a retelling and transfers to their ability to tell stories without using the guides. Other results from using story guides are revealed in a meta-analysis of 11 studies of young children's story retellings, where Dunst, Simkus, and Hamby (2012) found that story retellings influenced story-related comprehension and expressive vocabulary as well as nonstory-related receptive language and early literacy development.

2. *Chinese Fables: "The Dragon Slayer" and Other Timeless Tales of Wisdom* by S. S. Nunes. Tuttle, 2014—Use a Determining the Theme Graphic Organizer to help students focus on the different elements of a story and select the theme. An example is found in Appendix 2.2. Aesop's fables have a stated moral but some fables from other traditions do not have explicit morals. Shiho Nunes's *Chinese Fables: "The Dragon Slayer" and Other Timeless Tales of Wisdom"* presents 19 different fables. Begin by reading a fable to the students and then involve them in filling out the sections for characters, setting, problem or goal, and the solution. Explain that theme is the story's message or moral in fables. Themes are best expressed in complete sentences. For instance, "Friends often sacrifice for one another" is more powerful than the one-word topic "friendship." While activities and discussions related to one-word topics may be entertaining and promote learning; these types of topics are not substantive enough for students to make deeper connections to their lives and the world around them, therefore perpetuating a superficial treatment of theme. Students familiar with Aesop's fables are familiar with the morals being in complete sentences so inferring theme from this is more direct. Model for them how to make inferences to come up with a theme. Gradually turn more of the responsibility to students where they work in small groups to infer the fable's theme.

3. *A Place for Bats* by Melissa Stewart, illustrated by Higgins Bond. Peachtree Publishers, 2012—Teaching about main ideas and supporting details holds a key role in teaching about informational text. Begin explaining the concept of main ideas and supporting details then read a nonfiction picture book to the class and let students suggest possible main ideas. Help them choose the sentence that best tells what a portion of the book was about. Finally, involve the students in listing the supporting details on a chart on graphic organizer. See Appendix 2.3 for an example.

4. *Gravity* by Jason Chin. Roaring Brook Press, 2014—Read the book aloud to students. First, involve the students in determining the book's topic by making inferences from the title and illustrations. Brainstorm what main ideas the author might cover given the broad topic. Then lead students to determine the main idea about the function of gravity that the author does cover in the text. Finally, guide students to list details that support what gravity does.

Integrated Unit Overview

Theme: East of the Sun West of the Moon

Potential Essential Questions
- What is the central message, moral, or lesson of a fairy tale?
- How do different versions change the central message, moral, or lesson?
- What kinds of problems do characters in fairy tales have? How do they respond to those problems?
- What is the theme of a fairy tale?
- What can we learn from fairy tales?
- How do fairy tales vary across cultures and time?
- How do different retellers change a fairy tale? How do they change a familiar story into something new by changing the plot, setting, or other textual elements?
- How do the details of a tale change it from one variant to another?

Primary Texts
East of the Sun and West of the Moon original text at http://www.pitt.edu/~dash/norway034.html
K–2:
East of the Sun and West of the Moon by Laszlo Gal. McClelland and Steward, 1993.
East of the Sun and West of the Moon by Kathleen and Michael Hague. Harcourt Brace Jovanovich, 1980.
East of the Sun & West of the Moon by Mercer Mayer. Four Winds Press, 1980.
East of the Sun and West of the Moon by Nancy Willard, illustrated by Barry Moser. Houghton Mifflin Harcourt Books for Young Readers, 1989.
East o' the Sun and West o' the Moon retold by Naomi Lewis, illustrated by P.J. Lynch. Candlewick Press, 2005.
The Lady and the Lion: A Brother's Grimm Tale by Jacqueline K. Ogburn, illustrated by Laurel Long. Dial, 2003.
The Princess and the White Bear King by Tanya Robyn Batt. Barefoot Books, 2004.
Snowbear Whittington: An Appalachian Beauty and the Beast by William H. Hooks, illustrated by Victorai Lisi. Simon & Schuster, 1994.
3–6:
East by Edith Pattou. Harcourt Children's Books, 2003.
Ice by Sarah Beth Durst. Margaret K. McElderry Books, 2009.
Sun and Moon, Ice and Snow by Jessica Day George. Bloomsbury, 2008.
West of the Moon by Margi Preus. Harry N. Abrams, 2014.

Supporting Texts	**Multimedia Texts**
Aarne–Thompson Tale Type Index: http://en.wikipedia.org/wiki/Aarne%E2%80%93Thompson_classification_system *Beauties and Beasts (The Oryx Multicultural Folktale Series)* by Betsy Herne. Greenwood, 1993. *East o' the Sun and West o' the Moon and other Norwegian Folk Tales* illustrated by Frederick Richardson: http://www.childrenslibrary.org/icdl/BookPreview?bookid=thoeast_00150021&route=text&lang=English&msg=&ilang=English The Snow Show a National Arts Centre English Theater Production Study Guide: http://www.artsalive.ca/pdf/eth/activities/snowshow.pdf	"East of the Sun and West of the Moon" sung by Ella Fitzgerald: https://www.youtube.com/watch?v=2NfgINK8fDg "The True Bride" from Jim Hensen's "The Storyteller" (DVD available from retailers in Jim Henson's "The StoryTeller: The Definitive Collection." The Polar Bear King directed by Ola Solum (available from streaming video services and on DVD)

Potential Assessments (Unit Projects)
- Have students create a cartoon or graphic novel that recounts the story with its key details.
- Have students read several variations of the tale. Have the students create a script for a play or readers theatre version that combines the key details of the versions of the tale. Make sure that the scenes fit together and flow well. Have the students perform the play.
- Have students read and connect culturally different variants of the tale; there are direct variants here from Norway, the Americas, and Germany. Determine how the theme varies from culture to culture. Determine why the variants might change theme. Have the students write their own variant (A.W.3) representing their own cultural perspective that connects a theme that is important to them or their culture.
- Have students do extended research projects (A.W.7) about culture, dress, or history of the tale's original country of origin, Norway, using multiple print and digital sources (A.W.8). Have the students compare what they found with one of the texts. How did the author or illustrator represent the country of origin in the text? What key details did the author use to represent the country? What did they do differently than might be expected?
- Have students extend their study of the tale into other variants of Beast and Beauty tales like this one. Have students describe the challenges that each character faces in the variants. Have the students use fairy tale classification systems like the Aarne–Thompson Tale Type Index to chart how different tale variants with the same classification deal with challenges for their characters. Explore: Why do the challenges vary? What is it about the tale that makes this change? How are the different variants the same? Different? Have students collaborate on the project (A.SL.1) and present their conclusions to the class.

Standard 3

A.R.3	Analyze how and why individuals, events, and ideas develop and interact
RL.K.3; RL.1.3	Identify characters, setting, major events
RL.2.3	Describe characters' response to events and challenges
RL.3.3	Describe characters (traits, feelings); how actions contribute to sequence of events
RL.4.3	Describe in depth character, setting, events using key details
RL.5.3	Compare and contrast character, setting, event using key details
RL.6.3	Describe plot and character development
RI.K.3; RI.1.3	Describe connections between individuals, events, ideas, or pieces
RI.2.3	Describe connection between historic events, scientific ideas, concepts, steps in technical procedure
RI.3.3	"" / using language that pertains to time, sequence, cause/effect
RI4.3	"" / what happened and why
RI5.3	Relationships and interactions between individuals, events, ideas, or pieces based on key details
RI6.3	Analyze individuals, events, ideas introduced, illustrated, elaborated

Texts

Standard 3 for literature focuses on the textual structure of characters. To connect with this standard some texts that have vivid characters are offered. Standard 3 for informational texts discusses making connections between historic events and individuals. While the intent here is to focus on how this happens in nonfiction texts, fictional texts can easily be brought into the mix to address this standard especially when they contain real people and events. To connect this standard in this broad way some fictional texts that portray real people are offered.

Vivid Characters

K–2 Texts

Betty Goes Bananas by Steve Antony. Schwartz & Wade, 2014.

Big Bad Baby by Bruce Hale, illustrated by Steve Breen. Dial, 2014.

Boot & Shoe by Marla Frazee. Beach Lane Books, 2012.

Little Elliot, Big City by Mike Curato. Henry Holt & Co., 2014.

Peggy by Anna Walker. Clarion Books, 2014.

Room for Bear by Ciara Gavin. Knopf Books for Young Readers, 2015.

Rupert Can Dance by Jules Feiffer. Farrar, Straus and Giroux, 2014.

Say Hello to Zorro! By Carter Goodrich. Simon & Schuster, 2011.

Sparky! by Jenny Offill, illustrated by Chris Appelhans. Schwartz & Wade, 2014.

The Year of Billy Miller by Kevin Henkes. HarperCollins, 2013.

3–6 Texts

Counting by 7s by Holly Goldberg Sloan. Dial Books for Young Readers, 2012.

Jake and Lily by Jerry Spinelli. Balzer & Bray, 2012.

Joey Pigza Swallowed the Key (Joey Pigza Books #1) by Jack Gantos. Farrar, Straus and Giroux, 1998.

Junonia by Kevin Henkes. Greenwillow Books, 2011.

The Mighty Miss Malone by Christopher Paul Curtis. Wendy Lamb Books, 2012.

Navigating Early by Clare Vanderpool. Delacorte Press, 2013.

The Scandalous Sisterhood of Prickwillow Place by Julie Berry. Roaring Brook Press, 2014.

The Summer of the Gypsy Moths by Sara Pennypacker. Balzer & Bray, 2012.

Ungifted by Gordon Korman. Balzer & Bray, 2012.

Wonder by R.J. Palacio. Alfred A. Knopf, 2012.

Real People as Characters

K–2 Texts

Abe's Fish: A Boyhood Tale of Abraham Lincoln by Jennifer Bryant, illustrated by Amy June Bates. Sterling Publishing Co., 2009.

Albie's First Word: A Tale Inspired by Albert Einstein's Childhood by Jacqueline Tourville, illustrated by Wynne Evans. Schwarz & Wade Books, 2014.

Chasing Degas by Eva Montanari. Abrams Books for Young Readers, 2009.

Georgia Rises: A Day in the Life of Georgia O'Keefe by Kathryn Lasky, illustrated by Ora Eitan. Farrar, Straus and Giroux, 2009.

Jackie's Bat by Marybeth Lorbiecki, illustrated by Brian Pinkney. Simon & Schuster, 2006.

Looking for Bird in the Big City by Robert Burleigh, illustrated by Marek Los. Harcourt Brace, 2001.

Moses: When Harriet Tubman Led Her People to Freedom by Carole Boston Weatherford, illustrated by Kadir Nelson. Hyperion Books for Children, 2006.

Salt in His Shoes: Michael Jordan in Pursuit of a Dream by Deloris Jordan, illustrated by Kadir Nelson. Simon & Schuster Books for Young Readers, 2000.

The Secret of the Great Houdini by Robert Burleigh, illustrated by Leonid Gore. Atheneum Books, 2002.

Stand Straight, Ella Kate: The True Story of a Real Giant by Kate Klise, illustrated by Sarah M. Klise. Dial Books, 2010.

3–6 Texts

Ashes by Kathryn Lasky. Viking, 2010.

Beethoven Lives Upstairs by Barbara Nichol. Orchard Books, 1993.

Cleopatra VII: Daughter of the Nile (The Royal Diaries) by Kristiana Gregory. Scholastic, 1999.

The Haunting of Charles Dickens by Lewis Buzbee. Feiwel and Friends, 2009.

I Am Rembrandt's Daughter by Lynn Cullen. Bloomsburry, 2007.

King of Shadows by Susan Cooper. Margaret K. McElderry Books, 1999.

The Lacemaker and the Princess by Kimberley Brubaker Bradley. Margaret K. McElderry Books, 2007.

Leonardo's Shadow: Or, My Astonishing Life as Leonardo da Vinci's Servant by Christopher Grey. Atheneum Books, 2006.

The Man Who Was Poe by Avi. Orchard Books, 1989.

Mary, Queen of Scots: Queen without a Country (The Royal Diaries) by Kathryn Lasky. Scholastic, 2002.

The Musician's Daughter by Susanne Emily Dunlap. Bloomsbury, 2009.

My Brother Abe: Sally Lincoln's Story by Harry Mazer. Simon & Schuster Books for Young Readers, 2009.

Quest for a Maid by Frances Mary Hendry. Farrar, Straus and Giroux, 1988.

Riding Freedom by Pam Munoz Ryan, illustrated by Brian Selznick. Scholastic, 1998.

Ripper by Stefan Petrucha. Philomel Books, 2012.

The Shakespeare Stealer (Shakespeare Stealer #1) by Gary L. Blackwood. Dutton Children's Books, 1998.

The True Adventures of Charley Darwin by Carolyn Meyer. Harcourt, 2009.

X: A Novel by Iiyasah Shabazz with Kekla Magoon. Candlewick Press, 2015.

Text Activities

1. *The Black Cauldron* by Lloyd Alexander. Holt, 1965—Use a response guide as a tool for inviting students to consider characters' attitudes, beliefs, and values in relation to their actions (Hadaway, Vardell, & Young, 2002). An example is found in Appendix 3.1. After students complete the guides independently, they discuss their responses with a small group of peers. The discussion is as valuable as the completion of the guide itself as it helps students hone their understanding and delve deeper into their ideas. When creating response guides teachers generally follow the following procedures:

   a) List the characters down the left side of the grid.
   b) List general statements that reflect issues, beliefs, and values that relate to the book. (Do not list characters' direct quotes.)
   c) Develop a key for students to use while completing the activity.
   d) Finally, include directions for students.

2. *Paperboy* by Vince Vawter. Delacorte Press, 2013—A polar opposites graphic organizer allows students to analyze the characters in a reading selection (Yopp & Yopp, 2014). An example is given in Appendix 3.2. Students rate the characters on various traits, and justify their response with evidence from the text.

3. *Harry Potter and the Sorcerer's Stone* by J. K. Rowling. A. A. Levine Books, 1997—Literary report cards provide students with another tool for analyzing characters (Yopp & Yopp, 2014). An example is given in Appendix 3.3. Teachers create the card and select the "subjects" to be graded—character attributes are used rather than traditional subjects. Students not only give the grades, but they also cite text evidence for each grade given. Later students can be invited to create their own "subjects."

4. *A Place for Bats* by Melissa Stewart, illustrated by Higgins Bond. Peachtree Publishers, 2012—Connection charts can be used to explain the connection between two or more individuals, events, or pieces of information, or ideas (Owocki, 2012). An example is given in Appendix 3.4. Students can work in pairs of teams to complete the charts.

Integrated Unit Overview

Theme: The Villain as Character

Potential Essential Questions
- Which character is the villain? Why?
- Why are villains important characters in stories?
- What characteristics do villains have? How does that contrast with the characteristics the hero has?
- How does the villain cause or help to cause the events that take place in the book? What role do they play in developing the plot?
- What role does the villain play in creating the challenges or problems for the character? How do the actions of the villain shape the way the characters respond to the events and challenges they face?
- How could the author have developed the villain differently? What would have made him/her the hero?
- What is the difference between a character who is a villain and a character who is merely an antagonist? What makes the difference?
- How do different genres portray villains?
- How do real villains compare to literary ones? How do authors of fiction use real villains to build their fictional characters?

Primary Texts
The Bad Beginning (A Series of Unfortunate Events #1) by Lemony Snicket, illustrated by Brett Helquist. Scholastic, 1999.
Cinderella illustrated by K. Y. Craft. Chronicle Books, 2000.
Harry Potter and the Sorcerer's Stone by J. K. Rowling, illustrated by Mary GrandPré. Scholastic, 1997.
The Lion, the Witch and the Wardrobe (The Chronicles of Narnia) by C. S. Lewis, illustrated by Pauline Baynes. HarperCollins, 2007.
Ozma of OZ (OZ #3) by L. Frank Baum. Reilly & Britton, 1907.
Robin Hood and the Golden Arrow by Robert D. San Souci, illustrated by E. B. Lewis. Orchard Books, 2010.
Snow White and the Seven Dwarfs: A Tale From the Brothers Grimm illustrated by Nancy Ekholm Burkert. Farrar, Straus and Giroux, 1972.
Spider and the Fly by Mary Howitt, illustrated by Tony DiTerlizzi. Simon & Schuster, 2002.
The Witches by Roald Dahl. Farrar, Straus and Giroux, 1983.
A Wrinkle in Time (A Wrinkle in Time Quintet #1) by Madeleine L'Engle. Dell, 1962.

Supporting Texts	**Multimedia Texts**
The Best Villains in Children's Books from Imagination Soup: http://imaginationsoup.net/2012/04/the-best-villains-in-childrens-books/ *Heroes and Villains* by Anthony Horowitz. Macmillan, 2011. *Top 10 Worst Vicious Villains You Wouldn't Want to Know!* by Jim Pipe, illustrated by David Antram. Gareth Stevens Publishers, 2012. "Villains" from author Ellen Jackson: http://www.ellenjackson.net/villains_61470.htm "Villain" from Wikipedia: http://en.wikipedia.org/wiki/Villain *Villains: Traitors, Tyrants and Thieves* by Richard Platt. DK, 2002.	American Film Institute's 100 Greatest Heroes & Villains: http://www.afi.com/100Years/handv.aspx Kids' Books: Heroes and Villains: http://tvo.org/article/kids-books-heroes-and-villains Disney's Maleficent directed by Robert Stromberg. (Available on DVD from retailers.) Media Literacy: Heroes and Villains: https://www.youtube.com/watch?v=gRx6xmuF7uA#t=17

Potential Assessments (Unit Projects)
- Have students use a Character Traits Graphic Organizer such as the one found at http://www.scholastic.com/teachers/lesson-plan/character-sheet-and-traits-list to collect information about the villain's traits and feelings. Assess how the author uses these details to make the character seem real and to determine if the character is round or flat.
- Use a Character Comparison Graphic Organizer such as the one found at http://printables.scholastic.com/printables/detail/?id=35527 to describe the characters and then compare and contrast the hero and the villain of the story. How are they the same and how are they different?

- Have the students write a narrative (A.W.3) with an alternative ending to the story where the villain is redeemed or makes changes. Develop the character as the author would using key ideas and details of the character's traits and feelings from the text but change how their actions contributed to the sequence of events so they come out positively.
- Create a book advertisement or trailer (http://www.scholastic.com/teachers/classroom-solutions/2011/11/beyond-book-reports-%E2%80%94-book-trailers) that can be posted or shared (A.W.6) that features the actions of the villain and how they contribute to the plot or that describes or compares and contrasts the characters in some way.
- Lesson plans: Fantastic Characters: Analyzing and Creating Superheroes and Villains from read-writethink: http://www.readwritethink.org/classroom-resources/lesson-plans/fantastic-characters-analyzing-creating-30637.html?tab=5

Standards 4–6: Craft and Structure: What Authors Are Trying to Do
Standard 4

A.R.4	Interpret words and phrases, determine technical, connotative, and figurative meaning, analyze specific word choices
RL.K.4; RI.K.4	Ask and answer questions about unknown words
RL.1.4	Identify words and phrases that appeal to feelings or senses
RL.2.4	Identify how words and phrases supply rhythm and meaning
RL.3.4	Determine meaning of words and phrases / both literal and nonliteral
RL.4.4	"" / especially allusions to mythology
RL.5.4	"" / metaphors and similes
RL.6.4	"" / figurative and connotative meanings, impact of word choice on meaning and tone
RI.1.4	Ask and answer questions to clarify meaning
RI.2.4; RI.3.4; RI.4.4; RI.5.4	Determine meaning of words (academic, domain specific, etc.)
RI.6.4	"" / figurative, connotative, and technical meanings

Texts

Anchor Standard 4 focuses on the language used in a text. For this standard texts that use language in wonderful and unique ways will be the most useful. Here are some texts that offer great rhythm and rhyme and that use beautiful figurative language that will connect perfectly with this standard.

Great Rhythm and Rhyme

Fiction

A Boy Had a Mother Who Bought Him a Hat by Karla Kuskin, illustrated by Kevin Hawkes. HarperCollins, 2010.
Bugs Galore by Peter Stein, illustrated by Bob Staake. Candlewick Press, 2012.

Dancing Feet! by Lindsey Craig, illustrated by Marc Brown. Knopf Books for Young Readers, 2010.

Goodnight, Goodnight Construction Site by Sherri Duskey Rinker, illustrated by Tom Lichtenheld. Chronicle Books, 2011.

How Do Dinosaurs Say Goodnight? by Jane Yolen, illustrated by Mark Teague. Blue Sky Press, 2000.

I Ain't Gonna Paint No More by Karen Beaumont, illustrated by David Catrow. Houghton Mifflin Harcourt, 2005.

I Love My Hat by Douglas Florian. Two Lions, 2014.

Is Your Mama a Lama? by Deborah Guarino, illustrated by Steven Kellogg. Scholastic, 1989.

The Middle Child Blues by Kristyn Crow, illustrated by David Catrow. G. P. Putnam's Sons, 2009.

My Heart Is Like a Zoo by Michael Hall. Greenwillow Books, 2010.

One Big Pair of Underwear by Laura Gehl, illustrated by Tom Lichtenheld. Beach Lane Books, 2014.

The Pirates Next Door: Starring the Jolley Rogers by Jonny Duddle. Templar, 2012.

Silly Sally by Audrey Wood. Houghton Mifflin Harcourt, 1992.

When I Grow Up by Al Yankovic, illustrated by Wes Hargis. HarperCollins, 2011.

Nonfiction

Antarctic Antics: A Book of Penguin Poems by Judy Sierra, illustrated by Jose Aruego and Ariane Dewey. Harcourt Brace & Co., 1998.

Arithme-tickle: An Even Number of Odd Rhymes by J. Patrick Lewis, illustrated by Frank Remkiewicz. Harcourt, 2002.

Demolition by Sally Sutton, illustrated by Brian Lovelock. Candlewick Press, 2012.

Gobble it Up!: A Fun Song about Eating! by Jim Arnosky. Scholastic, 2008.

Have You Heard the Nesting Bird? by Rita Gray, illustrated by Kenard Pak. Houghton Mifflin Books for Children, 2014.

If You Were a Penguin by Wendell and Florence Minor. HarperCollins, 2009.

Jazz by Walter Dan Myers, illustrated by Christopher Myers. Holiday House, 2006.

Math Appeal by Greg Tang, illustrated by Harry Briggs. Scholastic, 2003.

One Nighttime Sea: A Ocean Counting Rhyme by Deborah Lee Rose, illustrated by Steve Jenkins. Scholastic, 2003.

Zin! Zin! Zin! A Violin by Lloyd Moss. Simon & Schuster, 1995.

Figurative Language

K–2 Texts

A Chocolate Mouse for Dinner by Fred Gwynne. Simon & Schuster, 1980.

Batter up Wombat by Helen Lester, illustrated by Lynn Munsinger. Houghton Mifflin Harcourt, 2006.

Grandfather's Journey by Allan Say. Houghton Mifflin, 1993.

Henry's Freedom Box by Ellen Levine, illustrated by Kadir Nelson. Scholastic, 2007.

My Best Friend Is as Sharp as a Pencil by Hanoch Piven. Schwarz & Wade, 2010.

Oh, No! by Candace Fleming, illustrated by Eric Rohmann. Schwartz & Wade, 2012.

The Other Side by Jacqueline Woodson, illustrated by E. B. Lewis. Putnam, 2001.

Red Sings from Treetops: A Year in Colors by Joyce Sidman, illustrated by Pamela Zagarenski. Houghton Mifflin Harcourt, 2009.

Sleep like a Tiger by Mary Logue, illustrated by Pamela Zagarenski. Houghton Mifflin Harcourt, 2012.

Spoon by Amy Krouse Rosenthal, illustrated by Scott Magoon. Disney-Hyperion, 2009.

Walter Was Worried by Laura Vaccaro Seeger. Square Fish, 2006.

Wilfrid Gordon McDonald Partridge by Mem Fox, illustrated by Julie Vivas, Kane/Miller Book Publishers, 1985.

3–6 Texts

Esperanze Rising by Pam Munoz Ryan. Scholastic Press, 2002.

The Evolution of Calpurnia Tate (Calpurnia Tate #1) by Jacqueline Kelly. Henry Holt, 2009.

The Lions of Little Rock by Kristin Levine. Putnam Juvenile, 2012.

Punished! by David Lubar. Darby Creek Publishing, 2006.

The Real Boy by Anne Ursu, illustrated by Erin Mcguire. Waldon Pond Press, 2013.

Savvy (Savvy #1) by Ingrid Law. Dial, 2008.

The Spindles by Lauren Oliver, illustrated by Iacopo Bruno. Harper, 2012.

Starry River of the Sky by Grace Lin. Little, Brown Books for Young Readers, 2012.

The Tale of Despereaux by Kate DiCamillo, illustrated by Timothy Basil Ering. Candlewick Press, 2003.

The Turtle of Oman by Naomi Shihab Nye. Greenwillow Books, 2014.

Text Activities

1. *Bats! Strange and Wonderful* by Laurence Pringle, illustrated by Meryl Henderson. Boyds Mills Press, 2000—Magic squares is an activity for reviewing vocabulary words related to a reading selection (Richardson, Morgan, & Fleener, 2012). An example is in Appendix 4.1. Students typically enjoy the self-checking activity. Students complete the magic squares by writing the number of the definition into the square with the correct term. Then they check their answers by adding the numbers across each row, down each column, and diagonally. Additional vocabulary magic square number combinations can be found online.

2. *Shark Attack!* by Cathy East Dubowski. Dorling Kindersley, 1998—Concept circles provide students with a format to study words critically and to learn how words conceptually relate to one another (Vacca, Mraz, & Vacca, 2014). An example can be found in Appendix 4.2. To construct a concept circle, divide a circle into four (or more) sections. In each section write a word or phrase related to the topic. Concept circles may be used in four ways:

   a) All of the words in the circle are related and the students must tell how they are related.

   b) All of the words in the circle are related except one. The student must identify the unrelated word and explain how the other words are related.

   c) One or more of the sections is left blank. Students must fill in the blank sections with words that are related to the other words in the circle and explain why they chose those words.

   d) Students are given a concept circle template and asked to create their own concept circles on the topic of study.

3. *The Many Faces of George Washington: Remaking a Presidential Icon* by Carla Killough McClafferty. Carolrhoda Books, 2011—Concept of definition maps helps students delve into the definitions of words and how they work. They focus on the category, characteristics, and examples of definitions, or in other words they focus on all the parts that appear in a traditional dictionary. To use the maps have students identify academic or domain-specific words in the text that they do not understand or that they feel they want more clarification on. Have the students fill out a concept of definition map. An example and samples of such a map can be found here: http://teacher.scholastic. com/reading/bestpractices/vocabulary/pdf/tr_AllConcept.pdf. After students have completed the map they should write up their own dictionary-type definition of the word using the information they found. Quotes from the text where the word appears can also be added next to the definition. All the students' work can be combined together to make a dictionary for many words the students encountered in the text.

4. *The Shadow Thieves (The Cronus Chronicles #1)* by Anne Ursu, illustrated by Eric Fortune. Atheneum Books for Young Readers, 2006—Have students extract from the text words and phrases

that contain allusions to mythology. Have students do research using both print and digital sources on the piece of mythology the text is referencing. Have the students use the references to create an online or paper board game that extends Ursu's characters and setting and has these structures interact at a different or deeper level than is offered in the text.

Integrated Unit Overview

Theme: Haiku

Potential Essential Questions
- How can poetry and figurative language help us understand the world around us?
- Why do poets use language in a way that appeals to a reader's feelings and senses? What does this kind of language supply to the poem?
- How do poets use words that have both literal and nonliteral meanings? What does this kind of language supply to the poem?
- How do the words poets choose impact the meaning and tone of the poem?
- How would this tone or meaning change if the poet chose different words?
- What is the poetry form of Haiku? How does it differ from other forms of poetry?
- How does Haiku appeal to the feelings and senses?

Primary Texts
GUYKU: A Year of Haiku for Boys by Bob Raczka, illustrated by Peter H. Reynolds. Houghton Mifflin Harcourt, 2010.
Hi, Koo!: A Year of Seasons by Jon J. Muth. Scholastic, 2014.
The Hound Dog's Haiku: And Other Poems for Dog Lovers by Michael J. Rosen, illustrated by Mary Azarian. Candlewick Press, 2011.
If It Rains Panckaes: Haiku and Lantern Poems by Brian P. Cleary, illustrated by Andrew Rowland. Millbrook Press, 2014.
If Not for the Cat: Haiku by Jack Prelutsky, illustrated by Ted Rand. Greenwillow Books, 2004.
I Haiku You by Betsy E. Snyder. Random House, 2012.
Wing Nuts: Screwy Haiku by J. Patrick Lewis and Paul B. Janeczko, illustrated by Tricia Tusa. Little, Brown, and Co., 2006.
Won-Ton: A Cat Tale Told in Haiku by Lee Wardlaw, illustrated by Eugene Yelchin. Henry, Holt & Co., 2011.
Won Ton and Chopstick: A Cat and Dog Tale Told in Haiku by Lee Wardlaw, illustrated by Eugene Yelchin. Henry Holt, & Co., 2015.
The Year Comes Round: Kaiku through the Seasons by Sid Farrar, illustrated by Llse Plume. Albert Whitman, 2012.

Supporting Texts	**Multimedia Texts**
Haiku by Patricia Donegan. Tuttle Publishing, 2003. Haiku from Wikipedia: http://en.wikipedia.org/wiki/Haiku *Haikus* by Valerie Bodden. Creative Education, 2008. Poetic Form: Haiku from Academy of American Poets: http://www.poets.org/poetsorg/text/poetic-form-haiku What Is Haiku? From Scholastic: http://teacher.scholastic.com/lessonplans/pdf/dec05_unit/whatishaiku.pdf The World of Haiku from the National Endowment for the Humanities: http://edsitement.neh.gov/lesson-plan/world-haiku	How To Haiku: https://www.youtube.com/watch?v=geSmDE57Amg How to Write Haiku Poems: http://www.watch-knowlearn.org/Video.aspx?CategoryID=1894&VideoID=12023

Potential Assessments (Unit Projects)

- Have students analyze the haiku texts to determine which words the author uses that appeal to the feelings or senses. Discuss why the author chose these words. Have the students rewrite the poem (A.W.3) using different words to appeal to different feelings or senses.
- Have students identify the five senses. Have them make posters or draw pictures that identify those senses. Place these pictures around the room. Have students collaborate (A.SL.1) to select words or phrases from the haiku texts that appeal to the senses. Have the students make quote sheets of those words or phrases and then place them under the correct poster for the sense they convey. Discuss as a class the reasoning (A.SL.3) the students had for placing that word in that place.
- Have students do in-depth research projects (A.W.7) on the origin and development of haiku poetry. Collect different samples of haiku from different times and cultures. Have students determine how the different pieces of poetry choose words to convey meaning and tone.
- Five Creative Ways to Teach Haiku from Scholastic by Carmella Van Vleet: http://www.scholastic.com/teachers/article/five-creative-ways-teach-haiku
- Haiku Graphic Organizer and Lesson Plans from readwritethink: http://www.readwritethink.org/classroom-resources/printouts/haiku-starter-30697.html

Standard 5

A.R.5	Analyze structure including sentence, paragraph, section, chapter, scene, stanza, and how they relate to the whole
RL.K.5	Recognize common types (stories, poems)
RL.1.5	Identify differences between fiction and nonfiction
RL.2.5	Describe story structure, beginning, and ending
RL.3.5	Refer to parts of stories, chapter, scene, stanza, show how parts build on each other
RL.4.5	Explain differences between poems, drama, and prose and their structures
RL.5.5	Explain how chapters, scenes, stanzas fit together
RL.6.5	"" / and contribute to the theme, setting, plot development
RI.K.5	Identify parts of a text (cover, title page, etc.)
RI.1.5; RI.2.5; RI.3.5	Use features to locate information (table of contents, headings, glossaries, index, hyperlinks, keywords, etc.)
RI.4.5	Describe structure of events, ideas, concepts, information (comparison, cause and effect, etc.)
RI.5.5	Compare and contrast structure of events, ideas, concepts, information (comparison, cause and effect, etc.) between two texts
RI.6.5	Analyze how sentence, chapter, paragraph, or section fits and contributes

Texts

Standard 5 calls directly for the use of drama, poetry, stories, fiction, and nonfiction. Here are some suggestions of favorites in each of these genres. For stories the selections will be picture books. For fiction the selections will be chapter books. For nonfiction the focus will be on texts that focus on comparisons and cause and effect.

Drama

Acting Out: Six One-Act Plays! Six Newbery Stars! Edited by Justin Chanda. Atheneum Books for Young Readers, 2008.

Good Masters! Sweet Ladies!: Voices from a Medieval Village by Laura Amy Schlitz ; illustrated by Robert Byrd. Candlewick Press, 2007.

Mozart, the Wonder Child: A Puppet Play in Three Acts by Diane Stanley. Collins, 2009.

Munsch at Play: Eight Stage Adaptations for Young Performers by Irene N. Watts, original stories by Robert Munsch. Annick Press, 2010.

My First Monologue Book: 100 Monologues for Young Children by Kristen Dabrowski. Smith and Kraus, 2007.

Now I Get It! 12 Ten-Minute Classroom Drama Skits for Science, Math, Language and Social Studies by L.E. McCullough. Smith & Kraus, 2000.

One Fine Day: A Radio Play by Elizabeth Van Steenwyk; illustrated by Bill Farnsworth. Eerdmans Books for Young Readers, 2003.

Roald Dahl's the BFG: A Set of Plays adapted by David Wood, illustrated by Jane Walmsley. Puffin Books, 2007.

Tales from Shakespeare: Seven Plays presented and illustrated by Marcia Williams. Candlewick Press, 1998.

Shakespeare Stories by Leon Garfield, illustrated by Michael Foreman. Houghton Mifflin, 1985.

William Shakespeare: A Midsummer Night's Dream adapted by Bruce Coville. Dial Books for Young Readers, 1996.

William Shakespeare: Macbeth adapted by Bruce Coville, illustrated by Gary Kelley. Dial Books for Young Readers, 1997.

William Shakespeare: Romeo and Juliet adapted by Bruce Coville, illustrated by Dennis Nolan. Dial Books for Young Readers, 1999.

William Shakespeare: The Winter's Tale adapted by Bruce Coville, illustrated by LeUyen Pham. Dial Books for Young Readers, 2007.

Poems

Cowpoke Clyde and Dirty Dawg by Lori Mortensen, illustrated by Michael Allen Austin. Clarion Books, 2013.

The Crossover: A Basketball Novel by Kwame Alexander. Houghton Mifflin Harcourt, 2014.

Digger, Dozer, Dumper by Hope Vestergaard, illustrated by David Slonim. Candlewick Press, 2013.

Firefly July: A Year of Very Short Poems by Paul B. Janeczko, illustrated by Melissa Sweet. Candlewick Press, 2014.

Forgive Me, I Meant to Do It: False Apology Poems by Gail Carson Levine, illustrated by Matthew Cordell. Harper, 2012.

Gone Fishing: A Novel in Verse by Tamear Will Wissinger. Houghton Mifflin Books for Children, 2013.

Grumbles from the Forest: Fairy-Tale Voices with a Twist by Jane Yolen, illustrated by Rebecca Kai and Matt Mahurin. WordSong, 2013.

In the Sea by David Elliott, illustrated by Holly Meade. Candlewick Press, 2012.

Little Poems for Tiny Ears by Lin Oliver, illustrated by Tomie dePaola. Nancy Paulsen Books, 2014.

Ode to a Commode: Concrete Poems by Brian P. Cleary, illustrated by Andy Rowland. Millbrook Press, 2014.

The Pet Project: Cute and Cuddly Vicious Verses by Lisa Wheeler, illustrated by Zacharaiah OHora. Atheneum Books for Young Readers, 2013.

Poem-Mobiles: Crazy Car Poems by J. Patrick Lewis and Douglas Florian, illustrated by Jeremy Holmes. Schwartz & Wade, 2014.

Pug: And Other Animal Poems by Valerie Worth, illustrated by Steve Jenkins. Farrar, Straus and Giroux, 2013.

The Red Pencil by Andrea Davis Pinkney, illustrated by Shane W. Evans. Little, Brown and Company, 2014.

Rutherford B., Who Was He?: Poems about Our Presidents by Marilyn Singer, illustrated by John Hendrix. Disney-Hyperion, 2013.

Sisters of Glass by Stephanie Hemphill. Alfred A. Knopf, 2012.

Stardines Swim High Across the Sky: and Other Poems by Jack Prelutsky, illustrated by Carin Berger. Greenwillow Books, 2013.

The Silver Moon: Lullabies and Cradle Songs by Jack Prelutsky, illustrated by Jui Ishida. Greenwillow Books, 2013.

UnBEElievables: Honeybee Poems and Paintings by Douglas Florian. Beach Lane Books, 2012.

Your Skeleton Is Showing: Rhymes of Blunder from Six Feet Under by Kurt Cyrus, illustrated by Crab Scrambly. Disney-Hyperion, 2013.

We Go Together!: A Curious Selection of Affectionate Verse by Calef Brown. Houghton Mifflin Harcourt, 2013.

The Weight of Water by Sarah Crossan. Bloomsbury, 2012.

Stories in Picture Book Form

The Adventures of Beekle: The Unimaginary Friend by Dan Santat. Little, Brown Books for Young Readers, 2014.

Battle Bunny by Jon Scieszka and Mac Barnett, illustrated by Matthew Myers. Simon & Schuster, 2013.

The Bear Ate Your Sandwich by Julia Sarcone-Roach. Knopf Books for Young Readers, 2015.

Imogene's Antlers by David Small. Crown Books for Young Readers, 1985.

Journey by Aaron Becker. Candlewick Press, 2013.

Mr. Tiger Goes Wild by Peter Brown. Hachette, 2013.

Ninja! by Arree Chung. Henry Holt and Co., 2014.

One Cool Friend by Toni Buzzeo, illustrated by David Small. Dial, 2012.

Princess Sparkle-Heart Gets a Makeover by Josh Schneider. Clarion Books, 2014.

Ribbit! by Rodrigo Folgueira, illustrated by Poly Bernatene. Knopf Books for Young Readers, 2013.

Room for Bear by Ciara Gavin. Knopf Books for Young Readers, 2015.

Russell the Sheep by Rob Scotton. HarperCollins, 2005.

Three Bears in a Boat by David Soman. Dial, 2014.

Two Bunny Buddies by Kathryn O. Galbraith, illustrated by Joe Cepeda. Houghton Mifflin Harcourt, 2014.

Fiction in Chapter Book Form

Another Day as Emily by Eileen Spinelli. Knopf Books for Young Readers, 2014.

The Boundless by Kenneth Oppel. Simon & Schuster, 2014.

Curiosity by Gary L. Blackwood. Dial, 2014.

Escape from Mr. Lemoncello's Library (Mr. Lemoncello's Library #1) by Chris Grabenstein. Random House, 2013.

Fly Away by Patricia MacLachlan. Margaret K. McElderry Books, 2014.

The Forbidden Stone (Copernicus Legacy #1) by Tony Abbott. Katherine Tegen Books, 2014.

I Kill the Mockingbird by Paul Acampora. Roaring Brook Press, 2014.

Jinx (Jinx #1) by Sage Blackwood. HarperCollins, 2013.

Liar and Spy by Rebecca Stead. Wendy Lamb Books, 2012.

The Night Gardener by Jonathan Auxier. Harry N. Abrams, 2014.

One Came Home by Amy Timberlake. Knopf Books for Young Readers, 2013.

Rain Reign by Ann M. Martin. Feiwel and Friends, 2014.

The True Blue Scouts of Sugar Man Swamp by Kathi Appelt, illustrated by Jennifer Bricking. Atheneum Books for Young Readers, 2013.

Nonfiction That Focuses on Comparison and Cause and Effect

Americas Great Disasters by Martin W. Sandler. HarperCollins, 2003.

The Beetle Book by Steve Jenkins. Houghton Mifflin Books for Children, 2012.

Body Bones by Shelley Rotner and David A. White. Holiday House, 2014.

Can You Tell a Tyrannosaurus from an Allosaurus? by Buffy Silverman. Lerner Publications, 2014.

Creep and Flutter: The Secret World of Insects and Spiders by Jim Arnosky. Sterling Children's Books, 2012.

Disasters by Ned Halley. Kingfisher, 1999.

Feathers: Not Just for Flying by Melissa Steward, illustrated by Sarah S. Brannen. Charlesbridge, 2014.

Giant Vehicles by Rod Green, illustrated by Stephen Biesty. Candlewick Press, 2014.

Global Warming by Seymour Simon. Collins, 2010.

How Big Were Dinosaurs? by Lita Judge. Roaring Brook Press, 2013.

Polar Bears' Search for Ice: A Cause and Effect Investigation by Gillia M. Olson. Capstone Press, 2011.

Tiny Creatures: The World of Microbes by Nicola Davies, illustrated by Emily Sutton. Candlewick Press, 2014.

Tooth and Claw: Bears, Big Cats, and Wolves by Jim Arnosky. Sterling Children's Books, 2014.

Volcano and Earthquake (Eyewitness books) by Susanna Van Rose. DK, 2014.

What's the Difference between a Frog and a Toad? by Mary Firestone, illustrated by Bandelin-Dacey. Picture Window Books, 2010.

What's the Difference between an Alligator and a Crocodile? by Lisa Bullard, illustrated by Bandelin-Dacey. Picture Window Books, 2010.

What was the Boston Tea Party? by Kathleen Krull, illustrated by Lauren Mortimer. Grosset & Dunlap, 2013.

Text Activities

1. *Alligators (Reptiles)* by Grace Hanson. ABDO Kids, 2014; *Crocodiles (Blastoff Readers Level 1)* by Megan Borgert-Spaniol. Bellwether Media, 2014; *Tell Me the Difference between an Alligator and a Crocodile* by Leigh Rockwood. PowerKids Press, 2013; *What's the Difference between an Alligator and a Crocodile?* by Lisa Bullard, illustrated by Debra Bandelin. Picture Window Books, 2010—When readers understand how text structures work they can more easily identify the key ideas and details in the expository texts they read (Dole, Donaldson, & Donaldson, 2014). Researchers have identified many different expository text structures, but the most common ones are cause/effect, compare/contrast, description, problem/solution, question/answer, and sequence. Students struggle with expository text structures for the following reasons (Dole et al., 2014):

   - some books, articles, and chapters may involve multiple text structures;
   - readers have little experience with expository text structures;
   - writers do not always utilize the signal words that alert students to the structure employed;
   - teachers do not always teach the structures; and
   - students sometimes become so overwhelmed with the vocabulary and content that they fail to consider the organizational structure of the text.

   To address these struggles expository text structures can be taught in the following manner:

   a) begin by reading many examples of a single text structure aloud to students;
   b) point out the signal words that are sometimes associated with the structure;
   c) model how students can use a graphic organizer for unpacking the information from the text. An example of one such organizer to help students compare and contrast information is provided in Appendix 5.1;
   d) demonstrate how to write a summary using a text frame; and
   e) let students work in pairs to repeat the process with a new book before asking them to do so independently.

2. *Froodle* by Antoinette Poris. Roaring Brook Press, 2014; *Bird Talk: What Birds Are Saying and Why* by Lita Judge. FlashPoint, 2012—Recently a teacher shared with the authors that one of her students became frustrated while reading an informational text and exclaimed, "There is no story in this book!" This reveals a common problem, in that many children cannot distinguish between the approaches fiction and nonfiction take. It cannot be assumed that all students understand the difference between the two types of texts. This is particularly true when it comes to understanding how fiction and nonfiction address and use the text structures. To remedy the situation invite students to browse through stacks of fiction and informational books placed on each table in the classroom. Provide students with an anchor chart like the one found in Appendix 5.2. Have students fill out the chart for a fiction text and a nonfiction text. Have students discuss the questions one by one in groups and then share teacher-crafted responses to the questions on the anchor chart. Activities like this can help students better understand the difference between story and informational text, and what to expect when reading each book type.

3. *Children Make Terrible Pets* by Peter Brown. Little, Brown, 2010—Students often need help in learning to distinguish between the narration and dialogue in a story. Taberski and Burke (2014) suggest that sharing a big book or projecting a book on a document camera can accomplish this. Different colors of highlighting tape can then be used to indicate what the narrator and key characters are saying. Taberski and Burke also recommend using books that use color-coded text to show what characters are saying. For instance, Peter Brown's *Children Make Terrible Pets* has the narration in green and the character dialog in color-coded speech bubbles.

4. *This Is a Moose* by Richard T. Morris, illustrated by Tom Lichtenheld. Little, Brown Books for Young Readers, 2014—In this text animals are trying to make a movie about a moose. They begin with the opening scene but things keep going wrong. Texts such as this that connect across forms, from text to film in this case, are useful when teaching how parts of a form fit together into scenes, chapters, and so on. Have students watch a nature documentary to determine how the director develops each scene. Determine what topics are covered in each scene and how this contributes to the overall cohesion of the film. Have students do research on moose and then create a PowerPoint or movie that conveys the real information that would have been made in the book if things did not keep going wrong.

Integrated Unit Overview

Theme: Cumulative Tales: "The House that Jack Built"
Potential Essential Questions • How are stories constructed? How are poems constructed? How are the two forms the same? How do the two forms differ? • How can the form of poetry be used to make a story? • What is the difference between chapters and stanzas? How are the two forms the same? How do the two forms differ? • What is the difference between fiction and nonfiction? How are the two forms the same? How do the two forms differ? • How can different forms be used to create nonfiction? What makes a story nonfiction? What makes a poem nonfiction? • Why would authors choose different forms (i.e., poems, drama, stories) to create fiction? Why would authors choose different forms (i.e., poems, drama, stories) to create nonfiction?

(Continued)

Primary Texts
Fiction:
All the World's a Stage by Rebecca Piatt Davidson, illustrated by Anita Lobel. Greenwillow Books, 2003.
The Book That Zack Wrote by Ethan Long. Blue Apple Books, 2011.
The Fort That Jack Built by Boni Ashvurn, illustrated by Brett Helquist. Abrams Books for Young Readers, 2013.
The House That Drac Built by Judy Sierra, illustrated by Will Hillenbrand. Harcourt Brace, 1998.
The House That Jill Built by Phyllis Root, illustrated by Delphine Durand. Candlewick Press, 2005.
This Is the House That Jack Built by Simms Taback. Putnam Juvenile, 2002.
The Tree House That Jack Built by Bonnie Verburg, illustrated by Mark Teague. Orchard Books, 2014.

Nonfiction:
The House That George Built by Suzanne Slade, illustrated by Rebecca Bond. Charlesbridge, 2012.
How the Dinosaur Got to the Museum by Jessie Hartlnad. Blue Apple Books, 2011.
How the Meteorite Got to the Museum by Jessie Hartlnad. Blue Apple Books, 2013.
The Pot That Juan Built by Nancy Andrews-Boebel, illustrated by David Diaz. Lee & Low Books, 2002.
The Prairie That Nature Built by Marybeth Lorbiecki, illustrated by Cathy Morrison. Dawn Publications, 2014.
The Swamp Where Gator Hides by Marainne Berkes, illustrated by Roberta Baird. Dawn Publications, 2014.
The Wright Brothers by Pamela Duncan Edwards, illustrated by Henry Cole. Hyperion Books for Children, 2003.

Supporting Texts	**Multimedia Texts**
Cumulative Tale from Wikipedia: http://en.wikipedia.org/wiki/Cumulative_tale	The House That Jack Built illustrated by Randolph Caldecott: https://www.youtube.com/watch?v=xDP-ZuimlDNA
Nursery Rhymes: Lyrics, Origins and History: http://www.rhymes.org.uk/	"The House That Jack Built" song sung by Aretha Franklin on the album *The Queen of Soul*. https://www.youtube.com/watch?v=CaSH59KgGIo
This Is the House That Jack Built from Wikipedia: http://en.wikipedia.org/wiki/This_Is_the_House_That_Jack_Built	Simms Taback's This Is the House That Jack Built: https://www.youtube.com/watch?v=GCEOnvlp6N8
Popular Cumulative Tales Books a list from Goodreads: https://www.goodreads.com/shelf/show/cumulative-tales	"This Is the House that Jack Built" Nursery Rhyme with Lyrics by HooplaKidz: https://www.youtube.com/watch?v=7sDSYVfnj_E

Potential Assessments (Unit Projects)
- Type or print out a copy of the tale. Have students mark the structure including the beginning and ending and the scenes and stanzas.
- Have the students do a short research project (A.W.7) on a historical event. Have the students write their own cumulative tale based on the formula they have discovered in the mentor texts. Make sure the tale is structured with a clear beginning, middle, and end and that the stanzas fit together to tell the whole story of the event.
- Use technology (A.W.6) such as PowerPoint or a video editing software and have students create their own fictional cumulative tale. Have the students use copyright-free visuals and music (A.W.8) to support their text. Structure the visuals so they support the stanzas of the story in an obvious way. Present the stories to the class and have them discuss how the stanzas of their stories fit together.
- Have the students memorize the story from one of the texts and perform it to the class or other group (A.SL.6). Have the students add visuals, movement, or music to show how the parts build on each other.
- Compare two versions of the story, one fiction and one nonfiction, using a Venn diagram that shows how the stanzas fit together or that shows how the stanzas contribute to theme and/or setting in similar or different ways. Have the students describe how the differences between the two tales indicate that it is fiction or nonfiction.

Standard 6

A.R.6	Assess purpose of point of view
RL.K.6; RI.K.6	Name author and illustrator and define their roles
RL.1.6	Identify who is telling the story
RL.2.6	Acknowledge differences in point of view
RL.3.6	Distinguish between the narrator and other characters' point of view
RL.4.6	Compare and contrast point of view in different stories and first and third person points of view
RL.5.6	Describe how point of view influences events
RL.6.6	Explain how point of view develops
RI.1.6	Distinguish between information in the text and in the pictures
RI.2.6	Identify the main purpose, what is the author explaining or describing
RI.3.6	Distinguish personal points of view from the authors
RI.4.6	Compare and contrast primary and secondary accounts of the same topic, describe differences in focus
RI.5.6	Analyze multiple accounts of the same topic for similarities and differences in point of view
RI.6.6	Determine author's point of view and explain how it is conveyed

Texts

Standard 6 focuses on point of view, so texts that use point of view in a unique way are particularly useful for this standard. Here are offered texts that connect to several aspects of point of view. First texts with direct first person point of view are given; these texts offer a basic introduction to point of view that can be used as the standard is introduced. Next texts that are told from multiple points of view are given. These texts present a more complex point of view and are good to use with more intricate or advanced activities connected to the standard. Lastly nonfiction text pairs are offered. These are two different texts on the same topic that offer different points of view that can be used in compare and contrast activities.

First Person

K–2 Texts

I Am Otter by Sam Garton. HarperCollins, 2014.
My Mom Is Trying to Ruin My Life by Kate Feiffer, illustrated by Diane Goode. Simon & Schuster, 2009.
Not Last Night but the Night Before by Colin McNaughton, illustrated by Emma Chichester Clark. Candlewick Press, 2009.
Penguin Problems (Life of Ty #1) by Lauren Myracle, illustrated by Jed Henry. Dutton Children's Books, 2013.
The Snow Day by Komako Sakai. Arthur A. Levine Books, 2009.
Song of Middle C by Alison McGhee, illustrated by Scott Menchin. Candlewick Press, 2009.
When You Are Happy by Eileen Spinelli, illustrated by Geraldo Valerio. Simon & Schuster Books for Young Readers, 2006.

Yuki and the One Thousand Carriers by Gloria Whelan, illustrated by Yan Nascimbene. Sleeping Bear Press, 2008.

3–6 Texts

The Great Trouble: A Mystery of London, the Blue Death, and a Boy Called Eel by Deborah Hopkinson. Alfred A. Knopf, 2013.

Homeroom Headhunters (The Tribe #1) by Clay McLeod Chapman. Hyperion, 2013.

Just Grace (Just Grace #1) by Charise Mericle Harper. Houghton Mifflin, 2007.

The Riverman by Aaron Starmer. Farrar, Straus and Giroux, 2014.

The Truth of Me: About a Boy, His Grandmother, and a Very Good Dog by Patricia MacLachlan. Katherine Tegen Books, 2013.

Welcome to Dog Beach (Seagate Summers Series #1) by Lisa Greenwald. Amulet Books, 2014.

Where I Belong Mary Downing Hahn. Clarion Books, 2014.

Zane and the Hurricane: A Story of Katrina by Rodman Philbrick. Blue Sky Press, 2014.

Multiple Points of View

Counting by 7s by Holly Goldberg Sloan. Dial, 2013.

Flipped by Wendelin Van Draanen. Knopf Books for Young Readers, 2001.

Ghost Hawk by Susan Cooper. Margaret K. McElderry Books, 2013.

Ice Whale by Jean Craighead George. Dial, 2014.

Leviathan (Leviathan #1) by Scott Westerfeld. Simon Pulse, 2009.

Loki's Wolves (Blackwell Pages #1) by K.L. Armstrong and M.A. Marr. Little, Brown and Company, 2013.

The Madman of Piney Woods by Christopher Paul Curtis. Scholastic Press, 2015.

Masterminds by Gordon Korman. Balzer and Bray, 2015.

The Misadventures of the Family Fletcher by Dana Alison Levy. Delacorte Press, 2014.

Mountain Dog by Margarita Engle, illustrated by Olga and Aleksey Ivanov. Henry Holt and Company, 2013.

A New Darkness (The Starblade Chronicles #1) by Joseph Delaney. Greenwillow Books, 2014.

Painting the Rainbow by Amy Gordon. Holiday House, 2014.

Road Trip by Gary Paulsen and Jim Paulsen. Wendy Lamb Books, 2013.

Running with Trains: A Novel in Poetry and Two Voices by Michael J. Rosen. Wordsong, 2012.

A Tanble of Knots by Lisa Graff. Philomel Books, 2013.

Wolf by Valerie Hobbs. Farrar, Straus and Giroux, 2013.

Wonder by R.J. Palacio. Knopf Books for Young Readers, 2012.

Nonfiction Text Pairs

1. Large Number Concepts:

How Much Is a Million? by David M. Schwartz, illustrated by Steven Kellogg. Mulberry Books, 1993.

Millions, Billions, and Trillions: Understanding Big Numbers by David A. Adler, illustrated by Edward Miller. Holiday House, 2013.

2. Gravity

Gravity by Jason Chin. Roaring Brook Press, 2014.

I Fall Down by Vicki Cobb, illustrated by Julia Gorton. HarperCollins, 2004.

3. Florence Nightingale

Florence Nightingale by Demi. Henry Holt and Co., 2014.

A Picture Book of Florence Nightingale by David A. Adler, illustrated by John Wallner. Holiday House, 1992.

4. Battle of Trenton, 1776

The Crossing: How George Washington Saved the American Revolution by Jim Murphy. Scholastic Press, 2010.

When Washington Crossed the Delaware: A Wintertime Story for Young Patriots by Lynne V. Cheney, illustrated by Peter M. Fiore. Simon & Schuster Books for Young Readers, 2004.

5. The Beatles

The Beatles Were Fab (and They Were Funny) by Kathleen Krull and Paul Brewer, illustrated by Stacy Innerst. Houghton Mifflin Harcourt, 2013.

How the Beatles Changed the World by Martin W. Sandler. Walker Books for Young Readers, 2014.

6. Black Holes

A Black Hole Is Not a Hole by Carolyn Cinami Decristofano, illustrated by Michael W. Carroll. Charlesbridge, 2012.

The Mysterious Universe: Supernovae, Dark Energy, and Black Holes by Ellen B. Jackson, illustrations by Nic Bishop. Houghton Mifflin Books, 2008.

7. Animal Behavior

Eat like a Bear by April Pulley Sayre, illustrated by Steve Jenkins. Henry Holt and Co., 2013.

Just One Bite: 11 Animals and Their Bite at Life Size by Lola Schaefer, illustrated by Geoff Waring. Chronicle Books, 2010.

8. Selma to Montgomery Civil Rights March

Because They Marched: The People's Campaign for Voting Rights That Changed America by Russell Freedman. Holiday House, 2014.

Marching for Freedom: Walk Together, Children, and Don't Grow Wary by Elizabeth Partridge. Viking, 2009.

9. Dogs in World War I

Rags: Hero Dog of World War I: A True Story by Margot Theis Raven; illustrated by Petra Brown. Sleeping Bear Press, 2014.

Stubby the War Dog: The True Story of World War I's Bravest Dog by Ann Bausum. National Geographic, 2014.

10. Bird Migration

Moonbird: A Year on the Wind with the Great Survivor B95 by Phillip M. Hoose. Farrar, Straus and Giroux, 2012.

On the Wing: American Birds in Migration by Carol Lerner. HarperCollins, 2001.

11. Nelson Mandela

Nelson Mandela by Kadir Nelson. Katherien Tegen Books, 2013.

Who Is Nelson Mandela by Pam Pollack and Meg Belviso; illustrated by Stephen Marchesi. Grosset and Dunlap, 2013.

12. Harry Houdini

Harry Houdini: The Legend of the World's Greatest Escape Artist by Janice Weaver, illustrated by Chris Lane. Harry N. Abrams, 2011.

Houdini: World's Greatest Mystery Man and Escape King by Kathleen Krull, illustrated by Eric Velasquez. Walker & Co., 2005.

Text Activities

1. *Nic Bishop Frogs* by Nic Bishop. Scholastic Nonficiton, 2008; *Frogs* by Gail Gibbons. Holiday House, 1993; *The Frog Scientist* by Pamela S. Turner. Houghton Mifflin Books for Children, 2009; *Frog Song* by Brenda Z. Guiberson, illustrated by Gennady Spirin. Henry Holt and Co., 2013—Over a few days read aloud an informational picture book to a group of students taking time each day to discuss what was learned from both the text and illustrations. Document what was learned from each on an anchor chart or graphic organizer. For younger students, you may read a book such as Nic Bishop's *Frogs* where the stunning photographs emphasize the amazing diversity in frogs

around the globe. This book could be followed up with *Frogs* by Gail Gibbons and discuss what can be learned from illustrations and techniques such as cutaways that cannot be observed in photographs. Older students would enjoy *The Frog Scientist* by Pamela Turner or *Frog Song* by Brenda Guiberson. The illustrations in both these texts provide details about frogs that will enchant readers.

2. Vardell, S. M. and Wong, Janet. (2015). *The Poetry Friday Anthology for Celebrations: Holiday Poems for the Whole Year in English and Spanish*. Princeton, NJ: Pomelo Books; Vardell, S. M. and Wong, Janet. (2014). *The Poetry Friday Anthology for Science: Poems for the School Year Integrating Science, Reading, and Language Arts*. Princeton, NJ: Pomelo Books; Vardell, S. M. and Wong, Janet. (2013). *The Poetry Friday Anthology 6–8: Poems for the School Year with Connections to the Common Core*. Princeton, NJ: Pomelo Books; Vardell, S. M. and Wong, Janet. (2012). *The Poetry Friday Anthology K–5: Poems for the School Year with Connections to the Common Core*. Princeton, NJ: Pomelo Books—The Core Standards provide a framework that informs instruction and also include a component focused on teaching children about poetry. Many educators, librarians, and parents are looking for guidance on how to share poetry with children and teach the skills within the curriculum as well. The authors have found that *The Poetry Friday Anthology* series by Vardell and Wong (2012, 2013, 2014, 2015) offers both shareable texts and classroom applications. With quality poetry plus curriculum-based suggestions for helping children enjoy and understand poetry more deeply for each week of the school year these anthologies are a great starting place. Here are some activities that are given for poems in this anthology. However, these activities can easily be adapted to use with other poems with the same form or topic or with distinctly different poems found in other sources.

A. "Who Invented Cookies?" by Joan Bransfield Graham (2012)
   1. Discuss possibly unfamiliar words (*clever, dabs, blossom, fragrant, savor*). Then, as you read the poem aloud, pantomime the actions in the poem.
   2. Invite students to join you in a second reading by pointing to their heads when you say the word *clever* and saying *WOW* in the final stanza. Pause before the word to cue them to their turn.
   3. For discussion: *What kinds of cookies are your favorites?*
   4. Talk about the steps for making cookies that are suggested in the poem (spooning dabs of dough on pans, popping them in the oven, eating them). The directions may be more exact in a recipe, but the rhyming of the poem makes it very fun to say over and over again.
   5. Connect this poem with a poem about birthday cakes, "Happy Birthday" by April Halprin Wayland (second grade, week 24, page 130), or with "Grandmother's Almond Cookies" by Janet Wong in *A Suitcase of Seaweed*.

B. "Catku" by Lee Wardlaw (2012)
   1. Point out the clever play on words in the title: *Catku* = haiku poems about cats. Then read the poems aloud in a kitty cat voice to convey the cat's point of view.
   2. Share the poems again, inviting students to say the quote in italics in the third stanza, "*Itty pwetty kitty!*" with exaggerated sweetness.
   3. For discussion: *If these are the elements of the "cat instruction book," what might a "dog instruction book" include?*
   4. This is an example of a poem form that usually does not rhyme, a haiku poem. Originally a Japanese form of poetry, a haiku focuses on nature in only three lines (generally five syllables, seven syllables, five syllables). Guide students in understanding the haiku form with these examples.

5. Follow up with another descriptive cat poem, "All Worn Out" by Kristy Dempsey (second grade, week 5, page 111), and with Lee Wardlaw's haiku picture book, *Won Ton: A Cat Tale Told in Haiku.*

C. "Wheel of Progress" by Juanita Havill (2012)

1. In this poem, the poet was inspired to have fun with the expression *don't put the cart before the horse.* Look and listen for it!

2. Display the words of the poem and ask for eight volunteers to help read the poem aloud, one volunteer for each line of the poem. Let them practice their lines softly with a partner, then read the poem aloud together.

3. Survey students collectively to see which of these transportation modes they have experienced (*cart, horse, log, wheel, car*).

4. Sometimes poets weave facts throughout their poems. Guide students in noting what information we learn about wheels and transportation from this poem, and talk about how the lines are arranged to dole out the facts bit by bit.

5. Connect this poem with another fact-filled poem by Juanita Havill, "Moon Buggy" (third grade, week 36, page 182).

D. "Leonardo Da Vinci" by Renee M. LaTulippe (2014)

1. Read this poem aloud pausing between stanzas for added effect. Then show pictures of da Vinci and some of his drawings and inventions found at drawingsofleonardo.org.

2. Share the poem again and invite students to read the first line of each stanza (*Far away and long ago / He was. . . / who built. . . / In fact. . .*) while you read the rest of the poem aloud.

3. Da Vinci was both an artist and a scientist. Talk about how drawing and inventing might go together.

4. Use the examples in this poem to talk with students about how information and critical thinking are used in scientific problem solving in Leonardo's time (in 1500) and now. What kinds of inventions might they imagine for the future? For background information, go to Legacy.MOS.org/sln/Leonardo/

5. For a poem about inventing things in the future, look for "Invention Intentions" by Kristy Dempsey (third grade, week 33).

E. "Invention Intentions" by Kristy Dempsey (2014)

1. Add some fun and share this poem with a "poetry prop"—hold a clipboard or notepad and a pen as if you're interviewing someone while you read this poem aloud.

2. Invite students to select their favorite question line and to chime in on that line only while you read the rest of the poem aloud.

3. Use the question lines in this poem as a prompt for class discussion. In particular, "what do you need, what do you wish? / would ma ke your life more simple-ish? / What products do you use the most? / Is there an item you can't stand?"

4. Much of scientific investigation and discovery is based on asking and answering questions, making inferences, and selecting and using equipment or technology to solve a specific problem. Model this process by identifying the steps discovery takes toward a solution or invention. Look for help here: KidsInvent.org.

5. For more poems about inventions and innovations, look for "Printing, Pressed Beyond Words . . ." by Robyn Hood Black (fifth grade, week 33 Computers) and "The Black Leonardo" by J. Patrick Lewis (first grade, week 32). Also, seek out selections from *Incredible Inventions* edited by Lee Bennett Hopkins and *A Burst of Firsts* by J. Patrick Lewis.

F. "Black History Month" by Charles Waters (2015)
1. If possible, project background images from the Smithsonian's new National Museum of African American History and Culture while reading this poem aloud slowly. Be sure to pause after the colon and at the end of each line.
2. Share the poem again and invite all the boys to chime in on the word "brothers" and all the girls to join in on the word "sisters" as you read the rest of the poem aloud.
3. Children may not be familiar with the phrase "racial divide," so talk with them briefly about our nation's history in separating or dividing people based on their race or skin color.
4. Pair this poem with this picture book: *We March* by Shane Evans (Roaring Brook, 2012). Read the book aloud and discuss how it takes all kinds of people (of many races, cultures, and ages) to stand together to push for change. Look for the resources for Teaching Tolerance at tolerance.org/article/dos-and-donts-teaching-black-history.
5. Pair this poem with "Martin's Birthday" by Nikki Grimes (third Monday in January: Martin Luther King Jr. Day) or with picture book adaptations of poems by Langston Hughes such as *I, Too, Am America* illustrated by Bryan Collier (2012).

Integrated Unit Overview

Theme: World War II
Potential Essential Questions • What different roles did people play during WWII? • What were the implications of WWII on people's lives? • How did both military and civilian personnel serve their countries and the people around them during WWII? • What was life like in America and/or in Europe during WWII? • What impact did the results/outcome of WWII have on the people of the time? • What can we learn today from the experiences of the people during WWII?
Primary Texts *K–2:* *Children of the World War II Home Front* by Sylvia Whitman. Carolrhoda Books, 2001. *First Dog Fala* by Elizabeth Van Steenwyk, illustrated by Michael G. Montgomery. Peachtree Publishers, 2008. *Irena's Jars of Secrets* by Marcia Vaughan, illustrated by Ron Mazellan. Lee and Low Books, 2011. *Mercedes and the Chocolate Pilot: A True Story of the Berlin Airlift and the Candy That Dropped from the Sky* by Margot Theis Raven. Sleeping Bear Press, 2002. *A Nation's Hope: The Story of Boxing Legend Joe Louis* by Matt de la Pena, illustrated by Kadir Nelson. Dial Books for Young Readers, 2011. *Sky High: The True Story of Maggie Gee* by Marissa Moss, illustrated by Carl Angel. Tricycle Press, 2009. *War Dogs: Churchill and Rufus* by Kathryn Selbert. Charlesbridge, 2013. *3–6:* *Beyond Courage: The Untold Story of Jewish Resistance during the Holocaust* by Doreen Rappaport. Candlewick Press, 2012. *Black and White Airmen: Their True History* by John Fleischman. Houghton Mifflin, 2007. *Candy Bomber: The Story of the Berlin Airlift's Chocolate Pilot* by Michael O. Tunnell. Charlesbridge, 2010. *Franklin and Winston: A Christmas That Changed the World* by Doug Wood. Candlewick Press, 2010. *Irena Sendler and the Children of the Warsaw Ghetto* by Susan Goldman Rubin, illustrated by Bill Farnsworth. Holiday House, 2011. *Pure Grit: How WWII Nurses in the Pacific Survived Combat and Prison Camp* by Mary Cronk Farrell. Abrams Books for Young Readers, 2014.

The Victory Garden by Lee Kochenderfer. Delacorte Press, 2001.
War, Women and the News: How Female Journalists Won the Battle to Cover World War II by Catherine Courley. Atheneum Books for Young Readers, 2007.
Yankee Doodle Gals: Women Pilots of World War II by Amy Nathan. National Geographic Society, 2001.

Supporting Texts	**Multimedia Texts**
Digital Public Library of America, Search the Library for World War II to find primary source documents: http://dp.la/ Famous People in World War II: http://www.biography.com/people/groups/world-war-ii Federal Registry for Educational Excellence, Search World War II: http://free.ed.gov/ The National World War II Museum: http://www.nationalww2museum.org/index.html A People at War: http://www.archives.gov/exhibits/a_people_at_war/a_people_at_war.html Women Airforce Service Pilots from Texas Women's University Libraries: http://www.twu.edu/library/wasp.asp World War II and Holocaust Resources: http://www.scholastic.com/teachers/collection/world-war-ii-and-holocaust-resources World War II: Everything You Need: http://www.scholastic.com/teachers/unit/world-war-ii-everything-you-need World War II Famous People: http://www.socialstudiesforkids.com/subjects/worldwariifamouspeople.htm	Inside WWII and Related Media (Maps, Videos, Photos, Speeches & Audio): http://www.history.com/interactives/inside-wwii-interactive WASP Pilot Violet Cowden: http://www.history.com/videos/wasp-pilot-violet-cowden#wasp-pilot-violet-cowden World War II (Interactive Maps and Audio): http://www.nationalarchives.gov.uk/education/worldwar2/default.htm WWII—American Gears Up for War: https://www.youtube.com/watch?v=VMz3e6ydNP0

Potential Assessments (Unit Projects)

- As students read the text or it is read aloud to them have them write down or draw a list of important information that the text offers. Have them draw this bulleted list or summary of the text from both the text and the illustrations. Have students identify which source the information comes from. Identify information that comes from one or another or both sources.
- Have students study two accounts of the same event. One could be a primary source and another could be a secondary source. Have the students create a Venn diagram comparing and contrasting the two sources. Indicate the information one provides but not the other and information that both provide.
- Select one of the people from the texts. Use character maps like the ones found here: https://www.risd.k12.nm.us/assessment_evaluation/Character%20Analysis.pdf to gather and articulate clues from the text that relate to that character. Fill in the holes left by what the author does not say with individual ideas that are consistent with what the author has revealed. Write a narrative (A.W.3) that recounts an event that is in the text(s) or one that is not in the text but is consistent with the text from that person's point of view.
- Use the Bio Cube interactive found on the readwritethink website (http://www.readwritethink.org/classroom-resources/student-interactives/cube-30057.html) to have students develop an outline based on the people studied in the text. As information is gathered distinguish between facts and personal points of view from the authors. Have the students use this outline to write a complete biography of the person (A.W.5; A.W.2). Have them add details from other primary or secondary sources to discuss events that may not have been noted in all the texts. Have students express their own point of view in their texts or maintain the point of view offered in one of the texts they read.
- Do short or long research projects (A.W.7) on one or more of the individuals in the texts by focusing on one or more of the essential questions. Have the students write an informative essay (A.W.2) on the topic.

Standards 7–9: Integration of Knowledge and Ideas: What the Text Means
Standard 7

A.R.7	Integrate and evaluate content from textual, visual, and quantitative media and other formats
RL.K.7; RI.K.7	Describe relationship between illustrations and words
RL.1.7; RI.1.7	Use illustrations and details to describe characters, setting, events, key ideas
RL.2.7	Use information for illustrations and words to understand characters, setting, events
RL.3.7	Explain how illustrations contribute to words (create mood, develop character or setting)
RL.4.7	Make connections between stories and their visual, dramatic, or oral versions
RL.5.7	Analyze how visual/multimedia contributes to tone, meaning, beauty
RL.6.7	Compare and contrast seeing and hearing with story, drama, poem in audio/video forms and print
RI.2.7	Explain how images contribute and clarify
RI.3.7	Use information from text and words to demonstrate understanding
RI.4.7	Interpret visual, oral, quantitative information and explain how it contributes
RI.5.7	Draw on multiple sources, both print and digital, to answer questions and solve problems
RI.6.7	Integrate visual, quantitative, and textual information to develop understanding

Texts

Standard 7 focuses on the visual aspects of texts. For this standard picture books provide a particularly good connection. Illustrations in a picture book can function in a variety of ways. Two important functions of the illustrations in a text are to help to establishing the setting and tone of a text. Texts that have illustrations that connect to these textual structures are offered first. Picture book illustrations, however, may not connect to the text at all; they may in fact tell an entirely different story altogether. Texts that have illustrations that tell another story from the text are then offered. While nonfiction of the past may have been dry and lifeless, today's informational texts are filled with color and wonderful visuals. Some of the authors' favorite nonfiction texts that have beautiful visuals are offered. Lastly standard 7 addresses the fact that stories can be told in both textual and visual versions. To connect with this aspect of the standard some of the authors favorite children's books that have been made into movies are offered.

Functions of Picture Book Illustrations

Establish Setting

Beauty and the Beast by H. Chuku Lee, illustrated by Pat Cummings. Amistad, 2014.
Blue on Blue by Dianne White, illustrated by Beth Krommes. Beach Lane Books, 2014.
The Fortune-Tellers by Lloyd Alexander, illustrated by Trina Schart Hyman. Dutton Children's Books, 1993.
I Need My Own Country! by Rick Walton, illustrated by Wes Hargis. Bloomsbury, 2012.
The Insomniacs by Karian Wolf, illustrated by Ben and Sean Hilts. Putnam Juvenile, 2012.

Journey by Aaron Becker. Candlewick Press, 2013.
Julia's House for Lost Creatures by Ben Hatke. First Second, 2014.
The Midnight Library by Kazuno Kohara. Roaring Brook Press, 2014.
Mr. Wuffles! by David Wiesner. Clarion Books, 2013.
This Moose Belongs to Me by Oliver Jeffers. Philomel, 2012.

Develop Tone

Baby Bear by Kadir Nelson. Balzer and Bray, 2014.
Bedtime at the Swamp by Kristyn Crow, illustrated by Macky Pamintuan. HarperCollins, 2008.
Black Dog by Levi Pinfold. Templar, 2012.
Bluebird by Bob Staake. Schwartz & Wade, 2013.
Lullaby (For a Black Mother) by Langston Hughes, illustrated by Sean Qualls. Houghton Mifflin Harcourt, 2013.
The Polar Express by Chris Van Allsburg. Houghton Mifflin, 1985.
Queen on Wednesday by Gabi Swiatkowska. Farrrar, Straus and Giroux, 2014.
Rules of Summer by Shaun Tan. Holder Children's Division, 2014.
Uni the Unicorn by Amy Krouse Rosenthal, illustrated by Brigette Barrager. Random House, 2014.
Unspoken: A Story from the Underground Railroad by Henry Cole. Scholastic, 2012.

Tell Another Story

Bamboozled by David Legge. Scholastic, 1994.
Come Away from the Water, Shirley by John Burningham. Crowell, 1977.
A Couple of Boys Have the Best Week Ever by Marla Frazee. Harcourt, 2008.
Hey, Al by Arthur Yorinks, illustrated by Richard Egielski. Farrar, Straus and Giroux, 1986.
Oh, Were They Ever Happy! by Peter Spier. Doubleday, 1978.
Rosie's Walk by Pat Hutchins. Macmillan, 1968.
Tough Boris by Mem Fox, illustrated by Kathryn Brown. Harcourt Brace Jovanovich, 1994.
The Troublemaker by Lauren Castillo. Clarion Books, 2014.

Visually Stunning Nonfiction

Abraham Lincoln and Frederick Douglass: The Story behind an American Friendship by Russell Freedman. Houghton Mifflin Harcourt, 2012.
A Leaf Can Be. . . by Laura Purdi Salas, illustrated by Violeta Dabija. Milbrook Press, 2012.
Almost Astronauts: 13 Women Who Dared to Dream by Tanya Lee Stone. Candlewick Press, 2000.
At the Same Moment, Around the World by Clotilde Perrin. Chronicle Books, 2014.
Ballet for Martha: Making Appalachian Spring by Jan Greenberg and Sandra Jordan, illustrated by Brian Floca. Roaring Brook Press, 2011.
Frog Song by Brenda Z. Guiberson, illustrated by Gennady Spirin. Henry Holt and Co., 2013.
My Country, 'Tis of Thee: How One Song Reveals the History of Civil Rights by Claire Rudolf Murphy, illustrated by Bryan Collier. Henry Holt and Co., 2014.
Nelson Mandela by Kadir Nelson. Katherine Tegen Books, 2013.
North: The Amazing Story of Arctic Migration by Nick Dowson, illustrated by Patrick Benson. Candlewick Press, 2011.
Sequoia by Tony Johnston, illustrated by Wendell Minor. Roaring Brook Press, 2014.
Snakes by Nic Bishop. Scholastic Nonfiction, 2012.
Tornadoes by Seymour Simon. HarperCollins, 2001.

Books Made Into Movies

Because of Winn-Dixie by Kate DiCamillo. Candlewick Press, 2000.
Beezus and Ramona by Beverly Cleary. Avon Books, 1990.

The City of Ember (Book of Ember, #1) by Jeanne DuPrau. Random House, 2003.

Cloudy with a Chance of Meatballs by Judi Barrett, illustrated by Ron Barrett. Atheneum, 1978.

Coraline by Neil Gaiman, illustrated by Dave McKean. HarperCollins, 2002.

Flipped by Wendelin Van Draanen. Knopf, 2001.

Holes by Louis Sachar. Farrar, Straus and Giroux, 1998.

Hotel for Dogs by Lois Duncan. Scholastic, 2008.

Howl's Moving Castle by Diana Wynne Jones. Greenwillow Books, 1986.

Inkheart by Cornelia Funke. Scholastic, 2003.

The Invention of Hugo Cabret by Brian Selznick. Scholastic, 2007.

The Lorax by Dr. Seuss. Random House, 1971.

Text Activities

1. Bang, M. *Picture This: How Pictures Work* by Molly Bang. Turtleback Books, 2000—For teachers who feel that both their and their students' abilities in reading illustrations can use some enhancement, Bang's work offers the perfect primer. She uses spare text to explain how the different elements of images and their components work. Bang uses the "Little Red Riding Hood" story to illustrate how shape, placement, color, composition, contrast, and space not only create tension and movement, but also shape emotions as they tell the story. After reading and discussing the book, share copies of "Little Red Riding Hood" books to have students identify how the illustrators used shape, placement, color, composition, and space in depicting the story. Students can also use the principles that Bang outlines to create their own illustrations for other tales.

2. *The Mitten* by Jim Aylesworth, illustrated by Barbara McClintock. Scholastic, 2009; *The Mitten* by Jan Brett. G. P. Putnam's Sons. 1989; *The Mitten: An Old Ukrainian Folktale* by Alvin Tresselt, illustrated by Yaroslava. HarperCollins, 1964—Stewig (1986) presents a nice three-step process to engage students with illustrations. In this process children first describe what they see, then compare illustrations across texts, and finally, express an opinion about which of the illustrations they prefer. This process is easily done in kindergarten and first grade as teachers share versions of "The Mitten" and provide students with a dye-cut paper mitten to decorate. The teacher can then post copies of the book jackets and the students then place their mittens on a bulletin board to create a graph indicating which one they like best.

3. *The Omnivore's Dilemma: The Secrets behind What You Eat* by Richie Chevat and Michael Pollan. Dial, 2009, or *Universe: Journey into Deep Space* by Mike Goldsmith, illustrated by Mark A. Garlick. Kingfisher, 2012, or any other informational text as appropriate—Create a large anchor chart to illustrate how visual features are used to convey information in informational trade books. An example of what a start to this chart might look like is given below. Under the heading "Visual Features" list terms such as charts, graphs, diagrams, and time lines. Model for students how the chart would be completed by explaining how the features work and then copy examples from texts to place under the examples column. After briefly explaining the features allow small groups of students to scan through informational picture books so they can find examples of one the features in the books. Ask each group to share examples found from the books, explain how the feature contributes to understanding the text, and recommend the best examples to place on the anchor chart.

Visual Features	Explain How the Feature Contributes to Understanding the Text	Examples
Time lines	They tell what happened when and how much time went by between events	

4. *A Baby Elephant in the Wild* by Caitlin O'Connell. Houghton Mifflin Harcourt, 2014, or *Little Rock Girl 1957: How a Photograph Changed the Fight for Integration* by Shelley Tougas. Compass Point Books, 2012, or *Picturing Lincoln: Famous Photographs That Popularized the President* by George Sulivan. Clarion Books, 2000, or any other nonfiction text with photographs—Creating Captions is an activity that requires students to look closely at an image and use precise language to convey its meaning to others (Owocki, 2012). Prepare the students by showing them examples of images with effective captions. Explain to students that captions have several functions (Mooney, 2001):
   a. to identify or summarize visual information;
   b. to expand visual information;
   c. to give another perspective;
   d. to explain the contents of an object or illustrative material; and
   e. to clarify.

   Then ask students to write captions for charts, diagrams, and other visual features using the most concise language possible.

Integrated Unit Overview

Theme: Little Red Riding Hood
Potential Essential Questions • What is the relationship between illustrations and words? • How do illustrations describe key events, setting, or character details? Why were these details in the illustrations and not in the words? • How do illustrations convey details of time, place, or culture that may not be in the words? • How do illustrations and words tell the same or different stories? • Why do illustrations tell a different story than the words? Why do the words tell a different story than the illustrations? • What can illustrations convey that words can't? What can words convey that illustrations can't? • How do illustrations develop the mood, character, or setting of a text? • How are stories in print, audio, and visual forms different from one another? Why are they different? • How do two different forms (print or visual) tell a story in different or similar ways? Why are they different or the same?
Primary Texts *Carmine: A Little More Red* by Melissa Sweet. Houghton Mifflin Harcourt, 2005. *Little Red: A Fizzingly Good Yarn* by Lynn Roberts, illustrated by David Roberts. Harry N. Abrams, 2005. *Little Red Riding Hood* retold and illustrated by Trina Schart Hyman. Holiday House, 1983. *Little Red Riding Hood* retold and illustrated by Jerry Pinkney. Little, Brown Books for Young Readers, 2007. *Little Red Riding Hood* retold and illustrated by Gennady Spirin. Marshall Cavendish, 2010. *Little Red Riding Hood: A Newfangled Prairie Tale* by Lisa Campbell Ernst. Simon & Shuster, 1995. *Little Roja Riding Hood* by Susan Middleton Elya, illustrated by Susan Guevara. Putnam Juvenile, 2014. *Lon Po Po: A Red-Riding Hood Story from China* by Ed Young. Philomel Books, 1989. *Ninja Red Riding Hood* by Corey Rosen Schwartz, illustrated by Dan Santat. Putnam Juvenile, 2014. *Petite Rouge: A Cajun Red Riding Hood* by Mike Artell, illustrated by Jim Harris. Dial, 2001. *Pretty Salma: A Red Riding Hood Story from Africa* by Niki Daly. Clarion, 2007. *Red Riding Hood* by James Marshall. Dial Books for Young Readers, 1987. *Ruby* by Michael Emberly. Little, Brown Books for Young Readers, 1991.

(Continued)

Supporting Texts	Multimedia Texts
Little Red Riding Hood from Wikipedia: http://en.wikipedia.org/wiki/Little_Red_Riding_Hood The Little Red Riding Hood Project from University of Southern Mississippi: http://en.wikipedia.org/wiki/Little_Red_Riding_Hood SurLaLune fairytales.com: The Annotated Little Red Riding Hood: http://www.surlalunefairytales.com/ridinghood/index.html	Into the Woods directed by Rob Marshall (available on DVD from retailers) Little Red Riding Hood App by Nosy Crow: http://nosycrow.com/apps/little-red-riding-hood Little Red Riding Hood—Story Time with Miss Booksy from Cool School: https://www.youtube.com/watch?v=yAyoE39cBvU Little Red Riding Hood sung by Sam The Sham and the Pharaohs: https://www.youtube.com/watch?v=_FA85RO89HA

Potential Assessments (Unit Projects)

- Using two different versions of the tale have students create a graphic organizer like the one found here http://www.readwritethink.org/files/resources/lesson_images/lesson275/compcon_chart.pdf to compare and contrast the illustrations for each story. Have students focus on the details the illustrator uses in the pictures to describe the key plot events. Have students write an informative essay (A.W.2) about the differences they found.
- Have students do short biographical research (A.W.7) on the illustrator of one of the versions of the tale. Have students compare the style that the illustrator uses in other texts they have illustrated. From the biographical research determine how the author's life impacts their style. Discuss how the illustrators' style conveys mood in all their texts. Discuss why the artist may have selected one style over the other for the particular text. Determine if there are any biographical connections to why the artist may have chosen one style over another. Have students write letters to the artist detailing how their illustrations added to the meaning or beauty of the text (A.W.1).
- Using two different versions of the tale in different mediums (i.e., versions illustrated in different ways or representing two different tones, moods, or cultures) have students create character graphic organizer like the one found here: http://www.readwritethink.org/files/resources/printouts/CharacterMap.pdf on the visual representation of the main character in each story. Focus only on the details the illustrator uses to convey the character. As individuals or in groups have the students write a biography for each of characters (A.W.2) drawing on the details they have found in the illustrations. Have them convey through their own style why the character is the same as well as different (A.W.4).
- Have students focus on the setting, plot, main idea, mood, tone, or character in one version of the tale. Have students make lists of key details relating to the chosen textual structure. List in one column details that convey information found only in the illustrations, in a second column list details found in both the text and the illustrations, and in a third column list details only in the text. Determine how the illustrations contribute to the text and vice versa and how both express meaning throughout the entire work. Have the students use the information to create charts or graphs that express their found data (A.SL.5) in a visual display.
- Have students select a time period or culture, doing short research as necessary (A.W.7) to get an idea of the time or place. Using that time or culture as a backdrop have the students illustrate their own short version of the tale (A.W.3). Help students use both words and images to convey the sense of time and place. Change the tale as necessary to use dialogue, themes, and other structures that relate to that particular time and place. Use culturally diverse texts to act as mentor texts as the students create their own.

Standard 8

A.R.8	Delineate and evaluate the validity and reasoning of claims
RI.K.8; RI.1.8; RI.2.8	Identify reasons the author uses to support points
RI.3.8	Describe connection between sentences, paragraphs (comparison, cause/effect, sequence)
RI.4.8	Explain how authors use reason and evidence

RI.5.8	"" / Identify which evidence supports which point
RI.6.8	Trace and evaluate arguments, find claims both supported and not supported by evidence

Texts

Standard 8 is entirely focused on nonfiction. While a wide range of nonfiction can be used to address this standard, including the cause/effect and comparison texts already offered, the main focus here is on persuasive and argumentative writing. Many texts in this style come in series. The good thing about these series is that they often offer texts on a wide range of topics. Here are offered some of those series with a few titles in each that the authors find to be useful in applying this standard.

Argumentative Nonfiction Series

Animals and Climate Change series published by Gareth Stevens Publishing
  Animals and Climate Change by Nicole Shea. 2013.
  Animals and Deforestation by Matteson Claus. 2013.
  Animals and Oil Spills by Jon Bogart. 2013.
  Animals on the Verge of Extinction by Karen O'Connor. 2013.

Essential Viewpoints series published by ABDO
  Advertising to Children by Marcia Amidon Lusted. 2008.
  The Causes of School Violence by Helga Schier. 2008.
  Gun Control by Kekla Magoon. 2007.
  Internet Piracy by Lee Hunnewell. 2007.

Global Viewpoints series published by Greenhaven Press
  Drugs edited by Maria Tenaglia-Webster, 2009.
  Famine edited by Diane Andrews Hennignfeld. 2009.
  Freedom of Expression edited by Alicia Cafferty and Adrienne Wilmoth. 2009.
  The War in Iraq edited by Tom Lansford. 2009.

Hot Topics in Media series published by Core Library
  Parental Guidance Ratings by Cassie Hermansson. 2013.
  Reality Television by Megan Kopp. 2013.
  Violence in Video Games by Diane Marczely Gimpel. 2013.
  Banned Books by Marcia Amidon Lusted. 2013.

Let's Think About . . . series published by Capstone Heinemann Library
  Let's Think about Animal Rights by Victoria Parker. 2014.
  Let's Think about Sustainable Energy by Victoria Parker. 2014.
  Let's Think about the Internet and Social Media by Alex Woolf. 2014.
  Let's Think about the Power of Advertising by Elizabeth Raum. 2014.

Lightning Bolt Books: Animals in Danger series published by Lerner Publications
  Endangered and Extinct Amphibians by Candice Ransom. 2014.
  Endangered and Extinct Birds by Jennifer Boothroyd. 2014.
  Endangered and Extinct Fish by Jennifer Boothroyd. 2014.
  Endangered and Extinct Reptiles by Jennifer Boothroyd. 2014.

Matters of Opinion series published by Norwood House Press
  Cheating by Bonnie Szumski. 2015.
  Food in Schools by Toney Allman. 2014.
  Recycling by Carla Mooney. 2014.
  Smoking by Peggy Parks. 2014.

Opposing Viewpoints Series published by Greenhaven Press
  Birth Defects edited by Noel Merino. 2014.
  Community Policing edited by Roman Espejo. 2014.
  Copyright Infringement edited by Carol Ullmann and Lynn M. Zott. 2014.
  Organized Crime edited by David Haugen, Susuan Musser, and Michael Chaney. 2014.

Science Gets It Wrong series published by Lerner Publications
  The Bull Is Seeing Red! Science's Biggest Mistakes about Animals and Plants by Christine
    Zuchora-Walske. 2014.
  Let's Make Some Gold! Science's Biggest Mistakes about Geology and Ecology by Christine
    Zuchora-Walske. 2014.
  We're the Center of the Universe! Science's Biggest Mistakes about Astronomy and Physics by
    Christine Zuchora-Walske. 2014.
  Your Head Shape Reveals Your Personality! Science's Biggest Mistakes about the Human Body by
    Christine Zuchora-Walske. 2014.

Text Activities

1. *Our Solar System* by Seymour Simon. HarperCollins, 2014—McLaughlin and Overturf (2012)
   suggest using the What—Why—How? Graphic Organizer as a tool to analyze an opinion by asking
   three questions while reading: (1) What does the author think? (2) Why does the author think this
   way? and (3) How do facts in the text support the author's thinking? The graphic organizer provides a place for students to record the answers to the questions in the process of analyzing the
   opinion. An example is found in Appendix 8.1.

2. *The Freedom Summer Murders* by Don Mitchell. Scholastic, 2014—Hillocks (2010) claims that in
   order to be ready for college and the workplace the kind of writing students need to do is argumentative. In order to teach students how to construct their own arguments they will need to become
   familiar with the basic components of an argument which include:

   • The claim ("What do I think?")
   • The reasons ("Why do I think this?")
   • The evidence ("How do I know this is the case?")

   After teaching the structure have students create a graphic organizer, similar to a Know-Wants to
   Know-Learned (KWL) Chart, with one column for claims, one for reasons, and one for evidence.
   Use close reading strategies to have students engage with the text. Have the students break down
   either the explicit or implicit arguments or claims that the author is making in a part of the text
   (paragraph or chapter) or overall in the whole text.

3. *First the Egg* by Laura Vaccaro Seeger. Roaring Brook Press, 2007—This text covers the sequence
   of events that makes animals and objects in nature change. Use the sequencing the author outlines
   in nature to show how she uses sentences and paragraphs to connect the sequences in the text.
   Use a graphic organizer like the one found here: http://www.readwritethink.org/files/resources/

printouts/SequenceEvents.pdf to have students track the sequence of events in the text while noting the sentences and paragraphs that connect the ideas.

4. *The Family Romanov: Murder, Rebellion, and the Fall of Imperial Russia* by Candace Fleming. Schwatz and Wade, 2014—Taberski and Burke (2012) note that it is important for teachers to model for their students how you read to find the main idea of a text. Teachers can do this by displaying a text on an overhead or documents camera. They can then model the process by thinking aloud about what the author is trying to convey while highlighting details that support the main idea. When students engage in this process a graphic organizer such as the one found here that allows students to outline main ideas and supporting details http://www.scholastic.com/teachers/sites/default/files/asset/file/graphic_organizers.pdf helps students support and document their own thinking for individual parts of the text or for the text as a whole.

Integrated Unit Overview

Theme: Global Warming
Potential Essential Questions • What is global warming? • How do humans impact global warming? What can humans do to stop or delay global warming? • How are different parts of the earth being affected by global warming? • How is global warming impacting animals and animal habitats? • What reasons are given in evidence of global warming? What reasons are given to dispute global warming? • Why do scientists and other professionals disagree about global warming? • How do we know what scientists say about global warming is true? • How do authors use reason and evidence to convince readers that global warming is a problem? • What kinds of claims do authors make that are supported or not supported by the evidence they give? • Are there other sources that contradict or support the evidence the author gives?
Primary Texts *K–2*: *Earth! Feeling the Heat* by Brenda Z. Guiberson, illustrated by Chad Wallace. Henry Holt and Co., 2010. *Global Warming (Green World, Clean World)* by Ellen Lawrence. Bearport Publishing, 2014. *Ice Bears* by Brenda Z. Guiberson, illustrated by Ilya Spirin. Henry Holt, 2008. *The Magic School Bus and the Climate Challenge* by Joanna Cole, illustrated by Bruce Degen. Scholastic, 2010. *Polar Bears* by Mark Newman. Henry Holt, 2011. *Waiting for Ice* by Sandra Markle, illustrated by Alan Marks. Charlesbridge, 2012. *Who Turned Up the Heat?: Eco-Pig Explains Global Warming* by Lisa S. French, illustrated by Barry Gott. Magic Wagon/ABDO Group, 2010. *Why Are the Ice Caps Melting?: The Dangers of Global Warming* by Anne F. Rockwell, illustrated by Paul Meisel. HarperCollins, 2006. *3–6*: *An Inconvenient Truth: The Crisis of Global Warming* by Al Gore. Viking, 2007. *Buried Sunlight: How Fossil Fuels Have Changed the Earth* by Molly Bang. Blue Sky Press, 2014. *Climate Change (in the News)* by Corona Brezina. Rosen Publishing, 2008. *The Down-to-Earth Guide to Global Warming* by Laurie David and Cambria Gordon. Orchard Books, 2007. *Earth in the Hot Seat: Bulletins from a Warming World* by Marfe Ferguson Delano. National Geographic, 2009. *Global Warming* by Amy Farrar. ABDO Publishing Co., 2008. *Global Warming* by Seymour Simon. HarperCollins, 2010. *Global Warming (Environment: Ours to Save)* edited by Michael Anderson. Britannica Educational Publishing, 2012. *Understanding Global Warming* by Rebecca L. Johnson. Lerner Publications, 2009.

(Continued)

Supporting Texts

Center for Climate and Energy Solutions Kids Corner: http://www.c2es.org/science-impacts/basics/kids
Climate Change Debate: Pros and Cons: http://climatechange.procon.org/
Climate Change from the White House: http://www.whitehouse.gov/energy/climate-change
Global Climate Change Vital Signs of the Planet: http://climate.nasa.gov/
Global Warming Conspiracy Theory from Wikipedia: http://en.wikipedia.org/wiki/Global_warming_conspiracy_theory
Global Warming from Polar Bears International: http://www.polarbearsinternational.org/about-polar-bears/global-warming
Natural Inquirer: Climate Change Edition: http://oceanservice.noaa.gov/education/pd/climate/teachingclimate/natural_inquirer_climate_change_curriculum.pdf
A Students' Guide to Global Climate Change from the US Environmental Protection Agency: http://epa.gov/climatechange/kids/index.html

Multimedia Texts

Arthur: George Reports on Global Warming: http://pbskids.org/video/?category=Arthur&pid=lxuOYcZ-mxRfI1kaxrhetwsgp1JhvAfRx
Climate Change 101 with Bill Nye the Science Guy: http://www.smithsonianmag.com/videos/category/3play_1/climate-change-101-with-bill-nye-the-science/?no-ist
Frontline: Climate of Doubt: http://www.pbs.org/wgbh/pages/frontline/climate-of-doubt/
Global Warming 101: http://video.nationalgeographic.com/video/101-videos/global-warming-101
Global Warming from Nick News: http://www.nick.com/videos/clip/global-warning-clip.html

Potential Assessments (Unit Projects)

- Conduct short or long research projects (A.W.7) on the issues of global warming brought up in the texts. Use scientific and popular sources to gather and evaluate evidence (A.W.8). Have the students write an explanatory essay (A.W.2) describing the evidence each source cites explaining why it may be supported, unsupported, difficult to understand, or why it may confuse the issue. Have the students use a bibliography generator (such as those in Microsoft Word, EasyBib, or BibMe) to cite their sources (A.W.7; A.W.8).
- Using two or more sources have the students create a compare and contrast map like the one found here http://www.readingquest.org/pdf/compare.pdf to compare how two different authors use reason and evidence to support the points they make. Discuss how the authors present information that is alike and different. Determine why the authors use the evidence they do. Discuss why authors may have chosen their evidence. Determine if other evidence would have been more convincing. Evaluate the arguments the authors make. Have students present (A.SL.4) their findings to the class.
- Craft an argumentative essay (A.W.1) discussing issues of global warming brought up in the texts where the student takes a stand on the issue and uses data and supportive points from their own research (A.W.7; A.W.8) to back up their claims (A.W.1).
- Research a company, business, or agency (A.W.7; A.W.8) that deals with the issue of global warming brought up in the texts. Create group wikis (http://www.wikispaces.com/content/teacher) to collect (A.W.8) and publish (A.W.6) the findings of what evidence the group is using to support their claims or devalue the claims of others. Write letters to the group presenting an argument (A.W.1) for what they could do to better support their points and claims.
- Supported by short or long research projects (A.W.7) and how the mentor texts effectively communicate information, create student-generated Glogs (interactive posters at: http://edu.glogster.com/) that use both visuals and text to effectively communicate an argument (A.W.1; A.W.6) for or against an issue. Focus the argument to address the concerns of a certain audience (A.W.4). Post these posters on a website and have classes, schools, or communities vote for their favorite (A.W.6).

Standard 9

A.R.9	Analyze two or more texts to compare and build knowledge
RL.K.9; RL.1.9	Compare and contrast characters (adventures, experiences, etc.)

RL.2.9	Compare and contrast versions for the same story (different authors or different cultures)
RL.3.9	Compare and contrast themes, settings, events in texts by the same author in a series
RL.4.9	Compare and contrast themes, topics, events in stories and myth from different cultures
RL.5.9	Compare and contrast themes and topics in texts in the same genre
RL.6.9	Compare and contrast themes and topics in texts in different genre
RI.K.9; RI.1.9	Identify similarities and differences between two texts on the same topic
RI.2.9; RI.3.9	Compare and contrast important points between two texts on the same topic
RI.4.9; RI.5.9	Integrate information from two (or more) texts to communicate knowledgably
RI.6.9	Compare and contrast two authors' depictions of events

Texts

Standard 9 is designed to expand students' understanding beyond the details and structures of a single text to engage with multiple texts. Any text that engages with a conversation with another text will address the needs of this standard. Here are offered four categories of texts that connect with one another. First versions of the same story that represent different cultures are offered. Second, texts that connect themselves through themes are given. Thirdly texts that address similar topics but come from two different genres are listed. Lastly a group of texts that pair fiction and nonfiction is given.

Versions of the Same Story Representing Different Cultures

Cinderella

Adelita: A Mexican Cinderella Story by Tomie dePaola. Puffin, 2004.
Cendrillon: A Caribbena Cinderella by Robert D. SanSouci, illustrated by Brian Pinkney. Simon and Schuster, 1998.
The Egyptian Cinderella by Shirley Climo, illustrated by Ruth Heller. HarperCollins, 1989.
Glass Slipper, Gold Sandal: A Worldwide Cinderella by Paul Fleischman, illustrated by Julie Paschkis. Henry Holt and Co., 2007.
The Golden Sandal: A Middle Easter Cinderella Story by Rebecca Hickox, illustrated by Wil Hillenbrand. Holiday House, 1998.
The Irish Cinderlad by Shirley Climo, illustrated by Loretta Krupinski. HarperCollins, 2000.
Mufaro's Beautiful Daughters by John Steptoe. Lothrop, Lee & Shepard, 1987.
The Rough-Face Girl by Rafe Martin. Putnam Juvenile, 1992.
Smoky Mountain Rose: An Appalachian Cinderella by Alan Schroeder, illustrated by Brad Sneed. Puffin, 2000.
Sootface: An Ojibwa Cinderella Story by Robert D. SanSouci, illustrated by Daniel San Souci. Dragonfly Books, 1997.
Yen-Shen: A Cinderella Story from China by Ai-Ling Louie, illustrated by Ed Young. Philomel, 1982.

Creation Myths

The Dog Who Walked with God by Michael J. Rosen, illustrated by Stanley Fellows. Candlewick Press, 1998.

In the Beginning: Creation Stories from Around the World by Virginia Hamilton, illustrated by Barry Moser. Houghton Mifflin Harcourt, 1991.

Lord of the Animals: A Miwok Indian Creation Myth by Fiona French. Millbrook Press, 1997.

The Star-Bearer: A Creation Myth from Ancient Egypt by Dianne Hofmeyer, illustrated by Jude Daly. Farrar, Straus and Giroux, 2001.

Sun Mother Wakes the World: An Australian Creation Story by Diane Wolkstein, illustrated by Bronwyn Bancroft. HarperCollins, 2004.

When the World Was Young: Creation and Pourquoi Tales by Margaret Mayo, illustrated by Louise Brierley. Simon & Schuster Books for Young Readers, 1996.

The Gingerbread Man

The Gingerbread Cowboy by Janet Squires, illustrated by Holly Berry. HarperCollins, 2006.

The Gingerbread Man by Jim Aylesworth, illustrated by Barbara McClintock. Scholastic, 1998.

The Matzo Ball Boy by Lisa Shulman, illustrated by Rosanne Litzinger. Dutton Children's Books, 2005.

The Runaway Rice Cake by Ying Change Compestine, illustrated by Tungwai Chau. Simon and Schuster Books for Young Readers, 2001.

The Runaway Latkes by Leslie Kimmelman. Albert Whitman & Co., 2000.

The Runaway Tortilla by Eric A. Kimmel, illustrated by Randy Cecil. Winslow Press, 2000.

The Stinky Cheese Man and Other Fairly Stupid Tales by Jon Scieszka, illustrated by Lane Smith. Viking, 1992.

Trickster Tales

Anansi and the Talking Melon by Eric A. Kimmel, illustrated by Janet Stevens. Holiday House, 1994.

Coyote Steals the Blanket: A Ute Tale by Janet Stevens. Holiday House, 1993.

Mrs. Chicken and the Hungry Crocodile by Won-Ldy Paye, illustrated by Julie Paschkis. Henry Holt, 2003.

A Ring of Tricksters: Animal Tales from America, the West Indies, and Africa by Virginia Hamilton, illustrated by Barry Moser. Blue Sky Press, 1997.

The Tale of Tricky Fox: A New England Trickster Tale retold by Jim Aylesworth, illustrated by Barbara McClintock. Scholastic, 2001.

The Tales of Uncle Remus: The Adventures of Brer Rabbit by Julius Lester, illustrated by Jerry Pinkney. Dial Books, 1987.

Zomo the Rabbit: A Trickster Tale from West Africa by Gerald McDermott. Harcourt Brace Jovanovich, 1992.

Thematically Connected Text Sets

Friendship

The Adventures of Beekle: The Unimaginary Friend by Dan Santat. Little, Brown and Company, 2014.

The Friendship Doll by Kirby Larson. Delacorte Press, 2011.

Nest by Esther Ehrlich. Wendy Lamb Books, 2014.

Picnic by John Burningham. Candlewick Press, 2014.

Two Bunny Buddies by Kathryn Osebold Galbraith, illustrated by Joe Cepeda. Houghton Mifflin Harcourt, 2014.

Good and Evil

Emma and the Blue Genie by Cornelia Funke, illustrated by Kerstin Meyer. Random House Children's Books, 2014.

The Iron Ring by Lloyd Alexander. Dutton Children's Books, 1997.

The School for Good and Evil by Soman Chainani, illustrated by Iacopo Bruno. Harper, 2013.

Splendors and Glooms by Laura Amy Schlitz. Candlewick Press, 2012.

Persistence

Ballerina Swan by Allegra Kent, illustrated by Emily Arnold McCully. Holiday House, 2012.
A Birthday for Bear by Bonny Becker, illustrated by Kady MacDonald Denton. Candlewick Press, 2012.
Brave Irene by William Steig. Farrar, Straus and Giroux, 1986.
The Great Race by Kevin O'Malley. Walker Books for Young Readers, 2011.

Prejudice

Bat 6 by Virginia Euwer Wolff. Scholastic Press, 1998.
East Dragon, West Dragon by Robyn Harbert Eversole, illustrated by Scott Campbell. Atheneum Books for Young Readers, 2012.
Fishing Day by Andrea Davis Pinkney, illustrated by Shaen Evans. Hyperion Books for Children, 2003.
The Hundred Dresses by Eleanor Estes. Harcourt, Brace, and Co., 1944.
Maniac Magee by Jerry Spinelli. Little, Brown, 1990.
Roll of Thunder, Hear My Cry by Mildred D. Taylor. Dial, 1976.

Self-Discovery

The Evolution of Calpurnia Tate by Jacqueline Kelly. Henry Holt, 2009.
Looking like Me by Walter Dean Myers, illustrated by Christopher Myers. Egmont USA, 2009.
Savvy by Ingrid Law. Dial Books for Young Readers, 2008.
There by Marie-Louise Fitzpartick. Roaring Brook Press, 2009.

Sharing

Frederick by Leo Lionni. Random House, 1967.
Hooray for Hat! by Brian Won. Houghton Mifflin Harcourt, 2014.
The Little Mouse, the Red Ripe Strawberry, and the Big Hungry Bear by Don Wood. Child's Play International, 1990.
Llama Llama Time to Share by Anna Dewdney. Viking Juvenile, 2012.
The Quiltmaker's Gift by Jeff Brumbeau, illustrated by Gail DeMarcken. Pfeifer-Hamilton Publishers, 2000.
Should I Share My Ice Cream? by Mo Willems. Hyperion Books for Children, 2011.

Text Sets That Cross Genres

19th-Century London

Constable & Toop by Gareth Jones. Amulet Books, 2013 (fantasy fiction).
The Great Trouble: A Mystery of London, the Blue Death, and a Boy Called Eel by Deborah Hopkinson. Alfred A. Knopf, 2013 (historical fiction).

Family Visits

Skies like These by Tess Hilmo. Farrar, Straus and Giroux, 2014 (realistic fiction).
The Watsons Go to Birmingham, 1963 by Christopher Paul Curtis. Delacorte Press, 1995 (historical fiction).

Magicians

The Magician's Boy by Susan Cooper, illustrated by Serena Riglietti. Margaret K. McElderry Books, 2005 (fantasy fiction).
The Vanishing Coin by Kate Egan, illustrated by Eric Wight. Feiwel and Friends, 2014 (realistic fiction).

Pirates

Magic Marks the Spot (Very Nearly Honorable League of Pirates #1) by Caroline Carlson. HarperCollins, 2013 (fantasy fiction).

The Pirate Meets the Queen: An Illuminated Tale by Matt Faulkner. Penguin Young Readers Group, 2005 (historical fiction).

Race Relations

Brotherhood by Anne Westrick. Viking Juvenile, 2013 (historical fiction).

The Cay by Theodore Taylor. Doubleday, 1969 (adventure fiction).

Treasure Hunting

Arthur and the Forbidden City by Luc Besson. HarperCollins, 2005 (fantasy fiction).

Three Bird Summer by Sara St. Antonie. Candlewick Press, 2014 (realistic fiction).

Fiction and Nonfiction Text Sets

Fiction: *The Berlin Boxing Club* by Robert Sharenow. HarperCollins, 2011.

Nonfiction: *Hitler Youth: Growing Up in Hitler's Shadow* by Susan Campbell Bartoletti. Scholastic, 2005.

Jazz Age Josephine by Jonah Winter illustrated by Marjorie Priceman. Atheneum Books for Young Readers, 2012.

A Nation's Hope: The Story of Boxing Legend Joe Louis by Matt de la Pena illustrated by Kadir Nelson. Dial, 2011.

Superman versus the Ku Klux Klan: The True Story of how the Iconic Superhero Battled the Men of Hate by Rick Bowers. National Geographic Children's Books, 2012.

Fiction: *Grave Images by* Jenny Goebel. Scholastic Press, 2013.

Nonfiction: *Encyclopedia of the End: Mysterious Death in Fact, Fancy, Folklore, and More* by Deborah Noyes. Houghton, Mifflin Harcourt, 2008.

How They Croaked: The Awful Ends of the Awfully Famous by Georgia Bragg, illustrated by Kevin O'Malley. Walker Childrens Books, 2011.

Fiction: *Hello, Moon!* by Francesca Simon, illustrated by Ben Cort. Orchard Books, 2014.

Nonfiction: *If You Decide to Go to the Moon* by Faith McNulty, illustrated by Steven Kellogg. Scholastic, 2005.

Sun, Moon, and Stars by Hannah Wilson. Kingfisher, 2014.

When the Moon Is Full: A Lunar Year by Penny Pollock, illustrated by Mary Azarian. Little, Brown, 2001.

You Can't Ride a Bicycle to the Moon by Harriet Ziefert, illustrated by Amanda Haley. Blue Apple Books, 2014.

Fiction: *Mississippi Trial, 1955* by Chris Crowe. Dial, 2002.

Nonfiction: *Simeon's Story: An Eyewitness Account of the Kidnapping of Emmett Till* by Simeon Wright and Herb Boyd. Lawrence Hill Books, 2010.

A Wreath for Emmett Till by Marilyn Nelson. Houghton Mifflin, 2005.

Fiction: *The Orchestra Pit* by Johanna Wright. Roaring Brook Press, 2014.

Nonfiction: *Meet the Orchestra* by Ann Hayes, illustrated by Karmen Thompson. Harcourt Brace Jovanovich, 1991.

Musical Instruments series published by Heinemann Library—includes *What in the World Is a Clarinet* by Mary Elizabeth Salzmann (2012) and *What in the World Is a Guitar?* by Mary Elizabeth Salzmann (2012).

The Story of the Incredible Orchestra by Bruce Koscielniak. Houghton Mifflin, 2000.

Fiction: *Rebel Fire (Young Sherlock Holmes #2)* by Andrew Lane. Farrar, Straus and Giroux, 2012.

Nonfiction: *Chasing Lincoln's Killer* by James L. Swanson. Scholastic, 2009.

Good Brother, Bad Brother: The Story of Edwin Booth and John Wilkes Booth by James Cross Giblin. Clarion Books, 2005.

Mr. Lincoln's High-Tech War by Thomas B. Allen and Roger MacBride Allen. National Geographic, 2008.

Fiction: *R Is for Robot: A Noisy Alphabet* by Adam F. Watkins. Price Stern Sloan, 2014.
Nonfiction: *Lightning Bolt Books: Robots Everywhere* series by Lerner Publications Company—includes *Helper Robots* by Nancy Furstinger (2014) and *Robots at Home* by Christine Zuchora-Walske (2014).
Pebble Plus: Cool Robots series by Capstone Press—includes *Animal Robots* by Erika L. Shores (2014) and *Robots in Space* by Kathryn Clay (2014).
Robots by Melissa Stewart. National Geographic, 2014.

Fiction: *Spell Robbers* by Matthew J. Kirby. Scholastic Press, 2014.
Nonfiction: *Albert Einstein and Relativity for Kids: His Life and Ideas with 21 Activities and Thought Experiments* by Jerome Pohlen. Chicago Review Press, 2012.
Max Planck: Revolutionary Physicist by Jane Weir. Compass Point Books, 2009.
Quantum Theory by Phillip Manning. Chelsea House, 2011.

Fiction: *Unicorn Thinks He's Pretty Great* by Bob Shea. Disney-Hyperion, 2013.
Nonfiction: *Behold . . . the Unicorns!* by Gail Gibbons. HarperCollins, 2002.
Unicorns (Bookworms Chapter Books: For Rea?) by Dana Meachen Rau. Marshall Cavendish Corporation, 2011.
Unicorns (Creatures of Legend) by Megan Atwood. ABDO Publishing Company, 2014.

Fiction: *Wanderville (Wanderville #1)* by Wendy McClure. Razorbill, 2014.
Nonfiction: *Orphan Train Rider: One Boy's True Story* by Andrea Warren. Houghton Mifflin, 1996.
Orphan Trains: An Interactive History Adventure by Elizabeht Raum. Capstone Press, 2011.
We Rode the Orphan Trains by Andrea Warren. Houghton Mifflin Co., 2001.

Text Activities

1. *Little Red Riding Hood*, retold by Jerry Pinkney. Little Brown, 2007; *Pretty Salma: A Little Red Riding Hood Story from Africa*, by Niki Daly. Clarion, 2007; *Little Roja Riding Hood*, by Susa Middleton Elya. Putnam, 2014; *Lon Po Po: A Red-Riding Hood Story from China*, retold by Ed Young. Philomel, 1989; *Carmine: A Little More Red*, by Melissa Sweet. Houghton Mifflin Harcourt, 2005—Comparing and contrasting is something that kids do naturally, as a teacher found when she read a variety of "Little Red Riding Hood" versions to her second-grade students. They discussed the books and loved to compare and contrast the different versions of the stories. To extend students' natural curiosity, use a chart for comparison, like the one found in Appendix 9.1. Remind students that each story comes from a different culture where there were differences in the beliefs and lifestyles. This is also an opportunity to instruct students in text structures and characteristics. Explain that the main characters are called protagonists and that their names are often in the title of the books. In this tale the protagonist wears special clothing that distinguished her from others. Explain that in "Little Red Riding Hood" the wolf was the antagonist who represented things that are dark and scary or unknown. Likewise tell them that the resolution was how the protagonist's problem was resolved. Instruction like this allows students to become very engaged while at the same time allowing them to learn a great deal about the texts by comparing the different versions of the story; and it also allows them to become quite proficient using literary terms.

2. *Tuck Everlasting* by Natalie Babbitt. Farrar, Straus and Giroux, 1974; *The Water Castle* by Megan Frazer Blakemore. Walker Children's Books, 2013—The structure of theme provides a good foundation for comparing and contrasting across texts. When connecting two texts across thematic lines it is best, as Owocki (2012), found to connect the selection of theme and texts as closely as possible to the aspects of interest and motivation from the reader's dimension. For the more interested students are in

a theme the more likely they will be motivated to engage with multiple texts so they can delve deeply into the aspects and comparison of the theme. *Tuck Everlasting* and *The Water Castle* have proven to be texts that are motivational because they address a theme that is of interest to students such as the nature of time, the connections of family, the meaning of friendship, and the importance of choices. To guide students' explorations use a graphic organizer like the one found in Appendix 9.2.

3. *Joey Pigza Swallowed the Key* by Jack Gantos. Farrar, Straus and Giroux, 1998; *The Lightning Thief* by Rick Riordan. Miramax, 2005—Texts that have characters who share one basic similarity provide a good foundation for students to start comparing and contrasting characters. For example, in these texts both of the main characters are boys who have been diagnosed with ADHD. Using a character comparison graphic organizer, like the one found at http://www.scholastic.com/teachers/lesson-plan/character-comparison-sheet, students can easily track character similarities and differences. Additionally, texts like these are a good way to compare and contrast texts across genres. Since *Joey Pigza Swallowed the Key* is realistic fiction and *The Lightning Thief* is fantasy this character comparison can also be extended to address how authors use characterizations differently in different genres.

4. *Loki's Wolves (Blackwell Pages #1)* by K. L. Armstrong and M. A. Marr. Little, Brown and Company, 2013; *Odin's Ravens (Blackwell Pages #2)* by K. L. Armstrong and M. A. Marr. Little, Brown and Company, 2014—Texts in the same series by the same author will certainly have similarities but they will also have differences. Studies of these differences can certainly be engaging for students. Have students focus on one text structure such as character, plot, or setting to compare and contrast differences. Have students write an essay that compares and contrasts that element from the texts. Readwritethink offers a wonderful online interaction at http://www.readwritethink.org/classroom-resources/student-interactives/compare-contrast-30066.html that guides students through the process of making an outline for their essay. This is an activity that is easily done in groups with each group taking a different text structure to study cumulating in the group writing a group essay as well.

Integrated Unit Overview

Theme: Inventing and Inventions
Potential Essential Questions • What similarities and differences are there between people/characters who are inventors? • What kinds of traits do you share with inventors? • What have been some of the most significant inventions? How have they impacted the world? • How did their family, background, education, and other experiences prepare individuals to invent? • How did outside forces impact an inventor's process during inventing? • What obstacles do inventors overcome to create their inventions? • What role does history, culture, time, and place play in inspiring inventors to invent? • What information do different texts give us about inventors and their experiences? What are the similarities and differences between these texts?
Primary Texts **Fiction:** *Awesome Dawson* by Chris Gall. Little, Brown and Company, 2013. *The Extraordinary Mr. Qwerty* by Karla Strambini. Candlewick Press, 2014. *The Field of Wacky Inventions (Floors #3)* by Patrick Carman. Scholastic, 2013. *Junkyard Wonders* by Patricia Polacco. Philomel Books, 2010. *Melonhead (Melonhead Books #1)* by Katy Kelly. Delacorte Press, 2009. *The Most Magnificent Thing* by Ashley Spires. Kids Can Press, 2014. *Fosie Revere, Engineer* by Andrea Beaty, illustrated by David Roberts. Abrams Books for Young Readers, 2013.

Fandy Riley's Really Big Hit by Chris Van Dusen. Candlewick Press, 2012.
One Beastly Beast: Two Aliens, Three Inventors, Four Fantastic Tales by Garth Nix, illustrated by Brian Biggs. HarperCollins, 2007.
Sleepy Time Olie by William Joyce. Laura Geringer Books, 2001.
Sky Jumpers by Peggy Eddleman. Random House, 2013.
Tesla's Attic by Neal Shusterman. Disney-Hyperion, 2014.

Nonfiction:
The Boy Who Invented TV: The Story of Philo Farnsworth by Kathleen Krull, illustrated by Greg Couch. A.A. Knopf, 2009.
The Day-Glo Brothers: The True Story of Bob and Joe Switzer's Bright Ideas and Brand New Colors by Chris Barton, illustrated by Tony Persiani. Charlesbridge, 2009.
Eureka! Poems about Inventors by Joyce Sidman, illustrated by K. Bennett Chavez. Millbrook Press, 2002.
The Genius of Islam: How Muslims Made the Modern World by Bryn Barnard. Random House, 2011.
Girls Think of Everything: Stories of Ingenious Inventions by Women by Catherien Thimmesh, illustrated by Melissa Sweet. Houghton Mifflin, 2000.
Leonardo da Vinci by Diane Stanley. Morrow Junior Books, 1996.
The Man Who Made Time Travel by Kathryn Lasky, illustrated by Kevin Hawkes. Melanie Kroups Books, 2003.
Mr. Ferris and His Wheel by Kathryn Davis. Houghton Mifflin Harcourt, 2014.
Now and Ben: The Modern Inventions of Benjamin Franklin by Gene Barretta. Henry Holt, 2006.
Queen Victoria's Bathing Machine by Gloria Whelan, illustrated by Nancy Carpenter. Simon and Schuster, 2014.
So You Want to Be an Inventor? by Judith St. George, illustrated by David Small. Philomel Books, 2002.
Timeless Thomas: How Thomas Edison Changed Our Lives by Gene Baretta. Henry Holt, 2012.
The Wright Brothers: How They Invented the Airplane by Russell Freedman. Holiday House, 1991.

Supporting Texts	**Multimedia Texts**
Black Inventors and Pioneers of Science: http://kids.nationalgeographic.com/explore/science/black-inventors-and-pioneers-of-science/	Best Apps for Young Inventors: https://www.commonsensemedia.org/lists/learning-tools-best-apps-for-young-inventors
Famous Black Inventors: http://www.biography.com/people/groups/famous-black-invento	PBS Inventors: https://www.youtube.com/user/inventorseries
Famous Inventors: http://www.biography.com/people/groups/famous-inventors	Whiz Kid Inventors Invade the White House: https://www.youtube.com/watch?v=c53QzWKuLpg
Innovative Lives: http://invention.smithsonian.org/centerpieces/ilives/	
Invention at Play from the Lemelson Center for the Study of Invention and Innovation: http://inventionatplay.org/	
Invention—Making the World a Better Place: http://www-tc.pbskids.org/designsquad/pdf/parentseducators/DS_Invent_Guide_Full.pdf	
Online Theme Unit: Inventions: http://teacher.scholastic.com/lessonrepro/lessonplans/theme/inventions.htm	
Spotlight Biography: Inventors: http://www.smithsonianeducation.org/spotlight/inventors1.html	

Potential Assessments (Unit Projects)
• Using an anchor text in addition to other sources, have students choose an inventor. Have students do some research (A.W.7; A.W.8), and then present a summary of the person's life and how he or she explored new frontiers or broke new ground. This presentation could be oral (a speech or slideshow presentation) (A.SL.3) or written (an informative biographical piece) (A.W.2) or take on another form (photo essay, wiki/encyclopedia entry, documentary, etc.) (A.W.1). Deeper meaning would be explored if students connect what they learn about this figure to any of the essential questions.

(Continued)

- As the students read about different inventors, have them record in a graphic organizer the specific qualities or ideas the authors choose to highlight in the text. Students can use word walls or notebooks to record their findings. Have students use dictionaries to define the terms they come up with from this work; they can expand on these definitions by writing their own definitions. Have students compare and contrast the various authors' depictions of the characters. Have them further explore the comparisons by writing short informative essays (A.W.2) about these inventors and their characteristics as presented by the texts; students can also connect the texts to their own lives by including in the essays ways they can develop these qualities in themselves.
- Compare different forms of information about inventors and inventing by having students explore different text forms including nonfiction, fiction, and multimedia texts. Have students determine how information is presented in each form and compare differences and similarities by studying the forms and what types of information they convey and at what depth it is conveyed. Students should determine why the different forms convey information in different ways by targeting certain audiences (A.W.4). Have students take information from one form and add information as needed to transfer the information into another form by writing their own news article, short informational essay, or movie script (A.W.1; A.W.2).
- Have students use the informational sources to write a piece of historical fiction that focuses on one person or event (A.W.3); this assignment should combine research strategy learning and creative writing (A.W.7; A.W.8). Encourage students to use information in a way that compares and contrasts all the texts they have read as they develop skills in creative expression, including incorporating the language standards (A.L.1; A.L.3). To add a reflective component, also allow students to explore how historical facts influence fiction writing.
- Develop an interactive time line (http://www.timetoast.com/). Have students gather information from and evaluate both primary and secondary sources (A.W.7; A.W.8) to consolidate the important events or facts about an inventor or an invention. Have students analyze the similarities and differences between the texts to compare and contrast the author's depiction of events.

Bibliography

Dole, J. A., Donaldson, B. E., & Donaldson, R. S. (2014). *Reading across multiple texts in the Common Core classroom, K–5*. New York: Teachers College Press.

Dunst, C., Simkus, A., Hamby, D. (2012). Children's story retelling as a literacy and language enhancement strategy. *CELLreviews, 5*(4). Retrieved from http://www.earlyliteracylearning.org/cellreviews/cellreviews_v5_n2.pdf

Hadaway, N. L., Vardell, S. M., & Young, T. A. (2002). *Literature-based instruction with English Language Learners, K–12*. New York: Allyn and Bacon.

Hillocks, G. (2010). Teaching argument for critical thinking and writing: An introduction. *English Journal, 99*(6), 24–32.

McLaughlin, M., & Overturf, B. J. (2012). *The Common Core: Teaching K–5 students to meet the reading standards*. Newark, DE: International Reading Association.

Mooney, M. E. (2001). *Text forms and features: A resource for intentional teaching*. Katonah, NY: Richard C. Owens.

Owocki, G. (2012). *The Common Core lesson book K-5: Working with increasingly complex literature, informational text, and foundational reading skills*. Portsmouth, NH: Heinemann.

Raphael, T. E., & Au, K. H. (2005). QAR: Enhancing comprehension and test taking across grades and content areas. *The Reading Teacher, 59*, 206–221.

Richardson, J. S., Morgan, R. F., & Fleener, C. (2012). *Reading to learn in the content areas*. Belmont, CA: Cengage.

Stead, T. (2009). *Good choice! Supporting independent reading and response K–6*. Portland, ME: Stenhouse.

Stewig, J. W. (1986). Books in the classroom. *Horn Book Magazine, 62*(3), 363–365.

Taberski, S., & Burke, J. (2014). *The Common Core companion: The standards decoded, grade K–2: What they say, what they mean, how to teach them.* Thousand Oaks, CA: Corwin.

Vacca, R. T., Mraz, M. E., & Vacca, J. A. (2014). *Content area reading: Literacy and learning across the curriculum.* Boston, MA: Pearson.

Whisler, N., & Williams, J. (1991). *Literature and cooperative learning: Pathway to literacy.* Sacramento, CA: Literature Co-op.

Yopp, H. K., & Yopp, R. H. (2014). *Literature-based reading activities: Engaging students with literary and informational text.* Boston, MA: Pearson.

1.1 Semantic Feature Analysis

Whales

by Seymour Simon (HarperCollins, 2006)

Directions: As you read this story, fill in the box with an "X" if the whale has the feature listed. Add names of other whales you find in the book.

Types of Whales:	Have Teeth	Have Baleen Plates	Bottom Feeder	Eat Fish	Eat Krill	Has Tusk	Rorqual	Sing Song	Bubble Netting	
Sperm Whale										
Narwhal										
Killer Whale (Orca)										
Baleen Whale										
Right Whale										
Gray Whale										
Fin Whale										

1.2 Anticipation/Reaction Guide for

Oh, Rats! The Story of Rats and People

by Albert Marrin

Circle T for True, F for False, or U for Unsure. Do not use Unsure more than twice. Then discuss your responses with your group. After you have read the text, go back and check your answers. Place the answers that agree with the text in the "after" column.

Before		After
T F U	1. Rats are eaten by people in some parts of the world, and rat meat costs more than chicken, pork, or beef.	T F U
T F U	2. Rats actually "fish" by dangling their tails in the water and pouncing on fish that bite.	T F U
T F U	3. Rats are fussy about washing and keeping clean.	T F U
T F U	4. Scientists found that rats actually survived the atomic bomb explosions.	T F U
T F U	5. A female rat can have as many as 381 pups per year. Thus, a single pair of rats could have 359 million descendants in three years.	T F U
T F U	6. A rat can be flushed down a toilet and live to climb up a drainpipe into another toilet bowl.	T F U
T F U	7. Rats can gnaw through iron and concrete.	T F U
T F U	8. Rats rely more on their hair than eyes to find their way.	T F U
T F U	9. Rats are important in fighting disease.	T F U
T F U	10. Some cultures have great respect for rats and consider them lucky animals.	T F U

List other important facts you learned about rats on the back of this paper.

1.3 We'd Rather

The Yellow Star: The Legend of King Christian X of Denmark

retold by Carmen Agra Deedy

Suppose you are the King of Denmark and Nazi soldiers are now occupying your country. You have committed yourself to keep all Danes safe from harm. Now the Nazis have ordered that all Jews must sew a yellow star onto their clothing. The people of your country are frightened. They have heard terrible stories about how Jews who wear yellow stars are taken away and never heard from again. What would you do?

WE WOULD DO _____ WE WOULD NOT DO

	Call the army to fight against the Nazis.	
	Smuggle all of the Jews to Sweden.	
	Hide the Jews.	
	Assist the Nazis in forcing the Jews to wear the yellow stars.	
	Tell the Danish people to ignore the Nazi orders.	
	Have a yellow star sewn onto your own clothes.	
	Seek help from the Allied Forces.	
	Wait one week to see what happens before making your decision.	

1.4 Question–Answer Relationship

Question Types and Sources of Information	
In the Book	**In My Head**
The answers can be found in the book.	The answers can be found in students' background knowledge and experiences.
Right There The answer is found directly in the text. Words from the question and words that answer the question are "right there" in the same sentence or two connected sentences.	**On My Own** The answer is not in the text. Readers need to use their own ideas and experiences to answer the question.
Think and Search The answer is in the text. Readers need to "think and search," or put together different parts of the text to answer the question. The answer can be within a paragraph, across paragraphs, or even across chapters in a book.	**Author and You** The answer is not in the text. Readers need to think about both the text and what they already know to answer the question.

Adapted from Raphael and Au, 2005.

Using QAR for Strategy Instruction	
In the Book	**In My Head**
Right There 1) Scanning to locate information 2) Using context clues for creating definitions	**On My Own** 1) Activate prior knowledge 2) Connect to the topic
Think and Search 1) Summarizing 2) Identifying important information 3) Using text organization (e.g., cause and effect, compare and contrast) to identify relevant information 4) Making inferences 5) Clarifying 6) Making text-to-text connections	**Author and You** 1) Predicting 2) Visualizing 3) Making inferences 4) Distinguishing between fact and opinion

Adapted from Raphael and Au, 2005.

2.1 *Retelling Guide for Zomo the Rabbit*

by Gerald McDermott

Retold by _____

Zomo
✧ **not big**
✧ **not strong**
Wanted wisdom
Sky God
3 impossible things
scales of Big Fish in the Sea
milk of Wild Cow
tooth of Leopard
played drum
Big Fish danced
scales fell off
climbed palm tree
insulted Wild Cow
hit tree
horns stuck
milked cow
scales and milk on path
hid behind rock
slipped, rolled down hill
Leopard hit rock
tooth popped out
Sky God
Wisdom
caution, courage, run fast
✧ **not big**
✧ **not strong**
wisdom
very fast

McDermott, Gerald. (1992). *Zomo the rabbit: A trickster tale from West Africa.* San Diego, CA: Harcourt Brace.

2.2 Determining the Theme Graphic Organizer

Name: <u>Adam Beus</u>

Title: <u>The Practical Bride</u>

Setting The countryside in China	Characters The bride and the four porters carrying her in a gaily-decorated chair to her new home.
Problem or Goal The chair broke and the bride fell to the ground.	**Solution** The bride decided to jog to her new home. Since canopy hangings covered her, nobody knew the difference.
Theme or Moral Make the best of a difficult situation so your life is not defined by an unfortunate event.	

Nunes, S. S. (2014). *Chinese fables: "The dragon slayer" and other timeless tales of wisdom*. Rutland, VT: Tuttle.

2.3 Main Ideas and Supporting Details

Name: <u>Mary Gale</u>

Book: <u>A Place for Bats</u>

Main Idea	Main Idea
Bats can make our world a better place.	There are many things that humans can do to protect bats.

Supporting Details	Supporting Details
Bats devour pesky insects all night long. Bats help pollinate many plants. Bats carry seeds to new places and help plants and trees grow. Bats are an important part of the food chain for many animals.	Bats can live and grow when people • turn off wind turbines on calm nights. • stop spraying harmful chemicals. • keep their pet cats indoors. • build bat-friendly gates for caves. • protect their habitats

Stewart, Melissa. (2012). *A place for bats*. Atlanta, GA: Peachtree.

From *Integrating Children's Literature through the Common Core State Standards* by Rachel L. Wadham and Terrell A. Young. Santa Barbara, CA: Libraries Unlimited. Copyright © 2015.

3.1 Response Guide for *The Black Cauldron*

by Lloyd Alexander

Directions: Listed across the page are nine statements about *The Black Cauldron*. Listed down the left side of the chart are the names of 10 characters involved in the plot of the story. In each box, indicate whether that character would agree or disagree with the words stated in the column above. Use the symbols provided in the key. You must make some inferences to answer all the questions. Be prepared to support your answer with examples from the book. It might be helpful to note page numbers from the book.

Key: A = Agree D = Disagree X = Doesn't Apply ? = Not enough information	Taran is ready to be part of the quest to destroy the Black Cauldron	The plan to steal the Black Cauldron from Arawn is wise.	The cauldron should be taken to Caer Dallben.	It is best to break into 3 parties To accomplish the mission.	It was right for Taran to give up the brooch to get the cauldron.	Crossing the river with the cauldron was a good decision.	Promising to lie about who found the cauldron was necessary.	The cauldron is a weapon of power to be used when it is offered.	Ellidyr was proud but also brave.
Taran									
Prince Ellydyr									
Prince Gwydion									
Gurgi									
Eilonwy									
Fflewddur									
Doli									
King Morgant									
Adaon									
Orddu									

From *Integrating Children's Literature through the Common Core State Standards* by Rachel L. Wadham and Terrell Young. Santa Barbara, CA: Libraries Unlimited. Copyright © 2015.

3.2 Polar Opposites

Book: Paperboy

Author: Vince Vawter

Victor is

Polite	✓					rude
Eloquent					✓	inarticulate
Courageous	✓					cowardly
Confident			✓			timid
Athletic	✓					unathletic

Victor always treated people with respect.

He was very smart but he stuttered a great deal and some people did not have patience with him.

Victor risked his life to protect Mam.

He was confident when it came to sports, but was timid when talking to people.

He could throw the meanest fastball in town.

3.3 Literary Report Card

Hogwarts School of Witchcraft and Wizardry

Student: Harry Potter		
Characteristic	Grade	Comment
Humility	A	He often attributes his strengths and successes to others rather than to himself.
Bravery	A	Harry often demonstrates his courage by standing up against evil and taking all challenges seriously.
Obedient	D–	Harry chooses which rules to follow. He did not receive an F because some good often comes from his disobedience.
Loyal	A	Harry stands up for his friends, Professors Dumbledore and McGonagal, and his parents' memory.
Generous	A	He uses his money to help others (e.g., his donations to St. Mungo's Hospital for Magical Maladies).
Studious	D	He doesn't always read his assignments and he often relies on Hermione to help him.

From *Integrating Children's Literature through the Common Core State Standards* by Rachel L. Wadham and Terrell A. Young. Santa Barbara, CA: Libraries Unlimited. Copyright © 2015.

3.4 Connection Chart

Text: *A place for Bats*, by Melissa Stewart				
	Hoary Bat	Gray Bat	Evening Bat	Connection
Why is the population of this bat in decline?	These bats fly through the low-pressure areas around wind turbine blades and their blood vessels around their lungs burst.	People disturb the bats in their caves and the mothers fly off and leave their babies to die.	Their woodland habitats are disappearing so they sleep in backyard trees. Cats eat the sleeping bats during the day.	Human actions are causing many bats to die.
What can humans do to help them?	Turn off wind turbines on calm nights.	Build bat-friendly gates that keep people out of some caves.	Keep their pet cats indoors during the day.	Human actions can also save bats.

4.1   *Magic Square for Bats! Strange and Wonderful*

by Laurence Pringle

Directions: Put the number of the definition listed below into the square with the correct term. Check your answers by adding the numbers across each row, down each column, and diagonally. The **MAGIC NUMBER** is the total you get each time.

beneficial _____	mammal _____	pollinate _____	_____
echolocation _____	vampire _____	roost _____	_____
colony _____	hibernation _____	rabies _____	_____
_____	_____	_____	_____

1. A warm-blooded animal that nurses milk from its mother's body.
2. A disease that bats can pass on to other animals with a bite.
3. The way bats find their way in the dark by using sounds and vibrations.
4. A large group of bats that live together.
5. A type of bat that does not catch insects, but instead drinks blood.
6. To carry or transfer pollen from one flower to another.
7. A safe place for bats to sleep.
8. Something that is good for you.
9. A deep sleep that saves energy.

The **MAGIC NUMBER** is _____.

4.2 Concept Circles

Name: _____

Date: _____

Shark Attack!

by Cathy East Dubowski

Dorling Kindersley Ltd, 1998

Directions: Read and think about the words and phrases in the concept circles. The words in each circle are directly related to a word or name in the Word Bank below. Determine which word each concept circle represents and write that word in the space provided by each concept circle. Be prepared to support your answers. You may refer to the book *Shark Attack!* by Cathy East Dubowski if necessary.

Circle 1:
- very rare
- Takes place in warm water
- Have occurred most frequently in Australia.
- May happen because people are mistaken for seals,

Circle 2:
- Survived the bite of a great white shark.
- Designed first shark cage.
- diver
- Trying to save sharks from extinction.

Circle 3:
- overfishing
- shark hunters
- fishing nets
- Consumers

Circle 4:
- meat eaters
- live, swim, and hunt alone
- slow to reproduce
- skeleton made of cartilage

	Weighed as much as 10,000 pounds	Jaws were over six feet wide		nets	chain-mail suits
	Grew up to 54-feet long	Lived millions of years ago		electrical beach barriers	shark screen bag
		Word	Bank		
Rodney Fox	attacks	protection	*Carcharodon megaloden*	sharks	extinction

5.1 H-Map for Compare/Contrast

Alligators	Both	Crocodiles
Blackish/grey		Brownish
Live in United States and China		Live in Africa, India, South America, and Southern United States
U-shaped rounded snout		V-shaped pointed snout
Can grow to 15 feet		Can grow to 20 feet
Teeth in lower jaw are not visible when mouth is closed	Reptiles live in tropical and semitropical regions	Teeth in lower jaw are visible when mouth is closed
Alligatoridae Family	Eat fish and nearby land animals	Crocodylidae Family
Have been known to live over 70 years	Can attack humans	Have been known to live over 100 years
Lay eggs in mounds of vegetation		Lay eggs in mud or sand
Live in freshwater		Live in brackish or salt water
Clutch size of 20–50 eggs		Clutch size of 30–70 eggs
Less aggressive		More aggressive

5.2 Comparing Stories and Informational Text Anchor Chart

	Stories	Informational Text
Where does the text content come from?	Based on the author's imagination	Based on the author's research
What is the purpose for reading?	Read for experience or pleasure	Read for information or pleasure
How is it organized?	Setting, characters, plot, theme	One particular topic, maybe narrative or expository
What do the illustrations do?	Extend the text	Clarify and explain

From *Integrating Children's Literature through the Common Core State Standards* by Rachel L. Wadham and Terrell A. Young. Santa Barbara, CA: Libraries Unlimited. Copyright © 2015.

8.1   What–Why–How? Graphic Organizer

Name: _____

Text: _Our Solar System_ _____

What does the author think?	Why does the author think this way?	How do facts in the text support the author's thinking?
Uranus is not boring like some scientists thought.	1. Uranus developed clouds	1. Hubble Space Telescope saw a change of seasons
		2. Storms developed just like the other planets
		3. Clouds developed
	2. Uranus has five large moons	1. Moons have strange surface features
		2. Gives a picture of Miranda one of the moons
		3. This moon has lots of features but is very small.
	3. Uranus has rings	1. It has 11 rings
		2. Has pieces or arcs of other rings
		3. The Black material spins like a merry-go-round

Adapted from McLaughlin and Overturf, 2012.

From *Integrating Children's Literature through the Common Core State Standards* by Rachel L. Wadham and Terrell A. Young. Santa Barbara, CA: Libraries Unlimited. Copyright © 2015.

9.1 *Little Red Riding Hood* Compare and Contrast Chart

Title & Reteller	Culture	Protagonist	Distinctive Clothing	Antagonist	Resolution
Little Red Riding Hood, retold by Jerry Pinkney					
Pretty Salma: A Little Red Riding Hood Story from Africa, by Niki Daly					
Little Roja Riding Hood, by Susa Middleton Elya					
Lon Po Po: A Red-Riding Hood Story from China, retold by Ed Young					
Carmine: A Little More Red, by Melissa Sweet					

9.2 Themes: Alike and Different Think Sheet

Name: _____

Book 1: _____

Book 2: _____

How does each author convey the theme?	
Book 1	Book 2

How are the books' themes alike?

How are the books themes different?	
Book 1	Book 2

Adapted from Owocki, 2012.

Index

Rachel L. Wadham, MLS, MEd, is the education and juvenile collections librarian at Brigham Young University, Provo, Utah. Her published works include ABC-CLIO's *This Is My Life: A Guide to Realistic Fiction for Teens* and *Integrating Young Adult Literature through the Common Core State Standards*. Wadham holds a master's degree in library science from University of North Texas and a master's in education from Pennsylvania State University.

Terrell A. Young, EdD, is professor of education, with an emphasis in literacy and children's literature at the David O. McKay School of Education at Brigham Young University. Young is a coauthor of *Children's Literature, Briefly*. He previously taught in public elementary schools in Utah and Wyoming and private elementary schools in Venezuela. He has also taught at the University of Texas-Arlington and at Washington State University. He holds a master's degree from Utah State University and a doctorate in education from Brigham Young University.

35234785R00106